LIPSMACKIN'
VEGETARIAN
BACKPACKIN'

LIPSMACKIN' VEGETARIAN BACKPACKIN'

Lightweight, Trail-Tested Vegetarian Recipes for Backcountry Trips

Second Edition

CHRISTINE AND TIM CONNERS

GUILFORD, CONNECTICUT
HELENA, MONTANA

FALCONGUIDES®

FalconGuides is an imprint of Rowman & Littlefield.

Distributed by NATIONAL BOOK NETWORK

Copyright © 2015 Christine and Tim Conners

Photos by Christine and Tim Conners, except for those by Ted Ayers, which appear on pages 42, 44, 58, 75, 119, 181, 213, 225, 230.

A previous edition of this book was published by Globe Pequot Press in 2004.

Library of Congress Cataloging-in-Publication data is available on file.

Conners, Christine.
Lipsmackin' vegetarian backpackin' : lightweight, trail-tested vegetarian recipes for backcountry trips / Christine and Tim Conners. — Second Edition.
pages cm
Includes index.
ISBN 978-0-7627-8502-5 (pbk. : alk. paper) — ISBN 978-1-4930-1489-7 (electronic)
1. Vegetarian cooking. 2. Outdoor cooking. I. Conners, Tim. II. Title.
TX837.C597 2015
641.5'636—dc23   2015011213

Printed in the United States of America

To the memory of Christine's Dad, Dr. David E. Yount, loving father, brilliant scientist, and a steadfast source of encouragement who helped set us on the path of book writing.

A Song of Ascents

I will lift up my eyes to the mountains;
From where shall my help come?
My help comes from the Lord,
Who made heaven and earth.

PSALM 121:1-2 (NASB)

CONTENTS

ACKNOWLEDGMENTS

This book, like others in the *Lipsmackin'* series, rests on the contributions from dozens of backpackers and outdoor chefs. The credits given at the bottom of the recipes don't do justice in demonstrating the gratitude we have for those who've helped us so generously along the way, both with the first edition and now this, the second. Our sincerest appreciation to you all.

We're indebted to two individuals, in particular, for their assistance with the second edition: Ken Harbison, recipe tester magnifico, the man by whom no cookbook of ours would be complete; and Ted Ayers, master outdoor photographer, whose friendship and photos grace the pages throughout this book. To Ken and Ted, thank you for the many years of vicarious adventures together through our writing.

And, finally, to our friends at FalconGuides, especially David Legere, Max Phelps, and Katie Benoit, who have yet again pulled us through another literary escapade. Your patience in the face of a rapidly changing publishing world has been appreciated.

INTRODUCTION

There was a time not long ago when just saying the word "vegetarian" was enough to earn a person rolling eyeballs, nervous silence, or an opinionated argument. Times have surely changed.

Practicing a vegetarian lifestyle is no longer considered an aberration by most people. In fact, these days, being vegetarian often garners positive interest from omnivores. It isn't hard to see why. Vegetarianism powerfully implies a healthier disposition and self-control in an area of lifestyle where, frankly, many people know they could use serious improvement.

And times have also changed in that a person is no longer expected to be a full-time vegetarian before preparing meatless dishes at home or ordering vegetarian items off the menu. Meat-free lunch and dinner entrees are increasingly common at restaurants, and grocery stores are packed with hearty and popular vegetarian options.

More people are making meat-free and animal-free selections for many of their meals, even if they aren't strict vegetarians or vegans. For example, while some of the meals we prepare at home aren't vegetarian, we often go a week or more without meat. And it isn't uncommon for either of us to avoid animal products altogether for even longer periods. We've always appreciated having vegetarian and vegan meal options for this reason, and we see an increasing fraction of the population showing the same sentiments.

When we wrote the first edition of *Lipsmackin' Vegetarian Backpackin'*, we wanted to provide backpackers with just such options. Our objective was to help fill what we saw as a large void in the lineup of really good vegetarian and vegan trail recipes. While they've long been a popular option for outdoor cooking, vegetarian and vegan backpacking meals are increasingly common choices, both for their longevity in the pack and because hikers tend to show a greater interest than the general population in healthier food options.

The first edition of *Lipsmackin' Vegetarian Backpackin'* was produced using many of the popular design elements found in our first outdoor cookbook, *Lipsmackin' Backpackin'*, and was well received by the trail community. But *Lipsmackin' Vegetarian*, like its older sibling, had aged to the point where it had earned a makeover, and this second addition is the result.

We've increased the number of recipes, keeping those that proved to be popular while adding many new ones. We've improved recipe layout for clarity and readability and updated reference and resource information. Finally, we've significantly expanded the material on tips and techniques found at the front of the book, sharing the additional experience we've been fortunate to glean over the years between editions.

As with all of our cookbooks, our sincere desire is that this thoroughly revised edition will do even more to reduce the anxieties and hassles that typically go with planning trail menus while, at the same time, greatly expanding your food choice options.

Christine and Tim Conners
Statesboro, Georgia

Planning and Preparing
Your Meals

The power of food over our physical health and well-being is obvious. However, its strong influence on the psyche is generally not as appreciated, especially by those new to backpacking. Food issues can easily make or break a long-duration backcountry outing.

Yet, despite the pitfalls of doing so, many backpackers relegate their menu to the last step in planning for the trail, or they treat their menu as an afterthought altogether. After all, what's the problem with just tossing a variety of food items straight into the pack? Well, nothing, as long as you're able to accurately estimate, while heading out the door, all your anticipated food requirements once you'll be on the trail! Some can actually pull it off. But most of us don't have that kind of acumen, even after thousands of miles of trail experience. The food equation is simply too complex.

It takes careful planning, and a lot of it, to predict how much food will be enough (many people, if not most, seriously overpack), how much spice and variety will be adequate (many trail menus end up grossly bland or monotonic), how durable the food should be for the trail conditions (ridiculously fragile items are commonly found in hikers' packs), how easy the food will be to prepare (complex, multistep recipes are a total drag before or after a long trail day), and the type of nutritional punch the meals should contain (in a nutshell, longer trips require higher quality fuel). Without much thought, it's left to chance to balance all of these variables. Ignore or misplan any one of them, and your expedition is guaranteed to become less enjoyable.

This all said, there is a somewhat obvious caveat to the above rule: For short-duration trips, spanning one or two nights on the trail, most folks, including those with little experience, can indeed throw together a menu on a whim that won't result in severe culinary misery. Even if far too much food is packed, it tastes lousy, it becomes crushed under the tent bag, it's too complicated for the trail, or it contains nothing but fiber, fat, or sugar, relief by way of civilization (and restaurants) can be measured in mere hours, not days. The predicament can be laughed off in the meantime.

However, for longer trips lasting several days to weeks or more, very few people are immune to the havoc wreaked by a poorly planned backpacking menu. It's no laughing matter when your food becomes repulsive or inedible and the ability to solve the problem is dozens of miles and days away by trail!

The recipes in *Lipsmackin' Vegetarian Backpackin'* have been selected and arranged to maximize the efficiency of the meal-planning process and steer backpackers around the usual pitfalls of trail cookery. Information is plainly presented to allow the reader to quickly judge the merits of a particular recipe while preparing for a backpacking trip, and each recipe is clearly structured for foolproof preparation once on the trail.

Ideal Attributes of Backpacking Food

The logic behind planning a great trail menu is straightforward and easy to master. In fact trail menu design becomes virtually foolproof when just a few key parameters are considered and carefully balanced.

Weight

Food obviously comprises a large fraction of total pack load, but many hikers don't realize that grub can easily exceed one-quarter of the total backpack weight on longer trips. Because of this, food weight becomes an increasingly important consideration as the length of a trip grows. For an overnight hike, for instance, canned goods, frozen vegetables, and fresh fruits are all possible options, even though they tend to be heavy for their nutritional value. But on longer trips, as pack load grows, an increasing fraction of dried food must be included because of the need for lighter weight and greater nutritional density.

Food is a security blanket, and nearly every backpacker finds it necessary, when loading a pack, to fight the urge to overfill it with rations. The key to knowing how much food to carry is to pay close attention to the quantity of food one normally consumes while on the trail. Ideally this can be done by weighing the food load before the trip, then doing the same with any leftovers afterward. The difference is then used for adapting the menu prior to the next outing.

Most hikers can expect to eat between 1 to 1½ pounds of packed food per day, assuming the bulk of it is dehydrated or freeze-dried in advance. It's a common, and easy, mistake to pack more than this. Consider the implications of overpacking by about 1 pound of food per day for a weeklong trip: you'll find yourself either overeating or needlessly carrying seven extra pounds on your back (equivalent to almost four fully filled one-quart water bottles).

As a caveat, keep in mind that the body's caloric burn grows with hiking distance and duration, with longer distance backpackers easily requiring twice the calories needed by a sedentary adult. So either the weight of food consumed per day, or the food's caloric density, will have to increase for very long trips. Pay close attention to your body's unique requirements and plan accordingly.

Food bulk is an interesting—and frustrating—parameter, because it tends to be inversely proportional to weight. Lightweight food items, including freeze-dried meals in presealed pouches, are often less dense, and generally pack less caloric punch, than heavier foods. To compensate, more lightweight items are usually carried, adding to the volume of the food cache and making it all the more difficult to cram into backpacks and bear canisters. Calorically dense foods make packing easier, provided one considers the extra calories per ounce during the planning process.

Each recipe in *Lipsmackin' Vegetarian Backpackin'* lists the trail-ready weight per serving. This is helpful for planning and estimating proper individual serving portions and total packed food weight. Note that the weight of any water required for reconstitution is not included in the listed weight data, as drinking and cooking water is usually found along the trail.

Nutritional Value

For backpackers, the nutritional quality of packed food becomes increasingly more important in proportion to the energy expended on the trail. The harder and longer the body works, the more critical it becomes to balance one's nutritional requirements, considering total calories, quality protein, complex carbohydrates and fiber, healthy fats, electrolytes, and vitamins and minerals. The body may be able to shrug off a significant deficiency in any of these categories during an average day at home. But on the trail, the effects of an imbalanced diet are easily felt and rapidly deleterious.

Don't immediately write off a food that's heavier than others per serving without considering what it offers in nutritional value. A heavier food item may provide exceptional nutritional density, making it especially ideal for powering the body during longer days on the trail. Conversely, foods that are featherlight per serving are often lacking in caloric density, complex carbs, or protein, so you should carefully scrutinize these foods before using them extensively in your meal planning.

Adequate consumption of electrolytes is essential while on the trail. Don't shift to a low-sodium diet at a time when your perspiration rate is going to skyrocket and your body will require a higher than normal level of electrolyte intake. On the other hand, if you are on a low-sodium diet, don't blindly switch to higher sodium foods! Talk to your doctor first about options for safely maintaining necessary levels of electrolytes while backpacking.

The nutritional data included with each recipe in this book are designed to help you tailor your backpacking trail menus to your individual dietary requirements. Use common sense: Balance the occasional decadent recipe with one of higher nutritional quality, and you'll find yourself able to go farther and faster when on the trail.

Taste

As we all know, the quality of "taste" is completely personal, with no objective characteristic with which to judge its merits. The problem is that if a food doesn't taste good, we don't want to eat it. This isn't a serious issue at home. If we don't like the food, we can select something else. However, taste, or lack thereof, can become a big issue in deep wilderness where alternate options don't exist. If you find you don't like the food you've brought along on the trail, you'll eat less, rapidly kick-starting a downward nutritional spiral.

For those new to backpacking, it may seem odd that the taste of food could even be a concern. After all, why would anyone bring along food that he or she doesn't like? Good question, but it's a remarkably common mistake, even among veteran outdoor folks. The simple reason is that recipes appropriate for backpacking aren't normally eaten off the trail. Backpackers will often throw together recipes on a whim, select and use recipes for the first time from a book such as this, or grab untried freeze-dried meals off the store shelf. In the mind's eye, we're convinced the food will taste good. Think about it: We do this all the time at the grocery store or in restaurants, then find—more often than we'd like—that our choices are disappointingly different from what we imagined.

If much of the food packed for the trail ends up being an unanticipated and nasty surprise, mealtime can quickly turn into a repulsive experience, with food being choked down instead of enjoyed. Poor-tasting food really puts a damper on a long trip. And for hapless hikers who didn't give their menu more thought, it can even end an excursion prematurely.

Taste testing your selections in advance and continuously taking note of the foods that you particularly enjoy while on the trail are two ways to build and improve your backpacking menu. And when selecting options from an outdoor cookbook, look for recipes that have been carefully tested, as they have been in this book. Taking these steps will help you avoid unpleasant revelations in the field.

Variety

When it comes to food quality, a close cousin to taste is variety. While some folks can eat the same type of food, or even the same exact recipe, meal after meal, day after day, even week after week, most of us like to mix up the menu. Even the best-tasting recipe can quickly grow tiresome on the trail.

Variety often falls victim to poor or last-minute planning. After all, it's easier to prepare and pack seven meals of spaghetti and sauce for a weeklong trip than it is to come up with something different for each night. But even if you're fond of Italian food, there's a good chance you'll be mighty tired of eating it after seven days. Don't underestimate this point. The mental demands on the trail can be incredibly challenging. If all you've brought are lentils and oatmeal, it won't be long before you're desperate to get off the path and into your favorite pizza parlor.

When packing foods new to you, it's particularly important to diversify the menu. In the event you don't like a meal, you won't have to wait too long before you'll be dining on something different. Imagine packing nothing but a week's worth of dried hummus for snacking only to find that it doesn't rehydrate as expected nor taste as you're used to. That's a lot of hummus to have to choke down before relief comes once you're home!

Simplicity

Some folks enjoy the challenge of preparing difficult, multipot masterpieces in the wild; but most backpackers seek an easier approach to mealtime, especially before or after the end of a long day of hard hiking. The same holds true for lunch and midday snacks; when forward progress is all-important and frequent, rapid food breaks are especially valued.

Simple meals mean less cookware, less fuel to burn, and less mess to clean up. Pack weight and volume decrease with the reduction in gear and fuel. The amount of effort required to prepare and recover from mealtime is reduced as well, as is the environmental footprint left behind. And simple is most definitely better when you have to cook in the dark or in foul weather. By primarily choosing one-pot meals and easier recipes, you'll spend less time cooking and cleaning and more time resting.

Don't be fooled into thinking that simple recipes are inherently loaded with heavily processed or unhealthy ingredients. On the contrary, precooked and dried ingredients give the backpacker an endless number of tasty and healthy options that result in simple recipes ideal for the trail. In fact, all recipes in *Lipsmackin' Vegetarian Backpackin'* have been selected with simplicity in mind, requiring no more than a single pot to prepare.

Durability

Rounding out the list of food qualities key to enjoyable backpacking is durability. Foods that are fragile, either in terms of spoilage or crushing, have limited use on the trail and are generally only appropriate for consumption on shorter trips, not far from the trailhead. They simply wouldn't reliably survive for much longer in the challenging environment found inside a backpack.

Few are the backpacks that aren't stuffed to the hilt or whose various items don't find themselves sandwiched at some point under the heavy weight of filled water bottles. Add constant movement for hours on end, and the pack can be likened to a rock tumbler. Imagine a bag of cookies in there after a few days!

Now add heat. Even in cooler weather some areas within a pack become roasting hot in direct sunlight. Ironically, the cooler regions of the pack, deep and buried, are the very places that fragile items should *not* be placed because of the weight of the gear that would rest on top of them.

You must carefully consider the warmth inside the pack if you want to bring along foods that are very perishable. Such foods *must* be eaten soon after you depart the trailhead, before they spoil. But the bulk of the food you carry on the trail for longer trips must be durable enough for the bruising environment of the pack. Well-packaged dried and dehydrated foods, tough-crust breads, hard cheeses, and vegetable oils sealed in containers are all examples of durable foods that carry well and resist spoilage.

All the recipes in *Lipsmackin' Vegetarian Backpackin'* were selected with durability in mind. Most can be assembled at home, then safely stored for months prior to use on the trail. This quality is of particular value to the very long-distance backpacker who has a great many meals to prepare well in advance of the expedition.

Recipe Categories

This section, along with the remaining portions of this chapter, explain the general layout of *Lipsmackin' Vegetarian Backpackin'* and how the information presented can specifically assist with trail meal planning and preparation.

Putting recipes into categories is not as easy as it might seem. There are as many ways to organize a cookbook as there are eating styles and preferences. The approach that appears to satisfy most people, and the one used in this book, is to begin by organizing entrees according to the meal category they best belong to: breakfast, lunch, or dinner. Those recipes that could not be tagged as "main dish" were grouped into three other primary categories: breads, snacks and desserts, and drinks.

The lunch section was constructed around the premise that fast and simple meals at noontime are particularly valued. It is time-consuming to break out the stove, heat the food, and then clean the gear, so we purposely minimized these types of recipes. Those that are included require only short cooking times and use foods that are easy to clean up. It is quite common for backpackers to simply snack on a variety of foods throughout the day, with no real differentiation between lunch and any other break. A number of such options, sometimes called "walking foods," have been included as well. Adapt and apply the lunch recipes according to your hiking preferences.

Three examples of meal systems are also provided, one each for breakfast, lunch, and dinner. Meal systems provide a flexible approach for using a fixed amount of basic staples and, when used judiciously, can simplify pre-trip menu planning while providing for substantial variety once on the trail.

Servings and Weights

Most of the recipes in this book require final preparation steps to be performed on the trail, with the number of resulting servings typically ranging from one to four. Because of practical limitations on the size of the gear that can be packed, the average backpacking cook pot is not much larger than 2-quart capacity. Four large servings can be comfortably prepared with such cookware.

It may seem odd that many of the recipes are written to produce only a single serving. There is good reason for this, the intent being that these dishes can be replicated as required to precisely meet the needs of your particular trip. One beauty of backpacking recipes is that they tend to be readily scalable in the number of servings, either up or down. So don't hesitate to scale as required. It's easy, and single-serving recipes provide even more flexibility to do so.

Many recipes in this book, especially lunch and snack items, require preparation only at home. These recipes often produce a large number of servings that can then be portioned, divided, and packed as required for the trail.

For consistency, the estimated number of servings included with each recipe assumes the target audience to be active adults on a moderate- to high-caloric intake, consistent with the exertion level expected when backpacking on rugged or long trails. Adjust these estimates for your specific situation, keeping in mind that activity level, richness of the meal, food preferences, snacking, weather, and altitude can all influence the optimum number of servings delivered by each recipe.

For estimating the total weight of your packed food, the dried weight per serving is also included for each recipe.

Challenge Level

A three-tier system has been used to assign a challenge level to each recipe: "easy," "moderate," or "difficult." The decision was based upon the *on-trail* preparation and cleanup effort required, the sensitivity of the cooking technique to variation, and the attention to care necessary to avoid injury. Most of the recipes in this book have been tagged as "easy," an important quality especially for the trail setting, where simplicity is definitely welcome.

Because cooking on the trail is often challenging enough, recipes considered "moderate" and "difficult" were purposely minimized. However, give careful consideration to those that have been included. As your skills grow, you'll find these worth the attempt.

Preparation Time

Total preparation time on the trail under pleasant weather conditions has been estimated for each recipe. This value includes time from turning on the heat through serving the dish. It is assumed that the cook will flow the preparation steps in parallel whenever possible. For instance, while water is being brought to a boil, other preparation tasks can often be accomplished simultaneously. The recipes are written to best take advantage of this.

Preparation Instructions

Instructions for each recipe include a list of ingredients along with step-by-step directions, each logically grouped and presented in numerical sequence. The use of numerical sequencing in the preparation steps is intended to help the chef stay focused and to assist in the assignment of specific tasks to any other backpackers able to lend a hand. All of the recipes require at least some preparation steps to be performed at home. These are clearly distinguished from final preparation steps required on the trail.

Remember to Pack the Instructions!

Don't make the mistake of packing your food without including instructions for what needs to be done once on the trail! Packable on-trail cooking instructions for each recipe can be found online, free of charge, at www.lipsmackincampin. com/packable/lvbp_2ed.pdf. Download the file, print the instructions for those recipes you'll be taking with you, and place the slips of paper along with your packed food.

Options and Tips

Interesting cooking options are provided for many of the recipes. An option differs from the main instructions and produces alternate endings to the recipe. Options included with a recipe are shown separately from the main preparation steps.

Likewise, contributors occasionally offered helpful tips to assist the trail cook with purchasing ingredients or preparing the recipe in some way. As with options, tips are listed separately from the main body of the recipe. Recommendations and tips of a more generic nature, or applicable to a wider range of recipes and situations, are presented separately in the following sections.

Equipment Requirements

Essential gear in any trail cooking kit, adequate for meeting the needs of several backpackers if traveling in a group, include the following:

- Backpacking stove with windscreen and fuel for the trip

- Small maintenance kit, appropriate for the stove type

- Lightweight cook pot with stowable handle

- Cook pot lid, preferably one that can double as a frying pan
- Short wooden or plastic stirring spoon
- Short plastic spatula, if foods requiring frying are on the menu
- Liquid measuring device, such as a water bottle with measurement indicator
- Ignition device, such as a lighter, and a waterproof backup, such as a spark igniter
- Small container of hand sanitizer
- Small container of biodegradable detergent
- Small scrub pad and camp cloth
- Mesh bags for storing and airing cooking kit items

In addition, each member of a hiking group should carry his or her own personal mess gear, which should include the following:

- Small, durable serving plate or cup
- Durable, heatproof drinking cup
- Lightweight spoon, fork, and knife (or spork, a utensil combo)
- Filled water bottles for cooking
- Mesh bag for storing personal mess kit items

If a recipe's equipment necessities go beyond the essentials noted here, those additional requirements are listed below the preparation steps to head off any mealtime surprises once on the trail.

Contributor Information

Rounding out each recipe is information about the contributors, the field experts who made the book possible. You'll learn their names, trail monikers, and place they call home. Many of our contributors included anecdotes and stories as well. Useful and often humorous, you'll find these at the top of the recipe.

All of our contributors have extensive experience in the long-trail or outdoor community. Most are accomplished long-distance backpackers.

Trail marker icons next to the contributor's names highlight the National Scenic Trails, the nation's grand long trails, with which these folks have been most connected, either through long-distance trekking or major involvement in preservation and protection.

Trail Marker Icon Key

AT – Appalachian National Scenic Trail

CDT – Continental Divide National Scenic Trail

FT – Florida National Scenic Trail

NCT – North Country National Scenic Trail

PCT – Pacific Crest National Scenic Trail

PHT – Potomac Heritage National Scenic Trail

PNT – Pacific Northwest National Scenic Trail

Category System

This book uses a category system to allow the cook to rapidly assess the most appropriate recipe options when planning a menu for the trail. The key attributes for backpacking recipes were already discussed. For the attributes of weight, nutritional value, simplicity, and durability, some level of objectivity can be used to identify the characteristics of each for each recipe. Taste and variety are obviously subjective; but the recipes in this book purposely span a wide range of tastes so that most any palate should find both covered.

Regarding the objective attributes, weight is obviously straightforward, and the trail-ready measure of weight in ounces is provided for each recipe. Nutritional data are included for each recipe, allowing you to build a menu appropriate for your personal dietary requirements and the anticipated demands of the trail you'll be traveling. Data are provided on a per-serving basis for the following common parameters: calories, protein, fat, carbohydrates, fiber, sodium, and cholesterol. Naturally occurring cholesterol in food is becoming less of concern because of its weak correlation to arteriosclerosis. However, it's a useful parameter for assessing vegan food options, and so we've retained it from the first edition.

Simplicity is addressed through the challenge level assigned to each recipe—"easy," "moderate," or "difficult." For durability, all recipes in *Lipsmackin' Vegetarian Backpackin'* are rugged enough to withstand the rigors of long-duration trips, and so a durability characteristic doesn't require noting.

In addition to the recipe attributes noted above, the trail chef must have a firm idea of the number of servings each recipe will produce so that the recipe can be scaled, if required. Explicit serving numbers are used for this purpose. Closely associated with challenge level, the preparation time is provided and generally rounded to the nearest quarter hour. These data are also useful for estimating fuel requirements, as cooking time usually scales with preparation time. To help ensure that the proper gear is packed along with the food, the required cooking method necessary *on the trail*—pot, frying pan, or no-cook—is indicated by the use of corresponding icons.

Because of their lightweight, durable nature, dehydrated ingredients are common in backpacking foods, and the recipes in this book include them as well. Many dried ingredients can be purchased commercially, but it's easy and inexpensive to do your own drying at home using a food dehydrator. Any additional effort spent in the home kitchen drying food is usually rewarded on the trail with easier preparation, improved durability, healthier options, and less fuel used. Nevertheless, to further simplify their food preparation options at home, some prefer not to use home-dehydrated foods. To quickly call attention to recipes that require such ingredients, an icon depicting a dehydrator is used.

To sort recipes, this book uses an approach specifically designed to assist with nearly any backpacking menu-planning scenario. Recipes are grouped at the top level by meal category, forming the main recipe chapters in the book. From there the recipes are subgrouped by cooking method. Recipes are then subgrouped by weight per serving. Number of servings, weight data, preparation time, and challenge level are summarized prominently at the top of each recipe.

Recipe Icons Category System
Required Equipment and Preparation Method

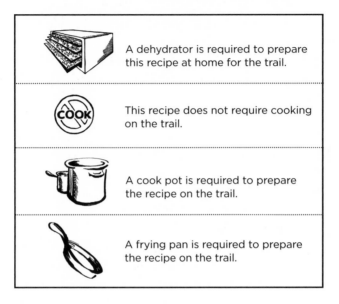

	A dehydrator is required to prepare this recipe at home for the trail.
	This recipe does not require cooking on the trail.
	A cook pot is required to prepare the recipe on the trail.
	A frying pan is required to prepare the recipe on the trail.

For backpackers looking specifically for vegan options, a **V** icon identifies the recipe as free of meat, dairy, and egg products. Otherwise, a **V-LO** icon indicates the recipe is lacto-ovo vegetarian, meaning free of meat but containing dairy and/or egg products. Many of the lacto-ovo vegetarian recipes in this book are easily converted to vegan using simple ingredient substitutions.

Supplemental Information for the Trail Cook
Additional information is included in the front and back sections of this book to assist the backpacking chef with the challenge of cooking on the trail. An important chapter on safety highlights the most common risks associated with trail cooking and what can be done to help reduce the probability of an accident while far from a hospital. Please err on the side of caution and review this material, especially if you are new to trail cooking.

Hand in hand with safety comes skill. Expert trail chefs are far less likely to inflict injury or illness to either themselves or their fellow backpackers. A chapter on basic skills reviews the competencies that outdoor chefs should seek to understand and master, with an emphasis from the vantage of cooking on the trail. Tips and techniques for home dehydrating are covered in a chapter devoted to saving weight and improving durability through the use of dried foods.

The appendices cover a wide variety of helpful reference information, including measurement conversions, sources of trail-cooking equipment and ingredients, a bibliography of additional books and information on outdoor cooking, and techniques for reducing the environmental impact of cooking while on the trail.

Healthy Pairings

Wise choices and moderation are the two keys to maintaining a healthy diet while on the trail. If care is taken not to overpack, moderation will be guaranteed, since there will only be so much food to be found in your pack!

But regarding wise choices, these begin and end with the planning process. When choosing recipes that lean toward higher fats and sugars, balance your meals with healthier options the remainder of the day. This is especially critical on treks of longer duration, when high-quality fuel is what your body needs and craves. Sure, bring along a couple of king-size candy bars, but retain them as a reward for making it up and over those grueling mountain passes!

Drinks containing electrolytes can be appropriate when the weather is warm and the level of exertion very high. But otherwise make the bulk of your liquid intake pure, cool filtered water from wild streams and springs, a rare treat that few people in this day have the opportunity to experience.

Trail Cooking Safety

The process of cooking presents some of the more significant hazards that backpackers face during their stay outdoors. Most people have learned to successfully manage dangers in the home kitchen through caution and experience. But outdoor cooking introduces many new and unique hazards that, if not appreciated and controlled, can cause severe injury or illness. The following information on trail cooking safety highlights the most common risks and what can be done to help reduce the probability of an accident.

While the goal should always be zero accidents, minor injuries, including cuts and burns, are common while cooking outdoors. Keep the first-aid kit handy for these. Never acceptable, however, are more serious injuries or food-borne illness. Extreme care and caution should always be used to prevent accidents that could send you to the hospital. This point is even more important while on the trail, where the time to get to help can be measured in days.

Always be careful! A razor-sharp pocketknife can go deep into your body before your brain has time to register what is happening. Fuel leaking from a pack stove can explode into a fireball, burning your face. Harmful bacteria, left alive due to improper cooking, can leave you so ill that you can't even walk.

Learn to respect every step of the cooking process, from preparation at home to clean up on the trail. Always think through what you are about to do and ask yourself, "Is this safe?" If it isn't, or even if you are uncomfortable for reasons you don't understand, trust your instinct. Stop and determine how to do the job better, either by using more appropriate techniques and equipment or by asking others for assistance or advice. Move slowly and methodically. No matter how hungry you might be, no meal is worth compromising your health and well-being.

With care and attention, any cooking risk can be managed to an acceptable level. The following list of guidelines for safety will help you do just that.

Setup and Assistance

- When cooking on the trail, schedule pressure often occurs while you're trying to break camp in the morning, when foul weather is moving in quickly, or when nightfall is fast approaching. If you find yourself trailing, don't rush to catch up. The chances of an accident and injury will only increase. And don't be a martyr if you're cooking for more than one, silently suffering under the burden. You'll only fatigue yourself all the more quickly. Instead, immediately enlist help from others to get the meal preparation back on track.

- If traveling in a group, establish your cooking zone in an area away from the main traffic in your trail camp. Especially at the end of a long day, with the natural desire for camaraderie, it's tempting to cook in the middle of where the action is. But pack stoves sit naturally low to the ground and are prone to being inadvertently kicked asunder in areas with a lot of activity.

Food Poisoning

- To decrease the probability of illness from parasites, bacteria, or viruses, all water taken from natural sources must be properly purified while on the trail. Do not assume that the heat from the cooking process will be adequate to sanitize your water. It often is not! There are many reliable devices on the market designed for water purification while backpacking. The best choice for your situation will depend on the water quality in the area you'll be visiting as well as your personal preference on the method of purification.

- The inside of a backpack can become toasty over the course of a long day, especially when the weather is warm. However, the surface of a backpack becomes downright hot when exposed to direct sunlight. Store foods away from the surfaces of the backpack. Instead, place them deeper in the center of the pack to reduce the temperature that the food is exposed to and extend its shelf life.

- Do not bring raw eggs on the trail unless they are to be cooked and consumed soon after leaving the trailhead. This is especially true in warm weather. If eggs develop an off odor, do not use.

- Cold and wet weather significantly affect cooking time. High altitude will as well, because it lowers the boiling temperature of water. Consider these factors and plan to cook your food longer to be certain it is thoroughly heated throughout.

- All food should be packaged tightly and securely to reduce the risk of spoilage. Loose seals on containers or ziplock bags give entry to moisture and contaminants, both of which decrease the shelf life of food. This is especially important if packing for a trip lasting more than a day or two. Now is not the time to cut corners: Always use high-quality ziplock bags and containers. Heavy-duty ziplock bags are recommended for foods with a rough, jagged nature that might otherwise puncture thin walls of less expensive bags.

- Certain elements of backpacking, especially when answering nature's call, require fastidious attention to the cleanliness of one's hands. Bring a small container of hand sanitizer, enough to last the trip, for thoroughly cleansing hands before handling food at mealtime. This is particularly needed in areas where water for cleaning is in short supply.

- Carefully clean all cookware and utensils following each use. If they are greasy or smell strongly of the meal just prepared, then keep washing. Not only will you avoid unwanted animal interest by reducing odors, but you'll reduce the chances of any food remnants becoming spoiled and then creating a hazard the next time you cook. And don't make the common mistake of overlooking your pocketknife if you've used it to slice cheese. The blade slots, grooves, and joints of a knife collect food bits that must be cleaned carefully after such use. Wipe your cookware and utensils dry following cleaning to help remove any remaining protozoa, cysts, or other nasties that may have survived washing.

- A final line of protection: If any food smells or looks odd, or if you see signs of mold or patches of discoloration, discard it! Do not take the risk. Even the mildest case of food poisoning can be a miserable experience when you're deep in the wilderness.

Physical Dehydration

- Heavy exertion can rapidly dehydrate the body, placing it at increased risk of cramping, injury, and ailment. To stay properly hydrated, you'll easily require more than 1 gallon of water on hot days when trekking with a heavy backpack. When urine becomes a deeper shade of yellow, that's a sign to up your water intake pronto. Don't rely on your sense of thirst, which often only develops after your body has become dehydrated. Keep a water bottle or hydration pack filled and handy at all times, and get in the habit of taking frequent sips while on the trail.

- Electrolytes, such as sodium and potassium, are essential to the proper metabolic functioning of the body. When you drink large quantities of water on warm days, more electrolytes are flushed from the body through perspiration, and they require replacement. A typical diet will normally provide enough sodium, but supplementation is often required to maintain adequate reserves of other electrolytes, either through energy bars, sport drink mixes, or mineral tablets. Have these types of items available on the trail and use them, especially if you feel your energy reserves diminishing or begin to cramp.

Cuts and Burns

- With many backpacking recipes, much of the cutting and chopping occurs at home and not on the trail. But an occasional recipe does require knife work at mealtime. A kitchen knife is too large for the pack. Heavy folding knives are also inappropriate and unnecessary. A standard pocketknife should be adequate for accomplishing any food-preparation job on the trail.

- Cutting utensils are inherently dangerous, and it goes without saying that they should be handled with care. Dull knife blades unintentionally slip much more easily when you're slicing or chopping, and they can quickly end up in the side of your finger instead of in the food you're cutting. Maintain the sharpness of knife blades to help ensure they do what you expect them to. When slicing and chopping, always keep your hands and fingers away from the underside of the cutting edge and from in front of the blade tip.

- Backpacking stoves are small and lightweight for good reason, but that small size makes them somewhat unstable, especially when used with larger cook pots or skillets. Improve the stability by setting the stove on a solid, level surface such as the top of a flat rock. Before leaving for the trail, check to be sure that your cookware is not too large for the stove. If the stove or cookware may tip easily, look for a smaller pot or skillet. Use care while cooking by bracing the pot or skillet handle with one hand while stirring with the other. If your cookware is not properly stabilized, it—and the hot food inside—could end up tipping onto the ground or your unprotected skin.

- Handles are easy to inadvertently snag, and so they become a frustratingly simple way to accidentally tip a pot or skillet. Use cookware that has retractable or removable handles so that they don't get in the way while the pot or skillet is on the stove.

- Stoves become red hot during use. Fortunately, because of their small size, they take only a few minutes to cool off. But their small size also makes them easy to grab and move without giving it much thought. And that is where the danger lies. Inadvertently grabbing a searing-hot stove from the top will leave a spectacular pattern of burns on your fingers and palm. This is sure to impress your friends, but it won't be very fun while you wait for them to heal.

- Be extra cautious with plastic food bags containing hot water, as the bags can potentially tip or rupture, covering your skin in scalding liquid. Brace the bag, such as by placing it in an empty cook pot, before pouring hot water into the bag, then minimize handling of the bag until it cools to a safe temperature.

Fire Safety

- It is imperative that any applicable fire regulations be strictly adhered to. These are often posted at trailheads. But a surer way to gather this information is to contact the appropriate authorities for the area you plan to visit. It is not uncommon for campfires to be banned while the use of backpacking stoves is permissible. In very dry conditions, any type of open fire may be banned, including stoves. Ignorance is no excuse. Make no assumptions regarding the law. The potential legal, financial, and environmental consequences are enormous should you ignore the law or lose control of your fire.

- All cooking must be performed in a fire-safe area, clear of natural combustibles like dry leaves, grass, and trees. Instead of creating a human-made fire-safe zone about your cooking area, and potentially leaving behind the ugly evidence, take your cooking to a durable area naturally free of combustibles, such as the surface of a large flat rock or an area of bare soil or sand. Imagine the size of the fireball that might occur should your stove leak fuel and burst into flames, then place the stove at least that far from the nearest combustibles, including overhanging trees.

- Cooking fuel is an obvious hazard, both to you and to the environment. Care should always be taken when lighting a stove, no matter what its design. A stove that is leaking liquid or propane fuel under pressure can produce an impressive fireball that, if you're fortunate, won't do anything more than burn the hair off your forearms. But you shouldn't let the situation get that far. Before striking a match—and with the stove assembled, pressurized, and the valve off—listen and sniff for fuel leaks. If you note a problem, repair the stove, using a maintenance kit if necessary, before proceeding. If you are unable to repair the stove, do not use it! Better to eat a cold dinner than to burn either yourself or the forest. Finally, always use care when starting a normally functioning stove. A stove will often flash while lighting, so keep your face well away when doing so. Understand how to properly operate your stove before using it for the first time, and especially before using it on the trail.

- Many stoves come with a metal windscreen, and some also come with a base plate to go underneath. Both the windscreen and base plate are designed to help keep heat where you want it: on the pot. But both also serve an important safety function. A base plate can help prevent bits of duff from igniting under the stove while it is in use, while a windscreen can prevent windblown sparks or embers from reaching nearby combustibles. Use a base plate, if your stove comes with one, and always use a windscreen if the weather is breezy.

- Keep loose and combustible items, such as jackets, sleeves, towels, plastic bags, and hair, away from the stove when it is in operation or cooling down following cooking. Alcohol stoves burn with a colorless flame that is almost impossible to see in sunlight. Without the visual cue, these stoves are notorious for burning clothing (and skin), and extra care is required for their use.

- Avoid building campfires for the sole reason of cooking while on the trail. Bring a backpacking stove for this purpose. Used properly, a stove will not leave behind evidence of its use; and, compared to a campfire, a properly maintained stove poses less chance of creating a wildfire.

- Have filled water bottles at the ready to extinguish any flames that might otherwise threaten to escape your fire-safe zone.

- Never attempt to cook in a sleeping tent! The fully enclosed walls can concentrate deadly gases and cause asphyxiation. Or the tent walls or floor could rapidly catch fire, trapping the occupants. A flat tarp—set at an angle above head height to safely vent noxious fumes and positioned well out of range of the flames of the stove—can serve to protect the stove during rainy or snowy weather.

Allergies and Special Diets

When planning a menu for a group outing, ask your fellow hikers if they have food allergies or health issues that might require special dietary restrictions. Once on the trail and far from medical assistance, a severe allergic reaction could be life-threatening. At the least a dietary reaction can make the trip very uncomfortable for the poor soul struck with such a malady. Do not assume, just because they haven't told you, that none of your trail companions has such issues. Selecting foods that meet everyone's tastes and requirements might seem impossible in these circumstances, but many recipes can be modified for special dietary needs while satisfying everyone else in the group. This approach can be far easier on the cook than attempting to adhere to a parallel special-requirements menu.

Wild Animals

- Critters searching for food can pose a danger to backpackers either through aggression or disease. Food bags; odorous items such as toiletries; dirty cookware and utensils left unattended; and leftover food waste improperly disposed of all will eventually attract unwanted animal attention and can create a major problem when in bear country. Wildlife that gains access to such goodies will surely come back for more, placing these animals at risk of harm along with the people who must interact with or remove them. A camp that is neat and clean, with food and garbage properly stored and secured, is far less attractive to the local fauna. Practice low-impact principles and adhere to any food storage regulations unique to your area, such as a requirement for bear bagging.

- In areas with the potential for bear activity, cook and eat far downwind from your sleeping area to reduce the chance of it becoming of nocturnal interest to bruins looking to satisfy their incessant hunger. Better yet, pause for an early dinner while still on the trail, then walk the final mile or two to your stopping point for the day. By doing so you'll leave the enticing aromas well behind.

No list can cover every danger lurking in every situation, and the above is surely no exception. But by learning to cook with a mind fixated on safety, few circumstances will catch you ill prepared or by surprise.

Basic Skills and Equipment for the Trail Chef

Cooking a great meal out of a backpack might seem magical, perhaps impossible. It's neither, of course. And a strong foundation in the fundamentals of outdoor cooking in general, and trail cooking in particular, will make it all the more likely you'll be successful. With this in mind, the following section covers the essential skills for cooking when your kitchen is on your back.

Planning for the Obvious . . . and the Unexpected

- If you are new to trail cooking, keep your backpacking menu simple, especially for longer trips. Raise the challenge level only after you've become more skilled and confident in your abilities. Taking on more than one can manage is a common mistake, and the botched meal that results is sure to disappoint your famished stomach.

- Foul weather adds a powerful variable to the outdoor cooking equation. And bugs and wild animals further distract by keeping the cook on the defensive. Prior to any outing, weather and critters should be considered and appropriately planned for. Be realistic about what you can handle under the circumstances you're likely to encounter. The more trying the conditions, the simpler the menu should be.

- When traveling in a group, enlist help and divide cooking and cleanup duties among everyone in the group. The recipes in this book use numerical sequencing for the instructions. Use this feature to best assign tasks to helpers.

- Make sure you can manage the additional workload when assigning tasks to new chefs. If cooking in inclement weather or under an extreme time crunch, there will come a better time to engage the assistance of inexperienced cooks.

- Groceries account for a large fraction of cost on most outings, and it's natural to attempt to keep these expenses reasonable. However, cost cutting can be taken to an extreme, with ingredients of such low quality that it's painfully obvious, meal after meal. Be prudent about cost-cutting measures. Spend the extra money when it makes sense. Once on the trail the difference in quality will be appreciated.

- Any dish can end its short life tragically dumped in the dirt by fate or accident. Many miles from the nearest road, Plan B's are hard to come by in the wilderness. If mealtime goes awry, you'll have no choice but to replan the menu for the remainder of the trip to offset the lost food. One such event shouldn't cause undue hardship to you and any folks traveling with you.

- Now, if a bear happens to abscond with the entire food stash, or the meal bag is inadvertently dropped over a cliff into a raging river, that's another story. Quickly take stock of any remaining inventory. If reserves are low, carefully plan how to stretch the remaining food and be prepared to head straight back to civilization, recognizing that a couple of days without grub never hurt anyone. As your stomach grumbles, don't forget to stay properly hydrated. Your body needs the water more than the food, and it can help lessen the hunger pains until that wondrous moment when you finally make it off the trail and into the nearest restaurant.

Menu Selection and Preparation at Home
- The typical adult or older teen will eat no more than about 1½ pounds of packed food per day, assuming that most, if not all, of the food has been dried. This weight value easily doubles or even triples when you're carrying fresh foods or canned goods. For a long trek spanning a week, about 10 pounds of mostly dried food will be adequate for most hikers. (In contrast, if canned goods comprised most of the food items, the weight would increase to nearly 30 pounds!) Total pack weight should not exceed one-quarter of your body weight to avoid overstressing joints and muscles, and food should not exceed one-quarter to one third of pack weight to leave adequate room for other critical gear. For a 30- to 40-pound pack, then, foods other than dried generally become too heavy once the trip length exceeds a few days.

- One-pot meals are the backbone of most trail menus, because less equipment, fuel, and effort are required for preparation compared to multicourse meals. But don't think that one-pot recipes make meals boring. There are many very good one-pot recipes, including those in this book, that stand perfectly well on their own.

- It's easier to prepare for a backpacking trip by multiplying good recipes for use on more than one day instead of preparing a unique recipe for every meal. But even a great recipe can become tiring if eaten too often, so balance convenience with variety when planning your menu.

- Most backpacking recipes are easy to prepare on the trail; but even many of the easiest require fairly accurate measurements of water or oils for final preparation. For these in particular, it is important that the on-trail directions be included with the recipe. Don't forget them! See www.lipsmackincampin.com/packable/lvbp_2ed.pdf to print packable on-trail directions for all recipes in this book.

- For overnight trips, special food preparation is usually unnecessary. With plenty of room in the backpack, canned goods, fresh fruits and vegetables, and larger and heavier cooking gear can be managed. If you do bring canned goods on short trips, don't forget the can opener! Many are the stories of frustrated backpackers who've had to resort to opening their cans with blows from rocks.

- For longer trips spanning more than a few days, it becomes difficult to justify the substantial weight penalty associated with foods that have not been dried. A larger portion of your meals should consist of dried foods on treks like these. For trips spanning four days or more, almost all foods should be dried, for reasons of weight and durability.

- Water accounts for most of the weight of fresh fruits and vegetables, about 80 percent of which can be eliminated through drying. For canned goods, the fraction saved may be even higher; the can itself accounts for as much as one-quarter of the weight. By eliminating the can, draining the liquid, drying the contents in a dehydrator, and repackaging the food in a plastic food bag, as much as 90 percent of the initial weight can be removed.

- When bringing along dried foods originally prepackaged in boxes, such as rice mixes, repackage the contents in ziplock bags for the trail. By removing the packaging, trail trash can be reduced and some weight saved in the process. In addition, ziplock bags pack more efficiently than boxes, because the bags are free to conform to the confines of the pack. Be sure to clip any relevant directions from the box and place them along with the food in the ziplock bag.

- Package dry foods and ingredients in high-quality ziplock bags just large enough to do the job. Standard ziplock bags are usually appropriate, but for more aromatic or jagged foods—or for challenging duty, such as when used with warm water in rehydrating foods on the trail—heavy-duty freezer-type bags are a better choice. Less expensive or generic-brand bags tend to have thinner walls or less robust seals, so use these with caution.

- Once filled, squeeze as much air as possible from storage bags, then seal tightly. Recheck the seal to be sure it is securely shut, then store the bag in the refrigerator or freezer until ready to head to the trail. When it's time to load the backpack, ingredients packaged individually for a given recipe can be gathered together into a larger size bag to create a self-contained meal.

- Always label ziplock bags with the recipe name, number of servings, and date packaged. Other useful information to note could include simple instructions, such as the amount of water required.

- Lightweight and durable, condiment packets are an excellent way to liven up foods on the trail. Catsup, taco sauce, barbecue sauce, hot sauce, relish, mayonnaise, mustard, honey, syrups, jellies, lemon juice, grated Parmesan cheese, and dried red pepper are some of the choices available. Save any extras from restaurants that you frequent or purchase them online in bulk from wholesale suppliers.

- Fresh butter is suitable for short treks but lacks durability for longer trips. Dried butter substitutes, such as Butter Buds, are an easy, good-tasting, and durable alternative for many recipes.

- Soy milk powder can often be exchanged in like amounts for dairy milk powder; and olive oil can typically be exchanged for butter, ounce for ounce.

- Use an accurate kitchen scale when preparing foods for the trail. Be sure the final weight is close to that specified by the recipe. If it isn't, this is a telltale sign that something is amiss, either with the recipe or the preparation; troubleshoot the problem before you hit the trail. A bath scale is valuable for determining the combined weight of the packed gear, to help with keeping the total weight of the pack below target, and for equally distributing the gear and food load between other backpackers who may be traveling with you.

- When packing equipment for the trail, use a checklist. By doing so you are less likely to forget a critical piece of gear. Review the list after each trip and modify it as required as you gain experience. Checklists tend to be very personal, and you'll soon discover that no two ever seem to be the same.

- To decrease the risk of their failure in a situation when you can least afford it, test recipes at home or on short trips before relying on them during longer or more challenging expeditions.

- Don't neglect nutrition on the trail. It's important to balance fats, carbohydrates, and proteins while backpacking. Carbohydrates provide a more rapidly available source of energy than do fats, and by combining the two, short- and long-term energy levels are more likely to be sustained. Proteins are valuable for extending the utilization of carbohydrates. Fats at suppertime are particularly useful in cold weather, as they help the body sleep more warmly throughout the night. Constipation is a common problem on the trail, but a fiber-rich diet, along with plenty of water, will help maintain regularity. Choose healthier fats, such as olive oil, when cooking, and avoid filling up on empty calories from simple sugars.

- If a bear-proof food canister is not required for the area you'll be visiting, gather all meals together into a large sturdy food sack for the backpack. Avoid placing your food at the bottom of the backpack, where it will be subjected to weight from heavy items above it. Instead, position the bag in the center of the pack, close to the forward (strap-side) wall of the backpack. This positions the food in a less compressed and cooler area of the pack while keeping the center of gravity farther forward, a more comfortable location for the backpacker.

Preparation on the Trail

- Review and understand your recipes before commencing preparation in the field. You're less likely to make a critical mistake if you do. And be sure to have everything needed before starting to cook by first gathering together all ingredients and utensils.

- A lot of purified water is an obvious requirement during the high exertion of walking the trail. But a surprisingly large amount is also required in camp for cooking, cleaning, and replenishing the body's reserves. To minimize wilderness impact, a trail camp should never be established next to a water source unless a dedicated area has been created for the purpose. Of course, one drawback to camping away from water is the need to haul it from the source back to camp. For this reason, a collapsible plastic water carrier or dromedary bag, with a capacity of a gallon or more, is an ideal way of keeping a supply of water close at hand. The carrier can be quickly filled with raw water at the source, then purified as needed at camp.

- An extension of the previous point is to avoid the vicinity of water altogether when stopping for the night, and instead, look for out-of-the-way areas with incredible vistas . . . and fewer bugs. Often called "dry camping," the idea is to purposely tank up on water at the source, with reserves adequate for the night and following morning, then continue along the trail to a campsite with a grand view or other redeeming quality. This is a liberating technique, opening up a vastly larger world of camping opportunities along the trail, while moving campsite wear-and-tear away from the more heavily used water sources.

- Nonfat dry milk powders are notorious for lumping during reconstitution, more so when using water that is cold. Of course warm water, and therefore warm milk, does not make for a good bowl of cold cereal in the morning. A method for avoiding lumping is to first add a very small amount of water, warm or cold, to the powder in a drinking cup, stirring until it becomes a thick, smooth paste. The remainder of the water, even if cold, can then be added and blended with no resulting lumps.

- Whole-fat milk powders generally reconstitute with less clumping compared to nonfat varieties. Many people find the taste more pleasing as well. Whole milk powder, such as Nestle's Nido, can be found in the Hispanic food section at the grocery store. It is also widely available online.

- Carry a selection of favorite dried herbs and spices on the trail to satisfy individual preferences. Small containers specifically for this purpose are available from backpacking suppliers.

- Etch water bottles, containers, or mugs in measures of a cup and fractions of a cup for determining required amounts of water when cooking on the trail. Many transparent or translucent water containers come premarked with measuring lines specifically for this purpose. Learn to estimate one teaspoon and one tablespoon as measured using your backpacking spoon.

- Although often necessary when carrying fresh vegetables, chopping and slicing isn't required for most trail recipes using dried ingredients. However, when knife work is called for, the clean inside bottom of a bare-metal cook pot or lid makes an adequate substitute for a cutting board.

- With the type of cooking equipment and methods now available, it can be hard to imagine how much effort went into camp cooking in the not-too-distant past. Roasting pits and trenches, roaring fires, wooden tripods, and cooking boards all had a reason and a place at one time but left behind a scar in the wilderness that was slow to heal. With modern gear these damaging methods and techniques are no longer necessary on the trail. Use appropriate tools and equipment to minimize your impact to the trail environment and to truly leave no trace.

Managing the Heat

- Become familiar with your cooking stove and how much fuel is required to prepare a meal. Don't forget fuel required for heating water for coffee, tea, and other hot drinks. Bring extra for contingency, especially if the weather is to be wet or cold. Monitor fuel consumption while on the trail and adjust your use accordingly if burning too much too quickly. Test your cooking equipment before leaving home, looking for clogging or leaks. Be sure your gear is in good working order, and carry a repair kit for contingency. Maintenance kits are very lightweight and take little room in the pack.

- Use a windscreen and, if your stove comes with one, a base plate to improve fuel efficiency. Both reflect heat back onto the pot or skillet and should be employed to save fuel even if the weather isn't windy. Likewise, place the lid on your pot when cooking to help retain heat.

- Pack ovens are wonderful devices that open up a world of baked food options on the trail. If baking with a pack oven that uses water, never allow the oven to boil dry. Otherwise the plastic oven bag is likely to melt and create a truly nasty mess in your cook pot.

- For some recipes, ziplock food storage bags make attractive cooking containers because they can simplify food preparation and reduce the hassle of cleanup. However, some plastics used in food storage bags may begin to soften at temperatures close to the boiling point of water. There is growing debate over the safety implications of such. However, rehydrating foods in storage bags using hot water, as opposed to boiling the bag directly, is generally considered safe, because the temperature of boiled water very quickly drops once the water is removed from the heat source and introduced to the bag. If rehydrating foods in storage bags using hot water is a concern for you, stick with your cook pot instead.

- An alternative to rehydrating foods in plastic storage bags with hot water is to use roasting bags instead. These are specifically designed for use at temperatures much higher than the boiling point of water and are correspondingly more expensive. While these bags can't be sealed in ziplock fashion, the open necks can be twisted and tied, with the top of the bag positioned so as not to collect steam or water.

- The boiling point of water decreases with altitude, dropping, for example, by nearly 20°F at 12,000 feet elevation compared to sea level. With the decrease in water temperature, foods will take longer to cook, requiring more time on the stove and more fuel. Bring extra fuel for contingency at high altitude and be prepared to stir often and to sample your food more frequently to be sure it's ready to serve.

Dealing with the Weather

- Perhaps the most challenging of all outdoor cooking situations involves rain. In a heavy downpour, the only options may be to cease and desist and wait it out, serve no-cook foods, or move the stove under a fire-safe tarp if you're fortunate to have one. Never cook in a sleeping tent.

- In light rain the pot itself, along with a windscreen, is usually adequate for shielding the burner, allowing cooking to commence and continue. This is also the moment when you'll be glad to have brought along a box of waterproof matches!

- Snow presents its own unique challenges to cooking; usually the most difficult is locating a decent place to set the stove. In mountainous areas, the tops of large rocks or boulders can often be found free of snow, as can the ground along the downwind side of the same. In areas with rapidly changing topography, it usually is just a matter of time before a snow-free area can be found along the trail. If snow stretches as far as the eye can see, but isn't deep, a suitable spot can be cleared by hand and foot. Place the stove on a pot lid set into packed snow if it's deep.

Keeping It Clean While Cooking on the Trail

- Maintain a close eye on your food while cooking so that it doesn't burn. Charred grub is difficult to remove from cookware and requires much more time, water, and detergent during cleanup.

- Use dishwashing detergent sparingly during cleanup, just enough for the job. Only detergents that are biodegradable should be used outdoors. Bring a small piece of scrub pad for tackling stuck-on foods. Clean coarse sand or small rock scree, along with a little water, are also very effective for cleaning the insides of pots and pans, provided the cookware isn't coated in nonstick material, which would otherwise be damaged by the bits of rock.

- Grease and stuck-on food are cut more easily, and with less detergent, when you use warm water. If you can spare the fuel, throw a little water in the soiled pot or skillet, warm the water briefly, splash it around, then let the cookware sit for a few minutes before scrubbing.

- Dispose of wash and rinse water, also called "gray water," in a manner acceptable for your particular area. Never dump gray water directly into a stream or lake. If the rinse water contains large bits of food, strain these out and dispose of them with your pack trash. If the area you are visiting is particularly sensitive ecologically or contains wild animals that may be especially interested in your food, then gray water should be disposed of like fecal matter—in a cat hole covered with several inches of soil and located at least 200 feet from the nearest water source. Always follow any local regulations regarding waste disposal.

- Dirty cookware left to lie will eventually attract bugs and wild animals. To avoid such interest, ensure that all utensils have been washed and rinsed before leaving base camp during the day or when retiring for the evening.

- Minimize the use of aluminum foil, which tends to shred into small pieces that are easy to miss during cleanup and remain unsightly for years. Likewise, keep a close eye on smaller trash bits, such as empty condiment packs, bouillon cube wrappers, and the like. A good practice is to immediately place small trash items in a larger bag before they are dropped and possibly forgotten.

- Reclaimed ziplock bags, used to carry food for your trip but now empty following the meal, make excellent trash receptacles. Squeezed to remove air then sealed tightly, they can be placed bag in bag to isolate aromatic and rotting waste. If carrying your dried food in ziplocks, you are unlikely to find yourself short on trash containers.

- Bear-proof food canisters are the best option when visiting areas with high bruin activity. They are neither inexpensive nor lightweight, but the peace of mind and convenience they bring over conventional bear bagging can't be overstated. In fact in some areas and parks, their use is required by law.

- When bear bagging, use a large sack to pack all foods along with any aromatics that could attract animal attention, including trash and toiletries. All items should be in waterproof storage bags, such as ziplocks, to keep them dry in case of rain. Be sure to use a stout sack to hold your stash, beefy enough to suspend it all off the ground without rupturing like a piñata in the middle of the night. You also need a long, strong hanging rope, at least 40 feet in length, to hoist it all. As any experienced backpacker knows, the perfect bear-bagging tree is a cruel myth. But try to find it anyway, one with a thick tree limb 15 or more feet from, and parallel to, the ground. Toss the rope over the limb and hoist the food bag. The bag should hang at least six feet off the trunk of the tree so that a climbing bear can't reach out and grab it. Likewise, the bag should rest several feet under the branch from which it hangs. Securely tie off the loose end of the rope to a neighboring tree.

- In some areas the bears are smart enough to defeat the bagging techniques described, and the more-involved process of counterbalancing may be required. Even that may not stop Yogi. However, if the bears in the area are this intelligent, local regulations most likely require the use of a bear-proof container anyway.

Key Equipment for Trail and Home

- All backpackers seem to have a strong personal preference regarding stoves, and there are persuasive pros and cons for each design. There are four major classes of the most common trail stoves: gasoline, alcohol, propane canister, and solid fuel. Gasoline stoves, some of which also burn kerosene, diesel, or even jet fuel, operate under pressure, generate tremendous heat, and work well at all altitudes. Because of their stability, gasoline stoves are arguably the best option for frying, especially when using larger pans. Alcohol stoves operate unpressurized and are very compact and lightweight. They are most useful for preparing single servings in a small metal cup or pot and are not well suited for cooking for groups. Propane stoves are also very lightweight and compact, with good heat output and excellent simmering capability for more delicate foods, but they are generally less stable than gasoline stoves, and their fuel canisters are bulky for the amount of energy they pack. The fuel remaining in a canister can also be difficult to judge, making it more challenging to manage fuel reserves. Solid fuel stoves use combustible tablets and are perhaps the lightest and simplest system to use. But, like alcohol stoves, they work best for heating water in small quantities and not for cooking for long periods of time. Some fuel tablets have a strong, somewhat off odor requiring layers of packaging to prevent transfer to other gear.

- Your cookware should be well matched to your stove and the types of recipes you'd like to prepare. For a lightweight alcohol stove, for instance, a single-serving metal cup is all that would be required for cookware. However, for recipes that make more than one serving, a true pot and sturdy stove may be necessary. And if frying is on the menu, you'll also need a lid that can also serve as a skillet.

- The selection of backpacking cookware is large and somewhat bewildering, but if you plan to cook for more than yourself, and would like to occasionally do some frying, all you'll need is a simple pot and multifunction lid. For packability and safety, select gear that has retractable or removable handles. Pots of about 2½-quart capacity are very good for handling six-serving recipes or less. Pack a small pot or simply a large metal cup when cooking for only yourself or a couple of people at most. Larger pots are too massive and unstable for many stoves, unnecessarily large for most backpack recipes, and more difficult to pack.

- Cookware comes in an assortment of metals and coatings, and some is sold in sets specifically designed to work with certain stoves. Standard aluminum is the least expensive material, but it's also the least durable. Anodized aluminum is a tougher variant with modest nonstick quality, but it's more expensive. Stainless steel is rugged but tends to be heavier than other metals. Titanium alloys are extremely light and tough, but they are also significantly more expensive than the other options. Nonstick surfaces definitely make cleanup easier in the wilderness, but some coatings are prone to damage and can eventually begin to flake off. The final choice regarding materials and coatings comes down to personal preference and budget.

- A pack *oven,* as opposed to a pack *stove,* isn't required, but can definitely broaden your repertoire, as it offers many new baking options on the trail. A lightweight and inexpensive insert, the pack oven is an ingenious modification of the simple trivet. It turns a cook pot into a double-boiler oven in water-based units, like the BakePacker. Breads, pancakes, and desserts are baked in high-temperature roasting bags. Pack ovens can require a significant amount of time for baking, but if you have the fuel to spare, and don't mind the extra few ounces in weight, they are simple to use and a lot of fun.

- Don't forget cooking and serving utensils for the trail. A short wooden spoon is ideal for stirring. A small plastic spatula is a must for frying pancakes and other foods that require flipping. Pack all cooking gear into a mesh bag of appropriate size to allow the equipment to breathe and dry when it is in your backpack.

- At home, a blender is essential for pureeing chunky foods so they can produce smooth fruit and sauce leathers. A food processor is handy for slicing or chopping foods to a uniform consistency prior to drying. And a food scale is invaluable for weighing ingredients and evenly subdividing a recipe into smaller serving sizes.

- A food dehydrator is indispensable for vastly expanding the range of trail cooking options, adapting your favorite home recipes for the trail, and maximizing and customizing the nutrition content of your trail foods. It is a surprisingly easy appliance to use. For more information, see the next section, where dried foods and dehydration are given exclusive treatment.

Reducing Weight and Improving Durability with Dried Foods

Whether performed at a factory for common food items found at the grocery store, or done at home for use on the trail, the reasons for drying foods are the same: Water makes up most of the weight of many food items and is an essential prerequisite for spoilage. So by removing the water through the process of drying, the food becomes much lighter and lasts longer. Dried foods are also more resistant to rough handling than those with a high water content. For all of these reasons, the process of drying food provides benefits that are ideal for backpackers.

Freeze-drying and dehydrating are the two primary techniques used to dry foods for the trail. Reconstitution is the process of rehydrating dried food back to its original state. On the trail this is usually done with hot water, although cold water often works, given enough time.

Freeze-drying is performed commercially using industrial equipment to remove moisture through a rapid deep-freezing process. Most prepackaged meal options available at outfitters have been freeze-dried. Freeze-dried meals are a convenient option for the backpacker who is short on time or prefers to minimize the cooking effort. However, freeze-dried meals have some disadvantages: They are expensive per serving, the packages are often bulky for the quantity of food provided, and the serving sizes can be awkward for the actual group size. While many freeze-dried meals are quite tasty, many aren't; and costly surprises can await the backpacker on the trail, unless each menu selection is sampled previously. These disadvantages make freeze-dried meals less desirable, especially when packing for longer trips or preparing food for a group of backpackers.

On the other hand, *dehydrating* is the process of using low heat over a period of hours or days to slowly and gently remove moisture from food. It is a simple and inexpensive process, and it can be performed easily at home using an appliance called a food dehydrator. A new, high-quality home food dehydrator can be purchased for about the same cost as a good quality blender. Dehydrators come in two primary designs. One design uses stackable round trays with a blower at either the top or bottom of the unit, the other uses a rectangular cabinet and slide-out trays over which warm air is blown. Each design has its advantages, depending on the task, but either performs well in drying foods for the trail. All models provide some method for adjusting temperature; and fine-mesh screens are usually included to permit drying of small-size food items, such as rice, that would otherwise fall through the trays. Additional accessories can make the drying process more convenient, but they aren't required for the recipes in this book.

Dehydrating foods and ingredients at home allows you to customize an endless variety of your favorite recipes for the trail. Serving sizes and amounts can be tailored to your needs. And to top it off, the ingredients shrink dramatically in size once dry, taking up less volume in your pack. For all of these reasons, combined with the cost-effective nature of home drying, dehydrated foods are a great option for backpacking trips.

Entire books have been written about the art of food dehydrating, but that doesn't mean you have to read one to successfully dry foods. The finer points of drying food are certainly worth learning, but they often relate to preparing foods for very long storage times or to those foods that are less common on the trail. You should understand the nuances of your own dehydrator, of course, to help ensure safe use and predictable results, but by becoming familiar with the following list of drying tips and recommendations, you'll be ready to tackle most any backpacking menu.

Steps for Maximizing Shelf Life and Improving Food Quality

- To minimize the chance of contaminating your food, thoroughly clean and dry your hands, preparation surfaces, cooking utensils, and dehydrating trays before commencing.

- Properly dried and sealed fruits, vegetables, and grains can last a year or more on the shelf. Remember: The more moisture or oils remaining in a dried food, the shorter its shelf life. Refrigeration greatly extends the life of foods once they've been dried, freezing even more so. Sealing dried foods tightly in high-quality food storage bags is necessary to maximize the longevity and preserve the taste.

- In very humid kitchen environments, dry the foods as usual, place in airtight containers for a few days to give any remaining moisture time to redistribute, then return the food to the drying trays for another round. This is an effective way to reduce the probability of spoilage due to mold.

- Always closely inspect your dried foods before packing them for the trip and cooking on the trail. Any patches of discoloration or molding, or an odd aroma, is an indication that the food has begun to spoil and should be discarded.

Planning for Drying

- Many food items can be dried overnight, but some foods may need as much as a full day or more to dehydrate, especially thick purees or leathers. If a lot of drying will be required for an upcoming trip, consider the capacity of your dehydrator and be sure to set aside enough time to do the entire job. It can take more than a week to dry the food required for a long excursion.

- Dried foods tend to pack a lot of nutrients per ounce, and this is especially true of fruit leathers. Some fruits make better tasting leathers than others; and some combinations, apple-and-berry combos, for instance, are truly wonderful. Certain fruits, like blueberries, produce a better texture when blended with other fruits before drying.

- The kitchen oven is naturally attractive for drying because of its large capacity, provided that the door can be held open slightly to allow moisture to escape. But the lowest achievable temperature on many ovens is higher than that recommended for drying many fruits and vegetables.

- Foods that contain a large fraction of high-fructose corn syrup, such as some canned fruits or pie fillings, can be impossible to dry, forever remaining very sticky to the touch. If attempting to dehydrate these types of foods, the results may be disappointing.

Preparing Foods for Drying

- The more finely chopped the ingredients and the more consistent the sizes of the pieces, the more uniformly they will dehydrate and the better they will reconstitute on the trail. Also ensure that pieces are spaced evenly on the drying trays for better air circulation.

- Don't mix different types of highly aromatic foods in the same drying batch to avoid intermingling flavors. The same holds true when mixing odorous foods with less aromatic types. As an example, it would be unadvisable to dry garlic and onions with a batch of fruit leathers!

- When drying sauce for spaghetti or soup on the trail, use a blender to puree chunky blends into a smooth consistency before drying. Texture can be introduced back to the sauces and soups at camp by adding dried vegetables and the like at the time of cooking.

- Thick liquids, such as spaghetti sauces and purees, can be dried in shallow pools on parchment paper, cut to the proper shape for your trays, or on reusable liners specifically designed for this purpose. Depending on the design of your dehydrator, very runny liquids are sometimes best dried in solid plastic trays specially made for your unit.

- Darkening of fruit and vegetables during and following drying naturally occurs due to oxidation. This doesn't affect the taste of the food, but it can be surprising to the uninitiated. There are several ways to reduce or eliminate the occurrence of oxidation when drying, but a reasonably effective and easy method is to soak sliced fruits and vegetables for 5 minutes in a bath of ¼ cup lemon juice to 1 quart water prior to drying.

- Blanching is the process of lightly steaming or boiling, but not thoroughly cooking, fruits or vegetables prior to dehydrating. Blanching is helpful in that it can extend a food's shelf life and improve its appearance once dried. It can also help speed the rehydration process for some foods. But, while beneficial, blanching is not a requirement, especially if the trip you're preparing for will occur within the next couple of months. Blanching produces no benefit to onions, tomatoes, and mushrooms, which have naturally long shelf lives and stable appearance when dried.

- Precooking, or parboiling, pasta and rice, then drying in the dehydrator, will greatly reduce cooking and reconstitution time on the trail. When parboiling, it even becomes possible to have excellent cold pasta and rice salads on the trail, because many parboiled foods can fully reconstitute using only cold water.

- Corn, legumes (peas and beans, for example), and root crops (carrots, in particular) should always be thoroughly cooked before drying. They will not dry or reconstitute satisfactorily otherwise.

Maintaining the Proper Drying Environment

- Typical drying temperatures range from the upper 90s to low 100s°F for drying fragile leafy vegetables, through 125°F for most chopped or sliced vegetables, to 135°F for fruits and purees. Follow the specific guidelines and settings that come with your dehydrator.

- It may be tempting to crank the temperature beyond recommended to hasten the drying process, but there's a very good reason for keeping to the specified range. When setting the temperature too high with fruits and vegetables, not only are healthful enzymes potentially destroyed, but the outer surface of the food pieces can rapidly dry and harden, trapping moisture in the interior and leading to rapid spoilage. By drying at lower temperatures, the dehydration process progresses more uniformly from inside to out. But don't take the temperature below the recommended range: The dehydration process can take so long that your food items can actually begin to spoil before drying is complete.

- When drying foods that tend to clump, such as rice, break up the clusters after half a day or so of dehydrating, then redistribute. This will hasten the remaining process and help ensure more uniform drying. If your dehydrator is new to you, check the progress of the drying every few hours to learn the subtleties. Rotate or restack trays to keep the drying uniform.

- Some foods retain a leathery and pliable texture once fully dried, whereas other types of foods become very crisp. With a little experience you'll find that you rarely underdry food. The instruction manual that comes with your dehydrator can help you identify the drying characteristics of a large variety of foods to help you get it right the first time.

Packaging Dried Foods

- Once removed from the dehydrator, allow dried foods to cool, then immediately transfer them to tightly sealed storage bags or containers.

- Quality ziplock bags with a sturdy seal are excellent for storing dehydrated foods. Pack a few extra bags for the trail just in case a seal breaks or a seam ruptures on a bag holding your dried foods.

- Remove fruit leather while it is still warm and pliable but not sticky. If overdried or allowed to cool completely, the leather may become brittle and more difficult to roll, though certainly still edible. Fruit leathers can be individually rolled on sheets of wax paper to prevent sticking.

- Vacuum sealing has debatable value for extending the life of some packaged trail foods, because the jagged edges of dried foods often puncture the tightly compressed walls of the vacuum bag, defeating the original objective of an airtight seal and permitting the entry of moisture from the air.

Bringing Your Dried Food Back to Life on the Trail

- Some dehydrated foods can be slower to rehydrate than others while cooking. And dehydrated foods tend to rehydrate more slowly than their freeze-dried counterparts. Don't expect all dehydrated foods to return to the same predried state once rehydrated. Many do not, being slightly smaller or chewier in texture. This is inconsequential to most recipes, since the goal is soft and tasty, not pretty.

- The best method for reconstituting dried food depends on the specific item and how it was dried. An extended simmer is usually required for foods that were not thoroughly cooked prior to drying, such as fresh vegetables. Foods that were precooked prior to drying are often restored simply by pouring hot water over the dried food in a cup or pot, then setting it aside for an appropriate amount of time, covering it to help trap heat and moisture. Some precooked foods restore well using cold water, although the time for reconstitution takes longer than when using hot water. The recipes in this book specify the method most appropriate for the foods being rehydrated.

Not all trail recipes require dehydrating foods at home, but many require dried foods of some sort, whether purchased at the grocery store or online. There are several web-based retailers of dried ingredients, and the range of foods now available is truly incredible. Check out the list of suppliers in Appendix B and challenge your creativity.

Breakfast

NIAGARA BARS

V-LO

Total Servings: 16 (2 bars per serving)
As Packaged for the Trail: As required
Weight per Serving: 2 ounces
Preparation Time on the Trail: None
Challenge Level: Easy

Preparation at Home:
1. Preheat oven to 325°F.
2. In a large bowl, mix all dry ingredients together.
3. Heat oil, honey, and vanilla extract in a pan, then add to the dry ingredients in the bowl. Stir well.
4. Pat batter into a 9x13-inch parchment-lined pan. Batter should be about ½-inch thick in pan.
5. Bake for 30 minutes.
6. Cool, then slice into 32 bars.
7. Package bars for the trail, assuming 2 bars per serving.

Preparation on the Trail:
None

Sherry Bennett
Rochester, New York

2⅔ cups old-fashioned oats

½ cup plus 1 tablespoon whole wheat flour

6 tablespoons all-purpose wheat flour

½ cup sesame seeds

½ cup brown sugar

¼ teaspoon ground cinnamon

1½ teaspoons salt

⅓ cup instant dry nonfat milk

½ cup vegetable oil

¾ cup honey

2 teaspoons vanilla extract

Required Equipment on the Trail:
None

Nutritional Information per Serving:
Calories: 226
Protein: 4 g
Fat: 10 g
Carbohydrates: 30 g
Fiber: 2 g
Sodium: 234 mg
Cholesterol: 2 mg

GRIZZLY BERRY GRANOLA

Total Servings: 12
As Packaged for the Trail: 1 serving
Weight per Serving: 3 ounces
Preparation Time on the Trail: None
Challenge Level: Easy

¼ cup vegetable oil

1 (18-ounce) jar blackberry jelly

2 cups chopped, lightly salted cashews

1 (16-ounce) package Bob's Red Mill 5-Grain Rolled hot cereal

1 cup shredded sweetened coconut

1 ounce dried blueberries

1 ounce dried strawberries

1 ounce dried blackberries or raspberries

Optional: instant dry milk to taste

Required Equipment on the Trail:
None

Nutritional Information per Serving:
Calories: 473
Protein: 10 g
Fat: 19 g
Carbohydrates: 69 g
Fiber: 8 g
Sodium: 65 mg
Cholesterol: 0 mg

Preparation at Home:
1. In a large pot, heat oil and jelly over low heat until thin.
2. Add chopped cashews to pot along with the cereal and coconut.
3. Stir until liquid has evenly covered the mixture.
4. Evenly spread granola in a nonstick jelly roll pan.
5. Bake at 225°F for 2 hours, stirring periodically.
6. Remove granola from oven and allow to cool completely.
7. Add dried fruit to granola and stir.
8. Place about 1 cup granola into each of 12 quart-size ziplock bags. Each bag produces 1 serving.
9. Pack optional instant dry milk separately.

Preparation on the Trail:
For a single serving, eat straight from the bag or add optional milk, cold or warm.

Christine and Tim Conners
Statesboro, Georgia

ROCKHOUSE BASIN APPLE GRANOLA

Total Servings: 10
As Packaged for the Trail: 1 serving
Weight per Serving: 4 ounces
Preparation Time on the Trail: None
Challenge Level: Easy

"Something unexpected happened on Columbus Day, 1992, in the Rockhouse Basin of California's Domeland Wilderness. On what was just a simple day hike, I (Tim) wasn't interested in going and essentially had to be dragged along by friends. But as the day wore on, the beauty and wonder of this area began to work their magic, and I couldn't wait to return. Several weeks later, I did just that on what would become my first multi-day trip. Making all the mistakes a novice can, the die was nevertheless cast, and I was absolutely hooked on backpacking."

Preparation at Home:

1. In a large pot, heat oil and jelly over low heat until thin.
2. Add cereal, pecan pieces, and coconut to the pot.
3. Stir until liquid has evenly covered the mixture.
4. Evenly spread granola in a nonstick jelly roll pan.
5. Bake at 225°F for 2 hours, stirring periodically.
6. Remove granola from oven and allow to cool completely.
7. Add chopped dried apples to granola and stir.
8. Place about 1 cup granola into each of 10 pint-size ziplock bags. Each bag produces 1 serving.
9. Pack optional instant dry milk separately.

Preparation on the Trail:
For a single serving, eat straight from the bag or add optional milk, cold or warm.

Christine and Tim Conners
Statesboro, Georgia

¼ cup vegetable oil

1 (18-ounce) jar apple jelly

1 (16-ounce) package Bob's Red Mill 5-Grain Rolled hot cereal

1½ cups (about 6 ounces) pecan pieces

1 cup shredded sweetened coconut

5 ounces dried apple rings, chopped

Optional: instant dry milk to taste

Required Equipment on the Trail:
None

Nutritional Information per Serving:
Calories: 480
Protein: 8 g
Fat: 19 g
Carbohydrates: 77 g
Fiber: 8 g
Sodium: 121 mg
Cholesterol: 0 mg

MOUNTAIN MUESLI

Total Servings: 10
As Packaged for the Trail: As required
Weight per Serving: 4 ounces
Preparation Time on the Trail: None
Challenge Level: Easy

4 cups regular oats

½ cup wheat germ

½ cup shredded sweetened coconut

1 cup chopped honey-roasted peanuts

1 cup honey

Optional: salt to taste

1 cup dried cherries or your favorite dried fruit

Optional: instant dry soy or dairy milk to taste

Required Equipment on the Trail:
None

Nutritional Information per Serving:
Calories: 540
Protein: 16 g
Fat: 12 g
Carbohydrates: 95 g
Fiber: 5 g
Sodium: 70 mg
Cholesterol: 0 mg

Preparation at Home:
1. Preheat oven to 200°F.
2. In a large bowl, combine oats, wheat germ, coconut, peanuts, honey, and optional salt. Stir well.
3. Evenly spread mixture over a large baking tray, then toast in oven for 30 minutes.
4. Remove tray from oven and allow to cool.
5. Sprinkle dried cherries over oat mixture.
6. Package muesli in ziplock bags for the trail, according to the number of servings that will be needed, using a little less than 1 cup mixture per serving.
7. Carry optional instant dry milk separately.

Preparation on the Trail:
A little less than 1 cup of muesli mix provides 1 serving. Eat as is or serve with optional instant dry milk and water, cold or warm.

Heather Burror
Martinez, California

SEVEN HILLS MUESLI

Number of Servings: 13
As Packaged for the Trail: 1 serving
Weight per Serving: 4 ounces
Preparation Time on the Trail: None
Challenge Level: Easy

V-LO

"I (Christine) was introduced to this recipe during a trip to Rome, Italy. I'll admit to having initially cringed at the sight of chocolate mixed with oatmeal, but 'when in Rome...' So I gave it a try and was pleasantly surprised! The light use of chocolate adds a delicate sweetness to the oats."

Preparation at Home:
1. Combine chocolate, pecans, cherries or apricots, and rolled oats in a very large bowl. Stir well.
2. Place about 1 cup of granola into each of 13 pint-size ziplock bags. Each bag provides 1 serving.
3. Pack optional instant dry milk separately.

Preparation on the Trail:
For a single serving, eat straight from the bag or add optional milk, cold or warm.

Christine and Tim Conners
Statesboro, Georgia

4 ounces 60-percent cacao bittersweet chocolate bar, finely chopped

8 ounces pecans, finely chopped

8 ounces dried unsweetened tart cherries or apricots, finely chopped

2 pounds rolled oats

Optional: instant dry milk to taste

Required Equipment on the Trail:
None

Nutritional Information per Serving:
Calories: 562
Protein: 15 g
Fat: 22 g
Carbohydrates: 76 g
Fiber: 15 g
Sodium: 2 mg
Cholesterol: 4 mg

OL' KOOGER'S MOUNTAIN HIGH GRANOLA

V-LO

Total Servings: 14
As Packaged for the Trail: 1 serving
Weight per Serving: 5 ounces
Preparation Time on the Trail: 5 minutes
Challenge Level: Easy

6 cups rolled oats

1 cup wheat bran

2 cups wheat germ

½ cup shredded sweetened coconut

1 cup brown sugar

1½ cups chopped pecans

1 cup honey

¼ cup vegetable oil

1 tablespoon vanilla extract

1½ cups dried fruit (raisins, apricots, and dried cranberries, or your choice)

4⅔ cups instant dry nonfat milk

1 cup water per serving, added on the trail

Required Equipment on the Trail:
None

Nutritional Information per Serving:
Calories: 587
Protein: 19 g
Fat: 17 g
Carbohydrates: 96 g
Fiber: 9 g
Sodium: 141 mg
Cholesterol: 5 mg

Preparation at Home:
1. Preheat oven to 325°F.
2. In a large bowl, thoroughly mix oats, bran, wheat germ, coconut, brown sugar, and pecans.
3. In a pan over low heat, bring honey, oil, and vanilla extract to a slight boil.
4. Continue to simmer honey mixture on very low heat for 10 minutes.
5. Pour honey mixture over the dry mix in the bowl and stir thoroughly.
6. Pour granola mixture onto a cookie sheet coated with nonstick vegetable spray.
7. Bake for 30 minutes, stirring periodically until granola is a light golden brown.
8. Remove tray from oven and allow granola to cool completely.
9. Pour granola into a large bowl and stir in the dried fruit.
10. Place about 1 cup granola into each of 14 quart-size ziplock freezer bags.
11. To each bag add ⅓ cup instant dry milk. Each bag provides 1 serving.

Preparation on the Trail:
1. To prepare 1 serving, add 1 cup cold water to a bag of granola.
2. Knead bag to dissolve and mix milk powder, then serve.

Option: To serve warm, substitute hot water for the cold.

*Emmett "Ol' Kooger" Autrey
Amarillo, Texas*

PCT

KOOLAU RIDGE GRANOLA

Total Servings: 7
As Packaged for the Trail: 1 serving
Weight per Serving: 5 ounces
Preparation Time on the Trail: None
Challenge Level: Easy

"I (Christine) grew up in Hawaii and spent a great deal of time hiking in the Koolau Mountains of Oahu. The range runs north-south for almost the entire length of the island, offering a diversity of hiking experiences including majestic waterfalls and breathtaking views. I created this recipe to reflect the unique flavors of the islands."

Preparation at Home:

1. In a large pot, heat oil and preserves over low heat until thin.
2. Add chopped nuts to pot along with the cereal and coconut.
3. Stir until liquid has evenly covered the mixture.
4. Evenly spread granola in a nonstick jelly roll pan.
5. Bake at 250°F for 1½ hours, stirring periodically.
6. Remove granola from oven and allow to cool completely.
7. Add chopped mango pieces to granola and stir.
8. Place about 1 cup granola into each of 7 pint-size ziplock bags. Each bag provides 1 serving.
9. Pack optional instant dry milk separately.

Preparation on the Trail:

For a single serving, eat straight from the bag or add optional milk, cold or warm.

Christine and Tim Conners
Statesboro, Georgia

¼ cup vegetable oil

1 (12-ounce) jar pineapple preserves

1 cup lightly salted macadamia nuts, chopped

1 (16-ounce) package Bob's Red Mill 5-Grain Rolled hot cereal

½ cup shredded sweetened coconut

6 ounces dried mango slices, chopped

Optional: instant dry milk to taste

Required Equipment on the Trail:
None

Nutritional Information per Serving:
Calories: 618
Protein: 11 g
Fat: 21 g
Carbohydrates: 104 g
Fiber: 12 g
Sodium: 44 mg
Cholesterol: 0 mg

ORANGE SKY GRANOLA

Total Servings: 10
As Packaged for the Trail: 1 serving
Weight per Serving: 5 ounces
Preparation Time on the Trail: None
Challenge Level: Easy

"If you're looking for granola with a unique flavor, Orange Sky is it!"

¼ cup vegetable oil

1 (18-ounce) jar orange marmalade

1 (16-ounce) package Bob's Red Mill 5-Grain Rolled hot cereal

1 pound chopped hazelnuts

1 cup shredded sweetened coconut

1½ cups dried cranberries

Optional: instant dry milk to taste

Required Equipment on the Trail:
None

Nutritional Information per Serving:
Calories: 605
Protein: 12 g
Fat: 23 g
Carbohydrates: 89 g
Fiber: 5 g
Sodium: 19 mg
Cholesterol: 0 mg

Preparation at Home:

1. In a large pot, heat oil and marmalade over low heat until thin.
2. Add cereal, nuts, and coconut to the pot.
3. Stir until liquid has evenly covered the mixture.
4. Evenly spread granola in a nonstick jelly roll pan.
5. Bake at 225°F for 2 hours, stirring periodically.
6. Remove granola from oven and allow to cool completely.
7. Add cranberries to granola and stir.
8. Place about 1 cup granola into each of 10 pint-size ziplock bags. Each bag produces 1 serving.
9. Pack optional instant dry milk separately.

Preparation on the Trail:
For a single serving, eat straight from the bag or add optional milk, cold or warm.

Christine and Tim Conners
Statesboro, Georgia

TRAILSIDE BREAKFAST RICE

V-LO

Total Servings: 4
As Packaged for the Trail: 1 serving
Weight per Serving: 4 ounces
Preparation Time on the Trail: 15 minutes
Challenge Level: Easy

Preparation at Home:

1. Combine all dry ingredients together in a bowl. Mix well.
2. Divide mixture evenly into 4 pint-size ziplock bags, about ¾ cup for 1 serving into each.

Preparation on the Trail:

1. To prepare 1 serving, bring ¾ cup water to boil in a pot.
2. Add contents of a bag of rice mix to the pot, cover, and cook over medium heat for about 5 minutes.
3. Remove pot from stove and let stand for about 5 minutes or until rice is tender.
4. Stir and serve.

Heather Burror
Martinez, California

2 cups instant brown rice

1 (3.4-ounce) package vanilla-flavored instant pudding

¼ cup instant dry nonfat milk

½ teaspoon ground cinnamon

½ cup dried mixed berries

¼ cup chopped honey-roasted peanuts

¾ cup water per serving, added on the trail

Required Equipment on the Trail:
Cook pot with lid

Nutritional Information per Serving:
Calories: 400
Protein: 8 g
Fat: 5 g
Carbohydrates: 82 g
Fiber: 4 g
Sodium: 422 mg
Cholesterol: 21 mg

MULE FUEL

Total Servings: 2
As Packaged for the Trail: 1 serving
Weight per Serving: 4 ounces
Preparation Time on the Trail: 15 minutes
Challenge Level: Easy

1 (single-serving) packet spiced apple cider mix

1 cup old-fashioned oats

¼ cup slivered almonds

¼ cup dried cranberries, currants, raisins, or other chopped dried fruit

½ teaspoon ground cinnamon

1 cup water per serving, added on the trail

Required Equipment on the Trail:
Cook pot

Nutritional Information per Serving:
Calories: 355
Protein: 9 g
Fat: 12 g
Carbohydrates: 58 g
Fiber: 7 g
Sodium: 17 mg
Cholesterol: 0 mg

Preparation at Home:

1. Thoroughly mix all dry ingredients together in a bowl.

2. Evenly divide mixture between 2 pint-size ziplock bags, about ¾ cup for 1 serving into each.

Preparation on the Trail:

1. To prepare 1 serving, bring 1 cup water to boil in a cook pot.

2. Add contents from 1 bag of mix to the hot water. Stir.

3. Allow to stand for a few minutes before serving.

Barbara "Mule 2" Hodgin
Sacramento, California

ADIRONDACK APRICOT OATMEAL

V-LO

Total Servings: 1
As Packaged for the Trail: 1 serving
Weight per Serving: 4 ounces
Preparation Time on the Trail: 15 minutes
Challenge Level: Easy

Preparation at Home:
Package all dry ingredients in a pint-size ziplock bag.

Preparation on the Trail:
1. To prepare 1 serving, bring 1½ cups water to boil in a cook pot, then remove pot from heat.
2. Add contents from 1 bag of oatmeal mix to the hot water and stir.
3. Let stand for 5 minutes before serving.

Ken Harbison
Rochester, New York

¾ cup quick oats

1 teaspoon brown sugar

1 pinch salt

⅓ cup instant dry nonfat milk

2 dried apricots, chopped

3 tablespoons cashew nut pieces

1½ cups water per serving, added on the trail

Required Equipment on the Trail:
Cook pot

Nutritional Information per Serving:
Calories: 510
Protein: 21 g
Fat: 17 g
Carbohydrates: 74 g
Fiber: 7 g
Sodium: 370 mg
Cholesterol: 5 mg

KETCHIKAN COUSCOUS

V-LO

Total Servings: 1
As Packaged for the Trail: 1 serving
Weight per Serving: 5 ounces
Preparation Time on the Trail: 15 minutes
Challenge Level: Easy

⅓ cup whole wheat couscous

2 tablespoons instant dry nonfat milk

2 tablespoons chopped dates (or other dried fruit of your choice)

½ tablespoon brown sugar

1 pinch salt

1 dash ground cinnamon

⅔ cup water per serving, added on the trail

Required Equipment on the Trail:
Cook pot with lid

Nutritional Information per Serving:
Calories: 500
Protein: 14 g
Fat: 11 g
Carbohydrates: 78 g
Fiber: 11 g
Sodium: 450 mg
Cholesterol: 2 mg

Preparation at Home:
Combine all dry ingredients in a pint-size ziplock bag.

Preparation on the Trail:
1. To prepare 1 serving, heat ⅔ cup water to boiling in a pot.
2. Stir in contents from the bag of couscous mix and cook for 2 minutes.
3. Remove pot from heat. Allow pot to stand, covered, until liquid is absorbed and couscous is tender, about 5 minutes.

Option: A dried butter substitute, such as Butter Buds, can be added on the trail for a creamier taste.

Carole and Ken Harbison
San Francisco, California
and Rochester, New York

KALALAU QUINOA CEREAL

Total Servings: 5
As Packaged for the Trail: 1 serving
Weight per Serving: 5 ounces
Preparation Time on the Trail: 15 minutes
Challenge Level: Easy

Preparation at Home:

1. Add quinoa to 1 quart water in a pot and bring to a boil. Cover and reduce heat.
2. Continue to cook until all water is absorbed, about 10 to 15 minutes, stirring often toward end.
3. Dry cooked quinoa on lined dehydrator trays.
4. In a large bowl, combine dried quinoa with sunflower seeds, raisins, brown sugar, cinnamon, and optional salt to taste. Stir well.
5. Evenly divide cereal mixture between 5 pint-size ziplock bags, about 1 cup for 1 serving into each.

Preparation on the Trail:

1. To prepare 1 serving, bring ¾ cup water to boil in a cook pot, then remove pot from heat.
2. Add contents from 1 bag of cereal mix to the hot water and stir well.
3. Allow cereal to rehydrate for a few minutes before serving.

Option: Consider substituting the raisins if you'll be hiking in blueberry country. This cereal is very tasty as is. But fresh and ripe wild berries make it heavenly.

Jason Rumohr
Seattle, Washington

2 cups quinoa

1 quart water

1 cup raw sunflower seeds

1 cup raisins or your favorite dried fruit

¼ cup brown sugar

1 teaspoon ground cinnamon

Optional: salt to taste

¾ cup water per serving, added on the trail

Required Equipment on the Trail:
Cook pot

Nutritional Information per Serving:
Calories: 552
Protein: 14 g
Fat: 18 g
Carbohydrates: 87 g
Fiber: 9 g
Sodium: 12 mg
Cholesterol: 0 mg

NORTH WOODS OATMEAL

Total servings: 1
As Packaged for the Trail: 1 serving
Weight per Serving: 5 ounces
Preparation Time on the Trail: 15 minutes
Challenge Level: Easy

V-LO

¾ cup quick oats

1 teaspoon brown sugar

1 pinch salt

⅓ cup instant dry nonfat milk

2 tablespoons dried blueberries

1 (2-bar) package Oats 'N Honey Nature Valley granola bars

1½ cups water per serving, added on the trail

Required Equipment on the Trail:
Cook pot

Nutritional Information per Serving:
Calories: 550
Protein: 20 g
Fat: 10 g
Carbohydrates: 99 g
Fiber: 10 g
Sodium: 420 mg
Cholesterol: 5 mg

Preparation at Home:
1. Combine quick oats, brown sugar, salt, dry milk, and dried blueberries in a pint-size ziplock bag.
2. Carry granola bars separately.

Preparation on the Trail:
1. To prepare 1 serving, bring 1½ cups water to boil in a cook pot.
2. Add contents from 1 bag of oatmeal mix to the boiling water and stir.
3. Remove pot from heat and allow to rest for 5 minutes.
4. Crumble 2 granola bars over oatmeal before serving.

Ken Harbison
Rochester, New York

CHEESY BREAKFAST GRITS

V-LO

Total Servings: 1
As Packaged for the Trail: 1 serving
Weight per Serving: 6 ounces
Preparation Time on the Trail: 15 minutes
Challenge Level: Easy

"Here's a fast recipe that won't hold you back in the morning."

Preparation at Home:
1. Combine grits, dry milk, garlic powder, salt, and dried egg in a pint-size ziplock bag.
2. Carry cheese separately.

Preparation on the Trail:
1. To prepare 1 serving, stir contents of a bag of grit mix into 2¼ cups water in a cook pot.
2. Heat grit mix to boiling while stirring.
3. Remove pot from heat once boiling begins, then add cheese, sliced into small pieces.
4. Continue to stir grits until cheese melts and is fully blended.

Ken Harbison
Rochester, New York

⅔ cup quick grits

⅓ cup instant dry whole milk

1 pinch garlic powder

1 dash salt

1 tablespoon dried egg white powder

2 ounces jack or cheddar cheese from block (or 2 1-ounce cheese sticks)

2¼ cups water per serving, added on the trail

Required Equipment on the Trail:
Cook pot

Nutritional Information per Serving:
Calories: 746
Protein: 33 g
Fat: 27 g
Carbohydrates: 92 g
Fiber: 5 g
Sodium: 802 mg
Cholesterol: 80 mg

A quick breakfast idea: Combine a handful of dehydrated fruits (apples, peaches, bananas, raisins, pineapple, cranberries—whatever is available) in a pot with just enough water to cover. Bring to a boil and simmer to rehydrate. Add brown sugar to sweeten to taste.

Sherry Bennett
Rochester, New York

BLUE BEAR MUSH

V-LO

Total Servings: 2
As Packaged for the Trail: 1 serving
Weight per Serving: 6 ounces
Preparation Time on the Trail: 15 minutes
Challenge Level: Easy

1 cup Arrowhead Mills Bear Mush

½ cup dried blueberries

2 tablespoons brown sugar

¼ teaspoon salt

⅓ cup instant dry nonfat milk

1½ cups water per serving, added on the trail

Required Equipment on the Trail:
Cook pot

Nutritional Information per Serving:
Calories: 435
Protein: 12 g
Fat: 0 g
Carbohydrates: 103 g
Fiber: 7 g
Sodium: 358 mg
Cholesterol: 3 mg

Preparation at Home:
1. Thoroughly mix all dry ingredients together in a bowl.
2. Evenly divide mixture between 2 pint-size ziplock bags, about 1 cup for 1 serving into each.

Preparation on the Trail:
1. To prepare 1 serving, bring 1½ cups water to boil in a cook pot.
2. Add contents from 1 bag of mix to the hot water and stir well.
3. Allow mush to cool for a few minutes before serving.

Heather Burror
Martinez, California

PCT

OMEGA BREAKFAST

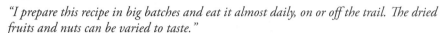

V-LO

Total Servings: 12
As Packaged for the Trail: 1 serving
Weight per Serving: 6 ounces
Preparation Time on the Trail: 15 minutes
Challenge Level: Easy

"I prepare this recipe in big batches and eat it almost daily, on or off the trail. The dried fruits and nuts can be varied to taste."

Preparation at Home:

1. In a large bowl, mix oats, rye, Grape-Nuts, sunflower seeds, cranberries, raisins, date pieces, soy nuts, walnut pieces, pumpkin seeds, and sesame seeds.
2. Evenly divide cereal mixture between 12 pint-size ziplock bags, a little less than ¾ cup into each.
3. To each single-serving bag also add ½ cup dry milk, ½ teaspoon cinnamon, ½ teaspoon nutmeg, and 1 tablespoon ground flaxseed.

Preparation on the Trail:

1. To prepare 1 serving, bring ¾ cup water to boil in a cook pot, then remove pot from heat.
2. Add contents from 1 bag of cereal mix to the hot water and stir well.
3. Let stand for 5 minutes before serving.

Tip: Flaxseed can be ground at home using a coffee grinder.

Richard "Ranger Rick" Halbert
Traverse City, Michigan

1 cup rolled oats

1 cup rolled rye

1 cup Post Grape-Nuts

1 cup raw sunflower seeds

1 cup dried unsweetened cranberries

1 cup raisins

1 cup date pieces

1 cup roasted unsalted soy nuts

1 cup walnut pieces

½ cup pumpkin seeds

½ cup sesame seeds

6 cups instant dry nonfat milk

2 tablespoons ground cinnamon

2 tablespoons ground nutmeg

¾ cup ground flaxseed

¾ cup water per serving, added on the trail

Required Equipment on the Trail:
Cook pot

Nutritional Information per Serving:
Calories: 603
Protein: 30 g
Fat: 26 g
Carbohydrates: 70 g
Fiber: 12 g
Sodium: 249 mg
Cholesterol: 6 mg

KEARSARGE PASS OATMEAL

Total Servings: 1
As Packaged for the Trail: 1 serving
Weight per Serving: 6 ounces
Preparation Time on the Trail: 15 minutes
Challenge Level: Easy

V-LO

½ cup instant dry nonfat milk

¾ cup old-fashioned oats

¼ cup toasted wheat germ

2 tablespoons raisins

1 tablespoon brown sugar

Slightly more than 1 cup water per serving, added on the trail

Required Equipment on the Trail:
Cook pot

Nutritional Information per Serving:
Calories: 525
Protein: 28 g
Fat: 7 g
Carbohydrates: 90 g
Fiber: 11 g
Sodium: 193 mg
Cholesterol: 6 mg

Preparation at Home:
Combine all dry ingredients together in a pint-size ziplock bag.

Preparation on the Trail:
1. To prepare 1 serving, bring slightly more than 1 cup water to boil in a cook pot, then remove pot from heat.

2. Add contents from 1 bag of oatmeal mix to the hot water. Stir.

3. Allow to rest for 5 minutes before serving.

Bill Albrecht
Lancaster, California

CRIMSON SKIES OATMEAL

Total Servings: 1
As Packaged for the Trail: 1 serving
Weight per Serving: 7 ounces
Preparation Time on the Trail: 15 minutes
Challenge Level: Easy

Preparation at Home:
Combine all dry ingredients in a pint-size ziplock bag.

Preparation on the Trail:
1. To prepare 1 serving, bring 1¼ cups water to boil in a cook pot.
2. Add contents from 1 bag of oatmeal mix to the hot water and reduce heat. Stir.
3. Continue to cook for a few additional minutes, stirring occasionally, then cover and remove from heat.
4. Allow to rest for a few minutes before serving.

Richard "Ranger Rick" Halbert
Traverse City, Michigan

½ cup old-fashioned oats

¼ cup Ocean Spray Craisins

2 tablespoons orange drink mix

¼ cup chopped walnuts

2 tablespoons instant dry soy milk mix

1¼ cups water per serving, added on the trail

Required Equipment on the Trail:
Cook pot with lid

Nutritional Information per Serving:
Calories: 606
Protein: 12 g
Fat: 20 g
Carbohydrates: 107 g
Fiber: 8 g
Sodium: 107 mg
Cholesterol: 0 mg

OLYMPUS OATMEAL

Total Servings: 1
As Packaged for the Trail: 1 serving
Weight per Serving: 7 ounces
Preparation Time on the Trail: 15 minutes
Challenge Level: Easy

V-LO

"This recipe is easy to replicate into multiple servings, as needed, and for adding variety on the trail through the use of easy-to-carry optional ingredients."

½ cup dried fruit pieces

1 cup old-fashioned oats

⅓ cup instant dry nonfat milk

Optional: sugar, cinnamon, allspice, wheat germ, salt, or Butter Buds to taste

2 cups water per serving, added on the trail

Required Equipment on the Trail:
Cook pot

Nutritional Information per Serving:
Calories: 620
Protein: 20 g
Fat: 6 g
Carbohydrates: 124 g
Fiber: 12 g
Sodium: 165 mg
Cholesterol: 5 mg

Preparation at Home:
Package dried fruit, oats, dry milk, and optional ingredients separately for the trail.

Preparation on the Trail:
1. To prepare 1 serving, add ½ cup dried fruit to 2 cups water and bring to boil in a cook pot.
2. Add 1 cup oats once water begins to boil vigorously. Stir and reduce heat.
3. Allow oats and fruit to simmer for 5 minutes.
4. Add 1/3 cup dry milk and any optional ingredients. Stir and serve.

Ramona Hammerly
Anacortes, Washington

DESERT GRUEL

Total Servings: 1
As Packaged for the Trail: 1 serving
Weight per Serving: 7 ounces
Preparation Time on the Trail: 15 minutes
Challenge Level: Easy

V-LO

"We once made a four-day backpack trip in Paria Canyon with two friends, one of whom brought along some really exotic food. I (Jo) was a little embarrassed the first time we poured up the gruel. But we ended up having to share for the rest of the hike!"

Preparation at Home:
1. Mix all dry ingredients together in a pint-size ziplock bag.
2. Package oil separately for the trail.

Preparation on the Trail:
1. To prepare 1 serving, add contents from 1 bag of gruel mix to a cook pot along with 1 tablespoon olive oil and 1½ cups water. Stir.
2. Warm mixture over medium heat, stirring occasionally. Ensure that the bouillon cube is dissolved before serving.

Options: The gruel can be made even tastier if the seeds and quinoa are toasted prior to packing. Chopped nuts can be substituted for the sesame seeds.

Jack Young and Jo Crescent
Winters, California

1 tablespoon nutritional yeast

1 tablespoon dried egg white powder

2 tablespoons sesame seeds

¼ cup quinoa flakes

1 (1.9-ounce) package Dr. McDougall's lower sodium vegan split pea soup

¼ cup rice flour

¼ cube vegan vegetable bouillon

1 tablespoon olive oil

1½ cups water per serving, added on the trail

Required Equipment on the Trail:
Cook pot

Nutritional Information per Serving:
Calories: 756
Protein: 29 g
Fat: 34 g
Carbohydrates: 70 g
Fiber: 20 g
Sodium: 1,215 mg
Cholesterol: < 1 mg

WOOD GNOME COBBLER

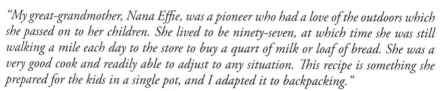

Total Servings: 1
As Packaged for the Trail: 1 serving
Weight per Serving: 7 ounces
Preparation Time on the Trail: 15 minutes
Challenge Level: Moderate

"My great-grandmother, Nana Effie, was a pioneer who had a love of the outdoors which she passed on to her children. She lived to be ninety-seven, at which time she was still walking a mile each day to the store to buy a quart of milk or loaf of bread. She was a very good cook and readily able to adjust to any situation. This recipe is something she prepared for the kids in a single pot, and I adapted it to backpacking."

½ cup dried mixed berries

2 tablespoons granulated sugar

1 teaspoon cornstarch

1 pinch ground nutmeg

½ cup Bisquick

1 cup and 3 tablespoons water per serving, added on the trail

Required Equipment on the Trail:
Cook pot with lid

Nutritional Information per Serving:
Calories: 620
Protein: 6 g
Fat: 10 g
Carbohydrates: 130 g
Fiber: 4 g
Sodium: 744 mg
Cholesterol: 0 mg

Preparation at Home:

1. Combine dried berries, sugar, cornstarch, and nutmeg in a pint-size ziplock bag.
2. Place Bisquick in a second pint-size bag.

Preparation on the Trail:

1. To prepare 1 serving, bring 1 cup water to boil in a cook pot.
2. Add contents of the bag of fruit mix to the boiling water.
3. Pour 3 tablespoons water into the bag of Bisquick and knead the mixture.
4. Snip a corner from the bottom of the Bisquick bag and squeeze spoonful-size dollops into the soup, pushing down the dumplings so they are immersed.
5. Cover pot to steam the mixture for about 5 to 7 minutes, with the heat just high enough to keep the liquid boiling.
6. Check occasionally, adding more water if needed to prevent scorching. The cobbler is ready once dumplings are fully cooked.

Traci Marcroft
Arcata, California

CHUCKWALLA CHOCOLATE CHIP PANCAKES

V-LO

Total Servings: 8
As Packaged for the Trail: 1 serving
Weight per Serving: 3 ounces
Preparation Time on the Trail: 15 minutes
Challenge Level: Moderate

Preparation at Home:

1. In a large bowl, mix together flours, salt, sugar, cocoa powder, baking powder, egg powder, dry milk, and chocolate chips. Stir well.
2. Evenly divide pancake mixture between 8 quart-size ziplock freezer bags, about ½ cup into each. Each bag provides 1 serving.
3. Package oil separately for the trail.

Preparation on the Trail:

1. To prepare 1 serving, warm 1 tablespoon oil in a frying pan over low heat.
2. Add ¼ cup water to 1 bag of pancake mix.
3. Knead pancake mix by squeezing bag to eliminate large chunks from batter.
4. Snip a corner from bottom of the bag and squeeze batter into pan.
5. Once batter begins to bubble, flip and brown the other side. Repeat until all batter is used.

Carole and Ken Harbison
San Francisco, California,
and Rochester, New York

1 cup all-purpose wheat flour

1 cup whole wheat flour

¼ teaspoon salt

¼ cup granulated sugar

¼ cup cocoa powder

1 tablespoon baking powder

¼ cup whole egg powder

½ cup instant dry whole milk

1 cup chocolate chips

1 tablespoon vegetable oil per serving

¼ cup water per serving, added on the trail

Required Equipment on the Trail:
Frying pan

Spatula

Nutritional Information per Serving:
Calories: 312
Protein: 9 g
Fat: 12 g
Carbohydrates: 48 g
Fiber: 4 g
Sodium: 301 mg
Cholesterol: 59 mg

BACKCOUNTRY BUTTERMILK PANCAKES

V-LO

Total Servings: 2
As Packaged for the Trail: 2 servings
Weight per Serving: 3 ounces
Preparation Time on the Trail: 15 minutes
Challenge Level: Moderate

1 cup Bob's Red Mill buttermilk pancake and waffle mix

3 tablespoons instant dry whole milk

2 tablespoons whole egg powder

1 tablespoon vegetable oil per 2 servings

1 cup water per 2 servings, added on the trail

Required Equipment on the Trail:
Frying pan

Spatula

Nutritional Information per Serving:
Calories: 438
Protein: 18 g
Fat: 14 g
Carbohydrates: 59 g
Fiber: 7 g
Sodium: 717 mg
Cholesterol: 121 mg

Preparation at Home:
1. Combine dry ingredients in a quart-size ziplock bag.
2. Pack oil separately for the trail.

Preparation on the Trail:
1. To prepare 2 servings, warm 1 tablespoon oil in a frying pan over low heat.
2. Add 1 cup water to the bag of pancake mix.
3. Knead pancake mix by squeezing bag to eliminate large chunks from batter.
4. Snip a corner from bottom of the bag and squeeze batter into pan.
5. Once batter begins to bubble, flip and brown the other side. Repeat until all batter is used.

Christine and Tim Conners
Statesboro, Georgia

SASQUATCH SCONES

V-LO

Total Servings: 4
As Packaged for the Trail: 1 serving
Weight per Serving: 4 ounces
Preparation Time on the Trail: 15 minutes
Challenge Level: Moderate

Preparation at Home:
1. Combine and thoroughly mix all dry ingredients in a bowl.
2. Divide mixture evenly into 4 pint-size ziplock freezer bags, a little more than ½ cup for 1 serving into each.
3. Pack oil separately for the trail.

Preparation on the Trail:
1. To prepare 1 serving, add 1 teaspoon oil and ¼ cup water to a bag of dry scone mix.
2. Seal bag and knead mixture until dough becomes uniformly stiff.
3. Warm 1 tablespoon oil in a nonstick frying pan over low heat.
4. Spoon two-inch blobs of the thick dough into pan and cook on low heat until bottoms are browned and the tops begin to lose their shine.
5. Flip scones with a spatula and continue cooking until bottoms are lightly browned.
6. Repeat steps 4 and 5 with any remaining batter.

Options: Ground cloves or cardamom make good spice alternatives. Dried lemon peel adds zing. Soy milk powder may be substituted for powdered dairy milk.

Suzanne Allen
Seattle, Washington

1½ cups all-purpose wheat flour

⅓ cup granulated sugar

2 teaspoons baking powder

¼ teaspoon baking soda

¼ teaspoon salt

1 tablespoon instant dry nonfat milk

¼ cup chopped walnuts

½ cup dried currants, raisins, cranberries, or blueberries

¼ teaspoon ground nutmeg

¼ teaspoon ground cinnamon

1 tablespoon and 1 teaspoon vegetable oil per serving

¼ cup water per serving, added on the trail

Required Equipment on the Trail:
Nonstick frying pan

Spatula

Nutritional Information per Serving:
Calories: 415
Protein: 6 g
Fat: 12 g
Carbohydrates: 67 g
Fiber: 2 g
Sodium: 410 mg
Cholesterol: 1 mg

SONORAN DESERT SCRAMBLED EGGS

Total Servings: 2
As Packaged for the Trail: 2 servings
Weight per Serving: 5 ounces
Preparation Time on the Trail: 15 minutes
Challenge Level: Easy

V-LO

¾ cup whole egg powder

1 dash salt

¼ teaspoon ground black pepper

½ teaspoon garlic powder

1 tablespoon dried chives

2 teaspoons Butter Buds Sprinkles

1 tablespoon vegetable oil per 2 servings

1 cup water per 2 servings, added on the trail

Required Equipment on the Trail:
Nonstick frying pan

Spatula

Nutritional Information per Serving:
Calories: 280
Protein: 8 g
Fat: 22 g
Carbohydrates: 5 g
Fiber: 0 g
Sodium: 400 mg
Cholesterol: 615 mg

Preparation at Home:
1. Combine dry ingredients in a quart-size ziplock bag.
2. Pack oil separately for the trail.

Preparation on the Trail:
1. To prepare 2 servings, add 1 cup water to bag of powdered egg mix.
2. Seal bag, knead contents, and set aside.
3. Warm 1 tablespoon oil in a nonstick frying pan over low heat.
4. Pour reconstituted egg mixture into pan.
5. Scramble, using a spatula to continually wipe the bottom of the pan to prevent eggs from burning.
6. Serve once eggs have a solid consistency.

Christine and Tim Conners
Statesboro, Georgia

68

PIKES PEAK PINEAPPLE PANCAKES

V-LO

Total Servings: 2
As Packaged for the Trail: 1 serving
Weight per Serving: 5 ounces
Preparation Time on the Trail: 45 minutes
Challenge Level: Moderate

Preparation at Home:

1. Dry pineapple along with its juice on a lined dehydrator tray.
2. Divide dried pineapple evenly into 2 separate quart-size ziplock freezer bags.
3. Add ¾ cup pancake mix to each of the bags. A single serving is provided by each bag.
4. Package oil and optional syrup or sugar separately for the trail.

Preparation on the Trail:

1. To prepare 1 serving, add ⅔ cup water to 1 bag of pineapple pancake mix.
2. Knead pancake mix by squeezing the bag to eliminate large chunks from batter.
3. Wait approximately 20 minutes, allowing pineapple to rehydrate.
4. Warm ½ tablespoon vegetable oil in a frying pan over low heat.
5. Snip a corner from bottom of the bag and squeeze some of the batter into pan.
6. Once batter begins to bubble, flip and brown the other side. Repeat until all batter is used.
7. Serve with optional syrup or sugar if desired.

Christine and Tim Conners
Statesboro, Georgia

1 (20-ounce) can crushed pineapple

1½ cups Arrowhead Mills Multigrain Pancake & Waffle Mix

½ tablespoon vegetable oil per serving

Optional: syrup or sugar to taste

⅔ cup water per serving, added on the trail

Required Equipment on the Trail:
Frying pan

Spatula

Nutritional Information per Serving:
Calories: 337
Protein: 4 g
Fat: 7 g
Carbohydrates: 64 g
Sodium: 303 mg
Fiber: 5 g
Cholesterol: < 1 mg

SAUCY SUMMER BREAKFAST BURRITOS

V-LO

Total Servings: 2
As Packaged for the Trail: 2 servings
Weight per Serving: 5 ounces
Preparation Time on the Trail: 30 minutes
Challenge Level: Moderate

1 (16-ounce) jar mild salsa

⅜ cup whole egg powder

1 tablespoon vegetable oil

2 ounces hard cheese from block, your choice

2 medium-size flour tortillas

1½ cups water per 2 servings, added on the trail

Required Equipment on the Trail:
Frying pan

Spatula

Nutritional Information per Serving:
Calories: 485
Protein: 21 g
Fat: 27 g
Carbohydrates: 41 g
Fiber: 1 g
Sodium: 1,300 mg
Cholesterol: 333 mg

Preparation at Home:

1. Dry salsa in a food dehydrator.
2. Tear dried salsa leather into small pieces and place in a quart-size ziplock freezer bag.
3. Pour egg powder into a pint-size ziplock bag. This bag along with the bag of dried salsa produces 2 servings.
4. Pack oil, cheese, and tortillas separately.

Preparation on the Trail:

1. To prepare 2 servings, bring ¾ cup water to boil in a frying pan.
2. Remove pan from stove and allow water to cool slightly.
3. Carefully pour hot water into bag of dried salsa. Seal and set bag aside for a few minutes.
4. Add ¾ cup cold water to bag of egg mix. Seal bag, then shake well to reconstitute.
5. Pour 1 tablespoon oil in pan and warm over low heat.
6. Add both the rehydrated salsa and egg mix to the pan. Scramble continuously with a spatula to prevent burning.
7. Slice 2 ounces of cheese into small pieces and divide onto each of 2 tortillas.
8. Once scramble mixture is heated through, divide mix onto both tortillas. Roll like a burrito and serve.

Heather Burror
Martinez, California

CHEWONKI MORNING BULGUR

Total Servings: 1
As Packaged for the Trail: 1 serving
Weight per Serving: 6 ounces
Preparation Time on the Trail: 15 minutes (plus overnight to rehydrate)
Challenge Level: Easy

V-LO

Preparation at Home:
1. Combine all dry ingredients in a quart-size ziplock freezer bag.
2. Pack cheese and oil separately for the trail.

Preparation on the Trail:
1. To prepare 1 serving, add 1 cup water to the bulgur mix in the ziplock bag the evening before breakfast.
2. Carefully seal bag and briefly knead contents.
3. In the morning, warm 1 tablespoon olive oil in a pan over medium heat
4. Pour rehydrated bulgur mix into pan and scramble with a spoon or fork until heated through.
5. Remove pan from heat, then add small pieces of string cheese to the top of the bulgur. Allow cheese to melt for a few minutes before serving.

Rachel Jolly / Chewonki Foundation
Burlington, Vermont

½ cup bulgur wheat
1 tablespoon dried onion flakes
1 dash salt
¼ teaspoon ground black pepper
¼ teaspoon ground oregano
¼ teaspoon ground cumin
¼ teaspoon garlic powder
1 (1-ounce) stick string cheese, your choice
1 tablespoon olive oil
1 cup water per serving, added on the trail

Required Equipment on the Trail:
Frying pan

Nutritional Information per Serving:
Calories: 503
Protein: 17 g
Fat: 21 g
Carbohydrates: 66 g
Fiber: 8 g
Sodium: 510 mg
Cholesterol: 15 mg

JENKINS JOURNEY CAKES

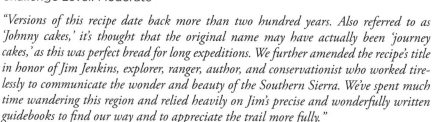

V-LO

Total Servings: 3
As Packaged for the Trail: 1 serving
Weight per Serving: 6 ounces
Preparation Time on the Trail: 15 minutes
Challenge Level: Moderate

"Versions of this recipe date back more than two hundred years. Also referred to as 'Johnny cakes,' it's thought that the original name may have actually been 'journey cakes,' as this was perfect bread for long expeditions. We further amended the recipe's title in honor of Jim Jenkins, explorer, ranger, author, and conservationist who worked tirelessly to communicate the wonder and beauty of the Southern Sierra. We've spent much time wandering this region and relied heavily on Jim's precise and wonderfully written guidebooks to find our way and to appreciate the trail more fully."

2 cups cornmeal

¼ cup all-purpose wheat flour

3 tablespoons whole egg powder

⅓ cup instant dry whole milk

½ cup brown sugar

½ teaspoon salt

½ teaspoon ground ginger

1 tablespoon vegetable oil per serving

⅓ cup water per serving, added on the trail

Required Equipment on the Trail:
Frying pan

Spatula

Nutritional Information per Serving:
Calories: 470
Protein: 11 g
Fat: 5 g
Carbohydrates: 102 g
Fiber: 8 g
Sodium: 340 mg
Cholesterol: 65 mg

Preparation at Home:
1. Combine and thoroughly mix all dry ingredients in a bowl.
2. Divide mixture evenly into 3 quart-size ziplock freezer bags, a little more than 1 cup for 1 serving into each.
3. Pack oil separately for the trail.

Preparation on the Trail:
1. To prepare 1 serving, add ⅓ cup water to a bag of journey cake mix.
2. Seal bag and knead mixture thoroughly.
3. Warm 1 tablespoon oil in a frying pan over medium heat.
4. Cut a corner from the bottom of the ziplock bag and squeeze several dollops of batter into pan.
5. Fry both sides as you would a pancake, flipping with a spatula and being careful to avoid overcooking.
6. Repeat steps 4 and 5 with any remaining batter.

Christine and Tim Conners
Statesboro, Georgia

FOUR-CORNERS FIESTA BURRITOS

V-LO

Total Servings: 2
As Packaged for the Trail: 2 servings
Weight per Serving: 6 ounces
Preparation Time on the Trail: 30 minutes
Challenge Level: Moderate

Preparation at Home:
1. Thaw stir-fry vegetables.
2. Chop vegetables into small pieces and dry in a dehydrator.
3. Place dried vegetables in a quart-size ziplock freezer bag.
4. In a pint-size ziplock freezer bag, add powdered egg and contents from packet of taco seasoning mix. This bag along with the bag of veggies produces 2 servings.
5. Pack oil, cheese, and tortillas separately.

Preparation on the Trail:
1. To prepare 2 servings, bring ¾ cup water to boil in a frying pan.
2. Remove pan from stove and allow water to cool slightly.
3. Carefully pour hot water into bag of dried vegetables. Seal and set bag aside for a few minutes.
4. Add ¾ cup cold water to bag of egg-seasoning mix. Seal bag, then shake well to reconstitute.
5. Pour 1 tablespoon oil in pan and warm over low heat.
6. Add both the rehydrated vegetables and egg-seasoning mix to the pan. Scramble continuously with a spatula to prevent burning.
7. Slice 2 ounces of cheese into small pieces and divide onto each of the 2 tortillas.
8. Once vegetable-egg mixture is heated through, divide mix onto both tortillas. Roll like a burrito and serve.

1 (16-ounce) package frozen stir-fry vegetables

⅜ cup whole egg powder

1 (1-ounce) package low-sodium taco seasoning mix

1 tablespoon vegetable oil

2 ounces hard cheese from block, your choice

2 medium-size flour tortillas

1½ cups water per 2 servings, added on the trail

Required Equipment on the Trail:
Frying pan

Spatula

Nutritional Information per Serving:
Calories: 480
Protein: 22 g
Fat: 22 g
Carbohydrates: 46 g
Fiber: 3 g
Sodium: 1,430 mg
Cholesterol: 333 mg

Heather Burror
Martinez, California

ARAPAHO APPLE PANCAKES

Total Servings: 2
As Packaged for the Trail: 1 serving
Weight per Serving: 7 ounces
Preparation Time on the Trail: 15 minutes
Challenge Level: Moderate

V-LO

1½ cups Bob's Red Mill 10 Grain Pancake & Waffle mix

3 ounces dried apple rings, finely chopped

1 (single-serving) packet spiced apple cider mix

1 tablespoon vegetable oil per serving

¾ cup water per serving, added on the trail

Required Equipment on the Trail:

Frying pan

Spatula

Nutritional Information per Serving:
Calories: 529
Protein: 12 g
Fat: 15 g
Carbohydrates: 90 g
Fiber: 9 g
Sodium: 996 mg
Cholesterol: 7 mg

Preparation at Home:

1. In a bowl, combine pancake mix, apple pieces, and apple cider mix. Stir well.

2. Divide mixture evenly into 2 quart-size ziplock freezer bags, about 1 heaping cup into each. Each bag provides 1 serving.

3. Pack oil separately.

Preparation on the Trail:

1. To prepare 1 serving, warm 1 tablespoon oil in a frying pan over low heat.

2. Add ¾ cup water to 1 bag of pancake mix.

3. Knead pancake mix by squeezing bag, breaking apart large lumps.

4. Snip a corner from bottom of bag and squeeze batter into pan.

5. Once batter begins to bubble, flip and brown the other side. Repeat until all batter is used.

Christine and Tim Conners
Statesboro, Georgia

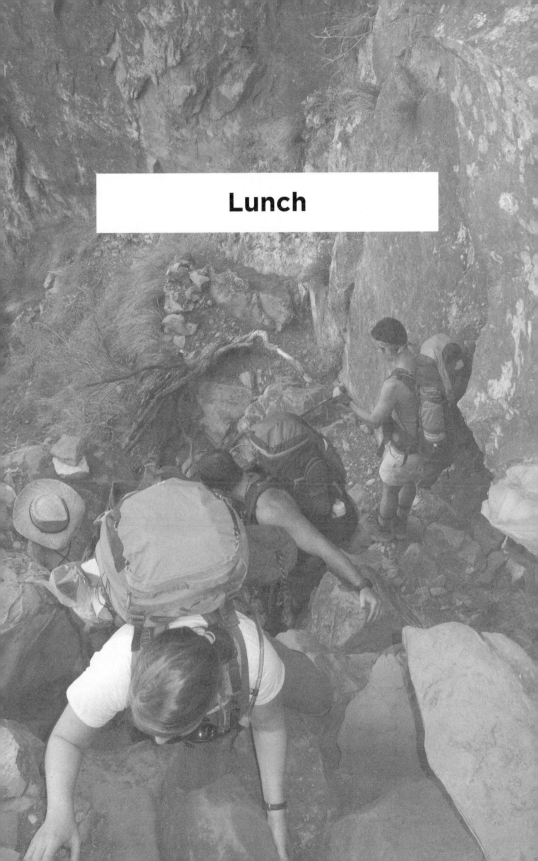

Lunch

ENERGY BALLS

V-LO

Total Servings: 16 (1 ball per serving)
As Packaged for the Trail: As required
Weight per Serving: 1 ounce
Preparation Time on the Trail: None
Challenge Level: Easy

1 cup peanut butter

½ cup quick oats

½ cup chocolate chips, crushed

½ cup flaked sweetened coconut

Required Equipment on the Trail:
None

Nutritional Information per Serving:
Calories: 153
Protein: 5 g
Fat: 11 g
Carbohydrates: 10 g
Fiber: 2 g
Sodium: 69 mg
Cholesterol: < 1 mg

Preparation at Home:
1. Combine and mix peanut butter, oats, and crushed chocolate chips in a bowl.
2. Form 16 balls and roll each in flaked coconut, thoroughly coating the exterior.
3. Package energy balls in a ziplock bag for the trail, assuming 1 ball per serving.

Preparation on the Trail:
None

Hannah Morris
Burlington, Vermont

CHEESE COINS

Total Servings: 30 (1 coin per serving)
As Packaged for the Trail: As required
Weight per Serving: 1 ounce
Preparation Time on the Trail: None
Challenge Level: Easy

V-LO

"If food can be considered a form of currency on the trail, then these 'coins' have the value of gold!"

Preparation at Home:
1. Combine butter, cheese, sauce, and sesame seeds in a bowl.
2. Add flour to the batter while kneading, a little at a time.
3. Form batter into a long roll, about 1 inch in diameter.
4. Cut batter into discs each about ¼-inch thick. About 30 "coins" should be produced.
5. Bake coins at 350°F for about 15 minutes.
6. Let cool, then package in quantity required for the trail, 1 coin per serving.

Preparation on the Trail:
None

Tip: Package carefully in the backpack to protect coins from crumbling.

Sherry Bennett
Rochester, New York

½ cup butter, softened

2 cups finely grated sharp cheddar cheese

½ tablespoon vegetarian Worcestershire sauce

1 tablespoon sesame seeds

1 cup all-purpose wheat flour

Required Equipment on the Trail:
None

Nutritional Information per Serving:
Calories: 72
Protein: 2 g
Fat: 6 g
Carbohydrates: 4 g
Fiber: 1 g
Sodium: 82 mg
Cholesterol: 16 mg

WALKING CARROT SALAD

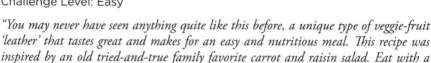

Total Servings: 12 (2 pieces per serving)
As Packaged for the Trail: 1 serving
Weight per Serving: 1 ounce
Preparation Time on the Trail: None
Challenge Level: Easy

"You may never have seen anything quite like this before, a unique type of veggie-fruit 'leather' that tastes great and makes for an easy and nutritious meal. This recipe was inspired by an old tried-and-true family favorite carrot and raisin salad. Eat with a handful of soy nuts or peanuts, and you have a complete meal."

2 cups grated carrot

2 cups applesauce

1 cup raisins

1 cup chopped walnuts

2 tablespoons agar powder

1 teaspoon ground cinnamon

¼ cup honey

Required Equipment on the Trail:
None

Nutritional Information per Serving:
Calories: 163
Protein: 2 g
Fat: 6 g
Carbohydrates: 25 g
Fiber: 2 g
Sodium: 70 mg
Cholesterol: 0 mg

Preparation at Home:

1. Combine all ingredients, except honey, in a saucepan. Stir well.

2. Allow mixture to sit for about 5 minutes to allow agar powder to congeal.

3. Cook over medium heat until carrots begin to soften and mixture thickens.

4. Remove pan from heat and add honey. Applesauce and carrots can differ in sweetness depending on brand or batch, so adjust quantity of honey accordingly, if desired, keeping in mind that the dehydrated product will have a more concentrated sweetness.

5. Drop ¼-cup dollops of the mixture onto lined dehydrator trays and flatten.

6. Dry to a leathery state, ensuring that no soft moisture pockets remain.

7. Package for the trail in ziplock bags, 2 dried dollop pieces for 1 serving to a bag.

Preparation on the Trail:
None

Options: *Vary the quantity or kind of nuts, maybe a spice other than cinnamon, or different fruits, such as pineapple in lieu of some or all of the raisins.*

Tip: Agar powder is a pure vegetable gelatin substitute that can be found at health-food stores.

Rosaleen Sullivan
Hudson, Massachusetts

ROARING MOUNTAIN KALE CHIPS

Total Servings: 4
As Packaged for the Trail: 1 serving
Weight per Serving: 1 ounce
Preparation Time on the Trail: None
Challenge Level: Easy

"Roaring with flavor and bursting with nutrients, kale chips make for a great mid-day food item, a healthy snack at any time, or a quick and easy way to add greens to a meal in a pot."

Preparation at Home:
1. Be sure raw kale leaves are free of surface water before proceeding.
2. Preheat oven to 300°F.
3. Trim kale leaves from any thicker stems, then place all leaves in a large bowl.
4. Sprinkle salt, curry powder, and oil, in that order, over kale leaves and toss well.
5. Cover 2 baking trays with parchment paper.
6. Evenly divide tossed kale leaves over the parchment paper.
7. Bake for 15 minutes, then redistribute kale leaves and rotate pans in the oven.
8. Continue baking for 10 minutes. Kale is ready once it's crisp but not burnt.
9. Remove trays from oven, allow kale to cool, then evenly divide among 4 small, tightly sealed ziplock bags, 1 serving per bag.

Preparation on the Trail:
None

1 (12-ounce) package prewashed and precut raw curly kale greens

½ teaspoon sea salt

2 teaspoons curry powder

1 tablespoon extra virgin olive oil

Required Equipment on the Trail:
None

Nutritional Information per Serving:
Calories: 78
Protein: 3 g
Fat: 4 g
Carbohydrates: 10 g
Fiber: 2 g
Sodium: 326 mg
Cholesterol: 0 mg

Options: Try grated parmesan cheese, cheese powder, or substitute your favorite spices for the curry powder.

Christine and Tim Conners
Statesboro, Georgia

TUMBLEWEED CORN LEATHER

V-LO

Total Servings: 6
As Packaged for the Trail: As required
Weight per Serving: 1 ounce
Preparation Time on the Trail: None
Challenge Level: Easy

1 (16-ounce) package frozen cut corn

1 (15-ounce) container Tostitos medium heat Salsa Con Queso dip

¼ cup water

Required Equipment on the Trail:
None

Nutritional Information per Serving:
Calories: 220
Protein: 4 g
Fat: 8 g
Carbohydrates: 33 g
Fiber: 1 g
Sodium: 887 mg
Cholesterol: 13 mg

Preparation at Home:
1. In a blender, combine corn, salsa con queso, and water. Blend well.
2. Pour about 1 cup pureed corn mix onto each of 3 lined dehydrator trays. Spread thinly. Each tray will produce 2 servings.
3. Dehydrate corn mix until thoroughly dry.
4. Tear dried corn mix into pieces and store in ziplock bags in quantity required for the trail.

Preparation on the Trail:
None

Christine and Tim Conners
Statesboro, Georgia

TERIYAKI TOFU JERKY

Total Servings: 2
As Packaged for the Trail: 1 serving
Weight per Serving: 2 ounces
Preparation Time on the Trail: None
Challenge Level: Easy

Preparation at Home:
1. In a bowl, prepare marinade sauce by combining all ingredients except tofu. Stir well.
2. Cut tofu into small cubes about ¼-inch thick on a side and add to bowl of marinade, ensuring that all pieces are coated.
3. Cover bowl and refrigerate tofu overnight.
4. Dry marinated tofu on lined dehydrator trays. Tofu is ready to package once it dries to a chewy consistency.
5. Divide dried tofu into 2 servings, packaging for the trail in small ziplock bags.

Preparation on the Trail:
None

Phil "Scodwod" Heffington
Edmond, Oklahoma

1 cup less-sodium teriyaki sauce

½ cup unsweetened pineapple juice

¼ cup brown sugar

1 tablespoon ginger powder

1 teaspoon garlic powder

12 ounces extra-firm tofu

Required Equipment on the Trail:
None

Nutritional Information per Serving:
Calories: 350
Protein: 22 g
Fat: 6 g
Carbohydrates: 50 g
Fiber: 3 g
Sodium: 800 mg
Cholesterol: 0 mg

BRAGG'S TOFU JERKY

Total Servings: 2
As Packaged for the Trail: 1 serving
Weight per Serving: 2 ounces
Preparation Time on the Trail: None
Challenge Level: Easy

1 cup Bragg's Liquid Aminos

1 tablespoon garlic powder

1 teaspoon ginger powder

12 ounces extra-firm tofu

Required Equipment on the Trail:
None

Nutritional Information per Serving:
Calories: 100
Protein: 16 g
Fat: 5 g
Carbohydrates: 5 g
Fiber: 0 g
Sodium: 1,380 mg
Cholesterol: 0 mg

Preparation at Home:

1. In a bowl, prepare marinade sauce by combining Liquid Aminos and seasonings. Stir well.
2. Cut tofu into small cubes about ¼-inch thick on a side and add to bowl of marinade, ensuring that all pieces are coated.
3. Cover bowl and let stand for 1 to 2 hours. The flavor will become more intense the longer the tofu marinates.
4. Dry marinated tofu on lined dehydrator trays. Tofu is ready to package once it dries to a chewy consistency.
5. Divide dried tofu into 2 servings, packaging for the trail in small ziplock bags.

Preparation on the Trail:
None

Mara Naber
Mountain Ranch, California

Try substituting kohlrabi, a member of the cabbage family, for tofu when making your favorite jerky recipe. Kohlrabi makes a great jerky because of its meat-like texture.

Matthew Farnell
Woodland, Washington

NORTHVILLE-PLACID TRAIL BALLS

V-LO

Total Servings: 12 (2 balls per serving)
As Packaged for the Trail: As required
Weight per Serving: 2 ounces
Preparation Time on the Trail: None
Challenge Level: Easy

Preparation at Home:
1. Combine peanut butter and honey in a bowl.
2. Add dry milk and oats to the bowl and thoroughly mix.
3. Shape mixture into 2 dozen balls.
4. Roll each of the pieces in wheat germ, thoroughly coating the exterior.
5. Set aside to rest for several hours.
6. Wrap pieces individually in wax paper.
7. Stored in a ziplock bag or plastic container for the trail, assuming 2 balls per serving.

Preparation on the Trail:
None

Sherry Bennett
Rochester, New York

½ cup peanut butter

½ cup honey

1 cup instant dry nonfat milk

1 cup old-fashioned oats

¼ cup toasted wheat germ

Required Equipment on the Trail:
None

Nutritional Information per Serving:
Calories: 156
Protein: 6 g
Fat: 6 g
Carbohydrates: 22 g
Fiber: 2 g
Sodium: 72 mg
Cholesterol: 2 mg

SPIRIT LIFTERS

Total Servings: 16 (1 bar per serving)
As Packaged for the Trail: As required
Weight per Serving: 2 ounces
Preparation Time on the Trail: None
Challenge Level: Easy

V-LO

"I like recipes that I can look forward to, that lift my spirit when I'm tired. This recipe goes a long way in doing that. Kind of like the feeling you have on a cold, windy day, when someone puts a hot cup of tea in your hands."

½ cup whole wheat flour

½ cup all-purpose wheat flour

½ cup brown sugar

½ cup quick oats

¼ cup wheat germ

1 tablespoon grated orange rind

½ cup (1 standard stick) butter, softened

2 eggs

1 cup slivered almonds

¼ cup raisins

¼ cup flaked sweetened coconut

½ cup semisweet chocolate chips

Preparation at Home:
1. Preheat oven to 350°F.
2. In a large bowl, combine flours, sugar, oats, wheat germ, and orange rind.
3. Beat butter, eggs, almonds, raisins, coconut, and chocolate chips into the flour mixture.
4. Line a 9x9-inch pan with parchment paper and pour batter into the pan.
5. Bake for 35 minutes.
6. Cool and cut into 16 bars. Each bar provides 1 serving.

Preparation on the Trail:
None

Sherry Bennett
Rochester, New York

Required Equipment on the Trail:
None

Nutritional Information per Serving:
Calories: 193
Protein: 4 g
Fat: 12 g
Carbohydrates: 19 g
Fiber: 2 g
Sodium: 86 mg
Cholesterol: 42 mg

BEAR BAIT

Total Servings: 4
As Packaged for the Trail: 4 servings
Weight per Serving: 2 ounces
Preparation Time on the Trail: None
Challenge Level: Easy

"Honey and nut butters make a wonderful combination that packs an energy wallop: carbs for the near term and fat for the long haul."

Preparation at Home:

1. Thoroughly mix honey and cashew butter in a small bowl.
2. Package honey-butter for the trail in a plastic squeeze tube or container. Storing in a pint-size ziplock bag placed securely within a second bag is also an option. Plan for about ¼ cup per serving.
3. Carry optional ingredients separately.

Preparation on the Trail:

For 1 serving (about ¼ cup), eat straight from the tube, container, or ziplock bag or spread on optional tortillas, pita bread, or crackers.

Tip: Honey is a great trail food because of its nutritional characteristics, but it's notoriously sticky. Premixing the honey with the oily nut butter helps reduce this annoying characteristic.

Richard "Ranger Rick" Halbert
Traverse City, Michigan

½ cup honey

½ cup cashew butter

Optional: tortillas, pita bread, or crackers

Required Equipment on the Trail:
None

Nutritional Information per Serving:
Calories: 300
Protein: 4 g
Fat: 16 g
Carbohydrates: 44 g
Fiber: 2 g
Sodium: 0 mg
Cholesterol: 0 mg

MUD

Total Servings: 10
As Packaged for the Trail: 10 servings
Weight per Serving: 2 ounces
Preparation Time on the Trail: None
Challenge Level: Easy

V-LO

"I once led a small group of women on a weekend canoe trip in the Adirondacks. While preparing, one of the ladies, the only one I didn't know personally, asked what kind of food she should bring. Well, as much as I like cooking and preparing food, I said half-jokingly, 'Don't worry about the food. Just bring the wine, and I'll see to it that no one goes hungry.' Well, this girl brought six bottles of wine and there were only four of us!"

¼ cup old-fashioned oats

¼ cup nonfat instant dry milk

¼ cup sunflower seeds

¼ cup raisins

¼ cup chopped walnuts

¼ cup mini chocolate chips

½ cup peanut butter

½ cup honey

Optional: bagels or crackers

Required Equipment on the Trail:
None

Nutritional Information per Serving:
Calories: 216
Protein: 6 g
Fat: 12 g
Carbohydrates: 26 g
Fiber: 2 g
Sodium: 92 mg
Cholesterol: 1 mg

Preparation at Home:
1. Thoroughly mix all ingredients in a bowl.
2. Package for the trail in plastic squeeze tubes or a container. Storing in one ziplock bag placed securely within a second bag is also an option. Plan for about ¼ cup per serving.
3. Carry optional ingredients separately.

Preparation on the Trail:
For 1 serving (about ¼ cup), eat straight from the tube, container, or ziplock bag or spread on optional bagels or crackers.

Option: Try peanut butter chips in place of the chocolate chips.

Sherry Bennett
Rochester, New York

GRUNCH

V-LO

Total Servings: 10
As Packaged for the Trail: 10 servings
Weight per Serving: 2 ounces
Preparation Time on the Trail: None
Challenge Level: Easy

Preparation at Home:

1. Thoroughly mix all ingredients in a bowl.
2. Package for the trail in plastic squeeze tubes or a container. Storing in one ziplock bag placed securely within a second bag is also an option. Plan for about ¼ cup per serving.
3. Carry optional ingredients separately.

Preparation on the Trail:

For 1 serving (about ¼ cup), eat straight from the tube, container, or ziplock bag or spread on optional tortillas, pita bread, or crackers.

Sherry Bennett
Rochester, New York

1 cup crunchy peanut butter

½ cup honey

½ cup finely crushed graham cracker crumbs

¼ cup nonfat instant dry milk

3 tablespoons ground cinnamon

1 tablespoon ground cloves

Optional: tortillas, pita bread, or crackers

Required Equipment on the Trail:
None

Nutritional Information per Serving:
Calories: 224
Protein: 8 g
Fat: 14 g
Carbohydrates: 22 g
Fiber: 2 g
Sodium: 126 mg
Cholesterol: 1 mg

WHOLE-FOOD GRANOLA BARS

V

Total Servings: 26 (1 bar per serving)
As Packaged for the Trail: As required
Weight per Serving: 2 ounces
Preparation Time on the Trail: None
Challenge Level: Easy

"This is a very flexible recipe because there are so many ways to modify it. For example, the applesauce can be replaced with bananas, and the combinations of dried fruit and nuts are endless. Have fun!"

2 cups raw almonds

1 cup applesauce

1½ teaspoons ground cinnamon

1½ cups water

1½ cups dried apricots, chopped

½ cup dried cranberries

½ cup chopped walnuts

½ cup ground flaxseed

½ cup whole wheat flour

5 cups old-fashioned oats

Optional: honey or agave to taste

Required Equipment on the Trail:
None

Nutritional Information per Serving:
Calories: 192
Protein: 6 g
Fat: 7 g
Carbohydrates: 26 g
Fiber: 5 g
Sodium: 8 mg
Cholesterol: 0 mg

Preparation at Home:

1. Soak almonds in water for at least 6 hours, then drain.

2. In a blender, combine almonds, applesauce, cinnamon, and water.

3. Thoroughly blend the mixture, then pour into a large mixing bowl.

4. Add remainder of ingredients to the bowl and mix into a batter.

5. Drop large balls of batter, each about ¼ cup in size, onto lined dehydrator trays. Flatten each ball into a bar or disc about ½-inch thick. There should be enough batter for about 26 bars.

6. Dry the bars in dehydrator until hard, then package for the trail. Each bar provides 1 serving.

Preparation on the Trail:
None

Matthew Farnell
Woodland, Washington

CABIN FEVER COOKIES

V-LO

Total Servings: 8 (1 bar per serving)
As Packaged for the Trail: As required
Weight per Serving: 2 ounces
Preparation Time on the Trail: None
Challenge Level: Easy

Preparation at Home:
1. Preheat oven to 350°F.
2. Combine rye flour, oats, salt, xanthan gum, and walnuts in a bowl.
3. In a separate bowl, beat oil, sugar, vanilla extract, and eggs.
4. Add dry ingredients from the first bowl to the second bowl and mix.
5. Pour batter into a greased 9x9-inch pan.
6. Bake for approximately 30 minutes. The cooked dough should pull away from the edges of the pan, and the surface will be somewhat resistant when poked.
7. Set pan aside to cool before cutting the 'cookie' dough into 8 bars. Each bar provides 1 serving.

Preparation on the Trail:
None

Ramona Hammerly
Anacortes, Washington

½ cup rye flour

½ cup old-fashioned oats

½ teaspoon salt

½ teaspoon xanthan gum or baking powder

¾ cup chopped walnuts

⅓ cup vegetable oil

1 cup brown sugar

1 teaspoon vanilla extract

2 eggs

Required Equipment on the Trail:
None

Nutritional Information per Serving:
Calories: 286
Protein: 6 g
Fat: 18 g
Carbohydrates: 28 g
Fiber: 3 g
Sodium: 172 mg
Cholesterol: 60 mg

DODIE-KAKES

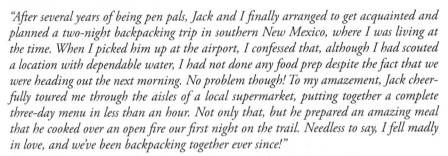

Total Servings: 8 (1 bar per serving)
As Packaged for the Trail: As required
Weight per Serving: 2 ounces
Preparation Time on the Trail: None
Challenge Level: Easy

"After several years of being pen pals, Jack and I finally arranged to get acquainted and planned a two-night backpacking trip in southern New Mexico, where I was living at the time. When I picked him up at the airport, I confessed that, although I had scouted a location with dependable water, I had not done any food prep despite the fact that we were heading out the next morning. No problem though! To my amazement, Jack cheerfully toured me through the aisles of a local supermarket, putting together a complete three-day menu in less than an hour. Not only that, but he prepared an amazing meal that he cooked over an open fire our first night on the trail. Needless to say, I fell madly in love, and we've been backpacking together ever since!"

½ cup roasted pumpkin seeds, chopped

½ cup raisins

½ cup quinoa flakes

2 tablespoons whole grain quinoa

2 tablespoons flax seeds

2 tablespoons sesame seeds, toasted

2 tablespoons honey

1 tablespoon rice bran

1 tablespoon red pepper flakes

1 tablespoon dried egg white powder

½ teaspoon xanthan gum

⅓ cup flour, your choice

4 tablespoons prepared hummus

6 tablespoons prepared tahini

6 tablespoons water

Required Equipment on the Trail:
None

Nutritional Information per Serving:
Calories: 244
Protein: 8 g
Fat: 13 g
Carbohydrates: 24 g
Fiber: 6 g
Sodium: 41 mg
Cholesterol: < 1 mg

Preparation at Home:
1. Preheat oven to 325°F.
2. Mix all ingredients in a bowl.
3. Form dough into a loaf, then slice into 8 bars.
4. Place bars on a greased cookie sheet and bake in oven for 20 minutes.
5. Pack for the trail, 1 bar providing 1 serving.

Preparation on the Trail:
None

Tip: Don't use dried hummus or tahini in this recipe. The moisture is necessary for proper mixing.

Option: For the flour, try a mixture of rice and rye.

*Jack Young and Jo Crescent
Winters, California*

CLEO'S COLESLAW

Total Servings: 1
As Packaged for the Trail: 1 serving
Weight per Serving: 2 ounces
Preparation Time on the Trail: 15 minutes
Challenge Level: Easy

"My youngest daughter named this recipe for Cleo's Bath, a beautiful waterfall near Pinecrest Reservoir in California, where we took her on her first backpack trip when she was seven years old."

Preparation at Home:
1. Mix all ingredients together in a bowl.
2. Dry mixture on a parchment-lined dehydrator tray.
3. Package dried slaw in a pint-size ziplock bag.

Preparation on the Trail:
1. To prepare 1 serving, add ⅓ cup cool water to a bag of slaw.
2. Allow slaw to rehydrate for 10 minutes before serving.

Option: *A squirt of lemon juice, such as from a condiment pack, makes for a nice variation.*

Mara Naber
Mountain Ranch, California

1½ cups fresh coleslaw vegetable mix

1 tablespoon chopped fresh chives

1 tablespoon chopped fresh mint leaves

1 tablespoon chopped fresh dill

2 tablespoons vinaigrette or Italian dressing

⅓ cup water per serving, added on the trail

Required Equipment on the Trail:
None

Nutritional Information per Serving:
Calories: 70
Protein: 1 g
Fat: 3 g
Carbohydrates: 11 g
Fiber: 2 g
Sodium: 200 mg
Cholesterol: 0 mg

CARTER NOTCH COLESLAW

Total Servings: 4
As Packaged for the Trail: 1 serving
Weight per Serving: 3 ounces
Preparation Time on the Trail: 30 minutes
Challenge Level: Easy

½ cup lemon juice

1 cup vinegar

1½ cups granulated sugar

1 teaspoon salt

1 teaspoon ground mustard seed

1 teaspoon celery seed

1 (16-ounce) package fresh coleslaw vegetable mix

1 carrot, peeled and shredded

1 medium sweet onion, chopped

1 small green bell pepper, chopped

Optional: ¼ teaspoon caraway seed or ½ teaspoon prepared horseradish

⅔ cup water per serving, added on the trail

Required Equipment on the Trail:
None

Nutritional Information per Serving:
Calories: 409
Protein: 4 g
Fat: 1 g
Carbohydrates: 100 g
Fiber: 4 g
Sodium: 639 mg
Cholesterol: 0 mg

Preparation at Home:
1. In a pot, heat lemon juice, vinegar, sugar, salt, mustard seed, and celery seed, stirring to dissolve sugar.
2. Immediately remove pot from heat once syrupy mixture reaches boiling.
3. Combine coleslaw mix, carrot, onion, bell pepper, and any optional ingredients in a large bowl.
4. Pour hot sugary syrup over vegetables in the bowl. Toss to coat all vegetables with the liquid.
5. Refrigerate vegetables, covered, for at least 8 hours, tossing at least once during the period.
6. Drain vegetables, then spread mixture thinly and evenly over lined dehydrator trays.
7. Dry, breaking up any lumps part way through the drying process.
8. Divide dried slaw mixture evenly into 4 quart-size ziplock bags, about ⅔ cup into each. Each bag provides 1 serving.

Preparation on the Trail:
1. To prepare 1 serving, add ⅔ cup water to a bag of slaw.
2. Allow slaw to rehydrate for about 30 minutes before serving straight from the bag.

Option: Add contents of a condiment packet of vinegar for additional tang.

Ken Harbison
Rochester, New York

RED HUSKY

V-LO

Total Servings: 1
As Packaged for the Trail: 1 serving
Weight per Serving: 3 ounces
Preparation Time on the Trail: 5 minutes
Challenge Level: Easy

"This is a very simple recipe that makes for a striking taste combination. The name was inspired by my dog, a red husky named Quinn."

Preparation at Home:
Package ingredients separately for the trail.

Preparation on the Trail:
1. To prepare 1 serving, cut 2 ounces of cheddar cheese into bite-size pieces.
2. Combine cheese with ¼ cup of almonds and serve.

Robert "Red Husky" Lauterbach
Rochester, New York

2 ounces sharp cheddar cheese, from block
¼ cup raw almonds

Required Equipment on the Trail:
None

Nutritional Information per Serving:
Calories: 390
Protein: 20 g
Fat: 33 g
Carbohydrates: 6 g
Fiber: 3 g
Sodium: 180 mg
Cholesterol: 30 mg

HIGH COUNTRY HUMMUS

Total Servings: 3
As Packaged for the Trail: 1 serving
Weight per Serving: 3 ounces
Preparation Time on the Trail: 5 minutes (plus 20 minutes to rehydrate)
Challenge Level: Easy

2 (16-ounce) cans garbanzo beans, one can of liquid reserved

½ cup lemon juice

¼ cup prepared tahini

2 gloves garlic, minced

1 tablespoon olive oil

½ teaspoon ground black pepper

Optional: pita bread, tortillas, or crackers

½ cup water per serving, added on the trail

Required Equipment on the Trail:
None

Nutritional Information per Serving:
Calories: 524
Protein: 15 g
Fat: 16 g
Carbohydrates: 67 g
Fiber: 13 g
Sodium: 896 mg
Cholesterol: 0 mg

Preparation at Home:

1. Drain liquid from 1 can garbanzo beans into a blender. Discard liquid from other can of beans.

2. Combine drained beans, lemon juice, tahini, minced garlic, olive oil, and black pepper in blender with the bean liquid from step 1.

3. Blend hummus until smooth.

4. Divide hummus onto each of 3 lined dehydrator trays, about 1 cup to each, then spread evenly.

5. Dry hummus until crumbly.

6. Place contents from each tray into its own pint-size ziplock bag, for a total of 3 bags. Each bag provides 1 serving.

7. Pack optional pita bread, tortillas, or crackers separately.

Preparation on the Trail:

1. To prepare 1 serving, add ½ cup water to a bag of dried hummus mix.

2. Seal bag and massage contents for a minute or so.

3. Allow bag to rest for about 20 minutes until moisture is absorbed.

4. Serve straight from the bag or on optional pita, tortillas, or crackers.

Christine and Tim Conners
Statesboro, Georgia

LOGGER'S GORP

Total Servings: 2
As Packaged for the Trail: 1 serving
Weight per Serving: 3 ounces
Preparation Time on the Trail: None
Challenge Level: Easy

"We ate this at home like popcorn when I was a kid. Dad learned the recipe while growing up in a logging camp. Takes some chewing, so it's good for killing time when you're stuck in your tent. An easy way to eat it is to simply lap it up with your tongue!"

Preparation at Home:
1. Mix raisins and oats together in a bowl.
2. Divide mixture evenly into 2 pint-size ziplock bags, about ¾ cup for 1 serving into each.

Preparation on the Trail:
None

Tip: Fresh and slightly sticky raisins work best because the uncooked oatmeal will cling to them more readily.

Ramona Hammerly
Anacortes, Washington

½ cup raisins, fresh and a bit sticky

1 cup old-fashioned oats

Required Equipment on the Trail:
None

Nutritional Information per Serving:
Calories: 280
Protein: 6 g
Fat: 3 g
Carbohydrates: 58 g
Fiber: 6 g
Sodium: 10 mg
Cholesterol: 0 mg

HORSE THIEF GORP

Total Servings: 20
As Packaged for the Trail: 1 serving
Weight per Serving: 4 ounces
Preparation Time on the Trail: None
Challenge Level: Easy

2 pounds salted roasted mixed nuts

12 ounces dried apricots, chopped

12 ounces dried pears, chopped

12 ounces raisins

6 ounces salted roasted sunflower seeds

10 ounces carob chips

Required Equipment on the Trail:
None

Nutritional Information per Serving:
Calories: 466
Protein: 12 g
Fat: 29 g
Carbohydrates: 41 g
Fiber: 6 g
Sodium: 124 mg
Cholesterol: 0 mg

Preparation at Home:
1. Combine all ingredients together in a bowl. Mix well.
2. Divide mixture evenly into 20 pint-size ziplock bags, about ⅔ cup for 1 serving into each.

Preparation on the Trail:
None

Matthew Farnell
Woodland, Washington

OREGON RAIN GORP

V-LO

Total Servings: 4
As Packaged for the Trail: 1 serving
Weight per Serving: 4 ounces
Preparation Time on the Trail: None
Challenge Level: Easy

Preparation at Home:
1. Mix all ingredients together in a bowl.
2. Divide mixture evenly into 4 pint-size ziplock bags, about ¾ cup for 1 serving into each.

Preparation on the Trail:
None

Beth Murdock
Portland, Oregon

1 cup dried cranberries

1 cup roasted hazelnuts

1 cup semisweet chocolate chips

Required Equipment on the Trail:
None

Nutritional Information per Serving:
Calories: 559
Protein: 6 g
Fat: 30 g
Carbohydrates: 69 g
Fiber: 3 g
Sodium: 1 mg
Cholesterol: < 1 mg

LEMBAS WAYBREAD

Total Servings: 6
As Packaged for the Trail: As required
Weight per Serving: 4 ounces
Preparation Time on the Trail: None
Challenge Level: Easy

"Inspired by the performance-enhancing elven food from J.R.R. Tolkien's classic, The Lord of the Rings.*"*

1 cup plain yogurt

3 cups old-fashioned oats

½ teaspoon salt

½ teaspoon baking soda

1½ cups all-purpose wheat flour

½ cup olive oil

Required Equipment on the Trail:
None

Nutritional Information per Serving:
Calories: 420
Protein: 10 g
Fat: 20 g
Carbohydrates: 53 g
Fiber: 4 g
Sodium: 330 mg
Cholesterol: 3 mg

Preparation at Home:
1. Preheat oven to 375°F.
2. Thoroughly mix yogurt and oats in a bowl.
3. In a separate bowl, combine salt, baking soda, and flour.
4. Add oil to the flour mix followed by the now-soggy oatmeal. Knead. Add a little water if needed, making note that the goal is to produce a consistency like that of pie dough, much more dry than runny.
5. Create a dough ball, then divide in half, forming two smooth, flat rounds.
6. Place each dough round in the middle of its own ungreased cookie sheet and roll dough until it is about ⅛-inch thick.
7. Score dough into squares about 2x2 inches on a side. A serrated pizza cutter works well for this.
8. Bake for about 15 minutes or until dough turns a golden brown.
9. Remove trays from oven and allow to cool.
10. Reduce oven temperature to about 170°F, corresponding roughly to the lowest heat setting.
11. Cut bread along the serrated lines, breaking into individual squares.
12. Once oven reaches the lower temperature, dry bread for about 3 hours, leaving the oven door slightly ajar.
13. Once bread is dry, remove from oven and cool.
14. If you have difficulty finding large, elven leaves, package the waybread instead in ziplock bags for the trail! Plan for about 4 ounces per serving.

Preparation on the Trail:
None

Ramona Hammerly
Anacortes, Washington

BAJA BURRITOS

V

Total Servings: 1
As Packaged for the Trail: 1 serving
Weight per Serving: 4 ounces
Preparation Time on the Trail: 15 minutes (plus several hours to rehydrate)
Challenge Level: Easy

Preparation at Home:

1. Pour salsa onto a lined dehydrator tray and dry.
2. Combine fresh coleslaw mix and onion, then dry on a second lined dehydrator tray.
3. Transfer dried coleslaw-onion mix to a quart-size ziplock freezer bag.
4. Pack the dry refried beans and dehydrated salsa in a second quart-size ziplock freezer bag.
5. Carry tortillas separately.

Preparation on the Trail:

1. To prepare 1 serving, pour ½ cup water, preferably warm, into the bag of dried beans and salsa early in the day.
2. Add ¼ cup of cool water to the bag of dried vegetable mix.
3. Carefully seal both ziplock bags and place in a safe location in your backpack. By midday, the foods will have rehydrated and will be ready to eat.
4. Snip a corner from the bottom of the ziplock bag containing the rehydrated bean and salsa mix.
5. Squeeze half of the beans and salsa onto 1 tortilla.
6. Add half of the coleslaw mix to the tortilla and roll it to serve.
7. Repeat steps 5 and 6 for the second tortilla.

Mara Naber
Mountain Ranch, California

¼ cup mild salsa

1 cup fresh coleslaw vegetable mix

½ onion, finely chopped

½ cup Fantastic World Foods instant refried beans

2 corn tortillas

¾ cup water per serving, added on the trail

Required Equipment on the Trail:
None

Nutritional Information per Serving:
Calories: 418
Protein: 17 g
Fat: 4 g
Carbohydrates: 78 g
Fiber: 22 g
Sodium: 1,215 mg
Cholesterol: 0 mg

ANASAZI TRAIL FOOD

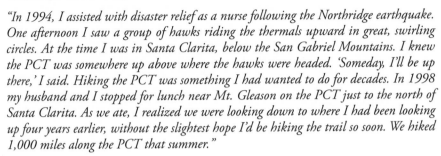

Total Servings: 2
As Packaged for the Trail: 1 serving
Weight per Serving: 4 ounces
Preparation Time on the Trail: 15 minutes (plus 1 hour to rehydrate)
Challenge Level: Easy

"In 1994, I assisted with disaster relief as a nurse following the Northridge earthquake. One afternoon I saw a group of hawks riding the thermals upward in great, swirling circles. At the time I was in Santa Clarita, below the San Gabriel Mountains. I knew the PCT was somewhere up above where the hawks were headed. 'Someday, I'll be up there,' I said. Hiking the PCT was something I had wanted to do for decades. In 1998 my husband and I stopped for lunch near Mt. Gleason on the PCT just to the north of Santa Clarita. As we ate, I realized we were looking down to where I had been looking up four years earlier, without the slightest hope I'd be hiking the trail so soon. We hiked 1,000 miles along the PCT that summer."

1 cup dry Anasazi beans, washed

1 onion, finely chopped

1 clove garlic, minced

1 tablespoon vegetable oil

1 (15-ounce) can diced tomatoes

1 teaspoon dried oregano

1 teaspoon ground cumin

½ to 1 chipotle chili in adobo sauce, mashed

½ teaspoon salt

Optional: crackers or tortillas

1 cup water per serving, added on the trail

Required Equipment on the Trail:
None

Preparation at Home:

1. In a pot, barely cover beans with water, then bring to a boil.

2. Reduce heat and simmer beans until fully cooked. Do not drain!

3. In a large frying pan, sauté onion and garlic in oil over medium heat until softened and translucent.

4. Add tomatoes, seasonings, chili, salt, and the cooked beans to the pan along with a little of the water the beans were cooked in, setting aside the remainder of the water used to cook the beans.

5. Bring bean mixture to simmer over very low heat to blend the flavors.

6. Remove pan from heat and allow bean mixture to cool.

7. Run bean mixture through a food processor until chopped but not pureed. Add bean cooking water, set aside earlier, in small amounts if mixture is too thick to pour.

8. Pour, then evenly spread bean mixture onto lined dehydrator trays.

9. Dry, then divide bean mix evenly between 2 quart-size ziplock freezer bags. Each bag provides 1 serving.

10. Package optional crackers or tortillas separately.

Preparation on the Trail:

1. To prepare 1 serving, add 1 cup water to contents of a bag of bean mix about an hour before lunch.
2. Seal bag, then knead bean mix for a few moments.
3. Hike on for a few miles, then stop and eat bean dip straight from the bag or spread on optional crackers or tortillas.

Beth Murdock
Portland, Oregon

Nutritional Information per Serving:
Calories: 372
Protein: 19 g
Fat: 7 g
Carbohydrates: 55 g
Fiber: 18 g
Sodium: 654 mg
Cholesterol: 0 mg

For vacuum-sealing oils and the like: Make small 1-inch by 3-inch packets using the seal strip on a vacuum sealer. Begin by sealing one narrow end, then both longer sides of each packet. Set a bunch of them, open end up, in the flatware holder of a dishwasher. Fill each packet with a tablespoon of oil or slightly heated ghee. Place packets in freezer, still upright and still unsealed. Once oil is solid, the packets can then be sealed without the vacuum sucking out the contents.

Dave "Chainsaw" Hicks
Dublin, Virginia

BOUNDARY WATERS HUMMUS ON RYE

Total Servings: 3
As Packaged for the Trail: 1 serving
Weight per Serving: 5 ounces
Preparation Time on the Trail: 15 minutes
Challenge Level: Easy

"Hummus and rye crisp will forever remind me of a sunny lunch by a waterfall in the middle of a long portage in the Boundary Waters Canoe Area Wilderness."

1 (6-ounce) package Fantastic World Foods Original hummus mix

1 (9.7-ounce) package rye crispbread

½ cup water per serving, added on the trail

Required Equipment on the Trail:
None

Nutritional Information per Serving:
Calories: 495
Protein: 15 g
Fat: 9 g
Carbohydrates: 84 g
Fiber: 14 g
Sodium: 1,067 mg
Cholesterol: 0 mg

Preparation at Home:
1. Into each of 3 separate pint-size ziplock bags, pour ⅓ cup firmly packed hummus mix.
2. For single servings, place 3 ounces of crispbread (about 6 pieces) into each of 3 pint-size ziplock bags. But if planning on using all 3 servings during the same trip, instead place the unopened package of bread into a gallon-size ziplock bag. This will help protect the bread and prevent crumbs once package is opened.

Preparation on the Trail:
1. To prepare 1 serving, add ½ cup cool water to a bag of hummus and knead mixture in the bag.
2. Allow hummus to rehydrate for about 10 minutes.
3. Snip a corner from bottom of bag and squeeze hummus onto each of 6 pieces of crispbread.

Ramona Hammerly
Anacortes, Washington

TREKIN' FUEL

Total Servings: 15
As Packaged for the Trail: 1 serving
Weight per Serving: 5 ounces
Preparation Time on the Trail: None
Challenge Level: Easy

V-LO

"The advantage of using candy corn in this recipe, instead of chocolate or carob, is that it doesn't melt while still providing lots of short-term energy. I sometimes use this mix for breakfast by just adding a little reconstituted milk, hot or cold. Gets me on the trail quickly with a burst of energy."

Preparation at Home:
1. Mix all ingredients together in a large bowl.
2. Divide mixture evenly into 15 pint-size ziplock bags, about 1 cup for 1 serving into each.

Preparation on the Trail:
None

Option: *Add a little reconstituted milk to eat like a cereal.*

Ted "Trekin' Ted" Ayers
Rapid City, South Dakota

1 (28-ounce) package Quaker Oats, Honey, Raisins, and Almonds granola

6 ounces dried sweetened cranberries

7 ounces dried apricots, chopped

10 ounces chopped dates

12 ounces candy corn

2 cups salted roasted peanuts

Required Equipment for the Trail:
None

Nutritional Information per Serving:
Calories: 538
Protein: 9 g
Fat: 15 g
Carbohydrates: 96 g
Fiber: 10 g
Sodium: 136 mg
Cholesterol: < 1 mg

JUST GORP

V-LO

Total Servings: 4
As Packaged for the Trail: 1 serving
Weight per Serving: 5 ounces
Preparation Time on the Trail: None
Challenge Level: Easy

"There are so many versions of gorp, but this is a favorite. It's tasty and provides quick energy."

1 cup low-fat granola

1 cup plain M&Ms

1 cup lightly salted dry-roasted peanuts

1 cup raisins

Required Equipment on the Trail:
None

Nutritional Information per Serving:
Calories: 593
Protein: 13 g
Fat: 24 g
Carbohydrates: 83 g
Fiber: 8 g
Sodium: 179 mg
Cholesterol: 5 mg

Preparation at Home:
1. Mix all ingredients together in a bowl.
2. Divide mixture evenly into 4 pint-size ziplock bags, about 1 cup for 1 serving into each.

Preparation on the Trail:
None

Liz Bergeron
Sacramento, California

HULA GORP

Total Servings: 7
As Packaged for the Trail: 1 serving
Weight per Serving: 5 ounces
Preparation Time on the Trail: None
Challenge Level: Easy

Preparation at Home:
1. Combine and mix all ingredients in a bowl.
2. Divide mixture evenly into 7 pint-size ziplock bags, about 1 cup for 1 serving into each.

Preparation on the Trail:
None

Christine and Tim Conners
Statesboro, Georgia

6 ounces dried mango, torn into bite-size pieces

8 ounces dates, chopped

6 ounces dried pineapple pieces

1 cup shredded sweetened coconut

2 cups salted roasted macadamia nuts

Required Equipment on the Trail:
None

Nutritional Information per Serving:
Calories: 605
Protein: 7 g
Fat: 32 g
Carbohydrates: 81 g
Fiber: 9 g
Sodium: 183 mg
Cholesterol: 0 mg

ZION GORP

Total Servings: 8
As Packaged for the Trail: 1 serving
Weight per Serving: 5 ounces
Preparation Time on the Trail: None
Challenge Level: Easy

"We were backpacking in Zion National Park one Christmas, at a time when Gloria weighed about one hundred pounds. We had almost topped a ridge to a fantastic view point when we met another group headed the opposite direction. We exchanged greetings and continued on our way. As we departed, a member of the other group was overheard to exclaim, 'Did you see that tiny lady with the giant backpack?' We attributed Gloria's endurance and strength to Zion Gorp."

1 cup pumpkin seeds (pepitas)

1 cup salted roasted peanuts

1 cup unsalted sunflower kernels

1 cup carob chips

1 cup soy nuts

2 cups raisins

Required Equipment on the Trail:
None

Nutritional Information per Serving:
Calories: 597
Protein: 21 g
Fat: 32 g
Carbohydrates: 61 g
Fiber: 10 g
Sodium: 151 mg
Cholesterol: 0 mg

Preparation at Home:
1. Combine and mix all ingredients in a large bowl.
2. Divide mixture evenly into 8 pint-size ziplock bags, about 1 cup for 1 serving into each.

Preparation on the Trail:
None

Option: This recipe serves great as a base, then adjusting as desired for different tastes.

Larry and Gloria Bright
John Day, Oregon

SPIDERMAN GORP

V-LO

Total Servings: 12
As Packaged for the Trail: 1 serving
Weight per Serving: 5 ounces
Preparation Time on the Trail: None
Challenge Level: Easy

Preparation at Home:
1. Combine and mix all ingredients in a large bowl.
2. Divide mixture evenly into 12 pint-size ziplock bags, about 1 cup for 1 serving into each.

Preparation on the Trail:
None

Mike "Spiderman" and
Sue "Ground Control" Reynolds
Columbus, Indiana

1 pound lightly salted roasted peanuts

24 (about 8 ounces) dried apricots, halved

5 ounces dried apples

9 ounces raisins

1 (19.2-ounce) package plain M&Ms

2 cups granola cereal

Required Equipment on the Trail:
None

Nutritional Information per Serving:
Calories: 653
Protein: 15 g
Fat: 29 g
Carbohydrates: 78 g
Fiber: 9 g
Sodium: 254 mg
Cholesterol: 6 mg

GREEK WAYFARING TORTILLA

V-LO

Total Servings: 1
As Packaged for the Trail: 1 serving
Weight per Serving: 5 ounces
Preparation Time on the Trail: 15 minutes
Challenge Level: Easy

10 sun-dried tomato halves, chopped

1 teaspoon dried basil

3 ounces feta cheese

1 tablespoon olive oil

1 small whole wheat tortilla

Required Equipment on the Trail:
None

Nutritional Information per Serving:
Calories: 614
Protein: 21 g
Fat: 38 g
Carbohydrates: 49 g
Fiber: 6 g
Sodium: 1,670 mg
Cholesterol: 45 mg

Preparation at Home:
1. Pack sun-dried tomatoes in a sandwich-size ziplock bag along with the basil.
2. Carry feta cheese and oil separately.
3. Wrap tortilla in foil and pack that separately as well.

Preparation on the Trail:
1. To prepare 1 serving, crumble feta cheese into bag of dried tomato-basil.
2. Add 1 tablespoon olive oil to the bag, then seal and shake the bag for a few moments.
3. Pour cheese-oil mixture over tortilla, then roll and serve.

Tip: Feta cheese does not keep long if it remains unrefrigerated, so use early in the trip or substitute with a more durable hard cheese.

Katarina "Katgirl" Sengstaken
Hollis, New Hampshire

Fresh veggies make a meal real.
Garlic, kale, and carrots pack well,
last a long time in cooler weather,
and are delicious.

Jason Rumohr
Seattle, Washington

TAPENADE

V-LO

Total Servings: 1
As Packaged for the Trail: 1 serving
Weight per Serving: 6 ounces
Preparation Time on the Trail: 15 minutes
(plus several hours to rehydrate)
Challenge Level: Easy

Preparation at Home:
1. Place sun-dried tomatoes, seasoning, and optional bell peppers in a pint-size ziplock bag.
2. Set bag in freezer for about 10 minutes to harden tomatoes.
3. Chop vegetables in a blender or food processor, then package for the trail in the ziplock bag.
4. Pack cheese and pita shells separately.

Preparation on the Trail:
1. Preferably several hours before lunch, but no less than 15 minutes prior, add 2 tablespoons water to the bag of dry vegetables and seasoning, then knead into a thick paste (tapenade).
2. When it's time for lunch, spread cream cheese into the pita shells, then add the now-rehydrated tapenade and serve.

Tip: Cheeses can often be found at the grocery store sealed in small 1-ounce packets. These pack and carry well on the trail.

Ken Harbison
Rochester, New York

½ ounce sun-dried tomatoes

½ teaspoon dry Italian seasoning

Optional: ¼ ounce dried bell peppers

3 ounces cream cheese

2 whole wheat pita bread shells

2 tablespoons water per serving, added on the trail

Required Equipment on the Trail:
None

Nutritional Information per Serving:
Calories: 680
Protein: 21 g
Fat: 29 g
Carbohydrates: 86 g
Fiber: 6 g
Sodium: 825 mg
Cholesterol: 120 mg

TABOULI SALAD

V-LO

Total Servings: 1
As Packaged for the Trail: 1 serving
Weight per Serving: 7 ounces
Preparation Time on the Trail: 30 minutes
Challenge Level: Easy

½ cup Fantastic World Foods tabouli

½ cup plain couscous

2 tablespoons chopped dried tomatoes

1 teaspoon dried cilantro

1 cup water per serving, added on the trail

Required Equipment on the Trail:
None

Nutritional Information per Serving:
Calories: 672
Protein: 32 g
Fat: 2 g
Carbohydrates: 145 g
Fiber: 16 g
Sodium: 1,149 mg
Cholesterol: 0 mg

Preparation at Home:
Combine all dry ingredients in a quart-size ziplock bag.

Preparation on the Trail:
1. To prepare 1 serving, add 1 cup water, cold or warm, to a bag of tabouli salad.
2. Allow contents to rehydrate for about 30 minutes before serving straight from the bag.

Ramona Hammerly
Anacortes, Washington

Why stand on tradition? Nori (dried seaweed) can be used as a wrapper for nontraditional fillings, such as polenta and sun-dried tomatoes. Traditional fillings, such as rice and veggies, can be spiced in new ways using nori.

Brandon "Uluheman" Stone
Honolulu, Hawaii

BLACK BEAR BEAN SPREAD

Total Servings: 4
As Packaged for the Trail: 1 serving
Weight per Serving: 2 ounces
Preparation Time on the Trail: 15 minutes (plus several hours to rehydrate)
Challenge Level: Easy

V

Preparation at Home:

1. Combine and mix all dry ingredients, except for crackers, in a bowl.
2. Divide mixture evenly into 4 quart-size ziplock freezer bags, about ½ cup into each. Each bag produces 1 serving.
3. Pack optional crackers and vegetable oil separately.

Preparation on the Trail:

1. To prepare 1 serving, bring ½ cup water to boil in a pot early in the day.
2. Allow boiling to subside for a few seconds, then carefully pour water into a bag of bean spread mixture. An optional 1 teaspoon oil can be added at this time, if desired.
3. Knead bean mixture in bag and stash away in a safe location in your pack.
4. When it's time for lunch, eat bean spread straight from the bag or add as a topping to optional crackers.

Suzanne Allen
Seattle, Washington

1 (7-ounce) package Fantastic World Foods instant black beans

¼ cup sesame seeds

1 teaspoon lemon pepper seasoning

¼ teaspoon garlic powder

½ teaspoon onion powder

¼ teaspoon ground cumin

Optional: crackers and 1 teaspoon vegetable oil per serving

½ cup water per serving, added on the trail

Required Equipment on the Trail:
Cook pot

Nutritional Information per Serving:
Calories: 237
Protein: 13 g
Fat: 6 g
Carbohydrates: 35 g
Fiber: 9 g
Sodium: 579 mg
Cholesterol: 0 mg

HEAVENLY HUMMUS

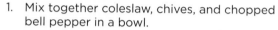

Total Servings: 1
As Packaged for the Trail: 1 serving
Weight per Serving: 4 ounces
Preparation Time on the Trail: 15 minutes
(plus several hours to rehydrate)
Challenge Level: Easy

"A great dip for carrots, celery, or crackers!"

1 cup fresh coleslaw vegetable mix

1 tablespoon chopped fresh chives

½ red bell pepper, chopped

¼ cup mild salsa

½ cup Fantastic World Foods Original hummus mix

Optional: mustard condiment packets and crackers

¾ cup water per serving, added on the trail

Required Equipment on the Trail:
Cook pot

Nutritional Information per Serving:
Calories: 284
Protein: 13 g
Fat: 8 g
Carbohydrates: 45 g
Fiber: 9 g
Sodium: 1,103 mg
Cholesterol: 0 mg

Preparation at Home:
1. Mix together coleslaw, chives, and chopped bell pepper in a bowl.
2. Dry vegetable mix on a lined dehydrator tray.
3. Pour salsa onto a separate lined dehydrator tray and dry as well.
4. Pack dried vegetable mix in a pint-size ziplock bag.
5. Pour hummus mix and dried salsa in a quart-size ziplock freezer bag.
6. Carry optional mustard packets or crackers separately.

Preparation on the Trail:
1. To prepare 1 serving, bring ½ cup water to boil in a pot early in the day.
2. Allow boiling to subside for a few seconds, then carefully pour water into a bag of hummus-salsa mixture.
3. Add ¼ cup cool water to the vegetable mix in its bag.
4. Carefully seal both ziplock bags and place in a safe location in your backpack. By midday, the foods will have rehydrated and will be ready to eat.
5. Combine vegetable mix with the hummus. Can be served as is or used as a dip for optional crackers. Optional mustard adds zing.

Mara Naber
Mountain Ranch, California

BASIC BACKPACKER'S SUSHI

Total Servings: 4
As Packaged for the Trail: 1 serving
Weight per Serving: 4 ounces
Preparation Time on the Trail: 15 minutes
(plus several hours to rehydrate)
Challenge Level: Difficult

"Special thanks to Marc Sherman with Outdoor Gear Exchange at gearx.com and Brandon Stone, who helped create this recipe."

Preparation at Home:
1. Prepare sushi rice according to package directions.
2. In a large bowl, combine sugar, rice vinegar, salt, and sesame seeds.
3. Once rice is ready, add it to the liquid in the bowl and stir until rice is evenly coated.
4. If using optional ingredients, process those that are vegetables, fruit, or roots in a food grinder, then add to the rice mixture at this time.
5. Place rice mixture on lined dehydrator trays and dry.
6. Break apart lumps, then place about 1 cup of dried rice mixture into each of 4 separate quart-size ziplock freezer bags. Each bag provides 1 serving.
7. Carry sheets of nori separately, packing 2 per serving.
8. Package optional soy sauce or powdered condiments separately for the trail.

Preparation on the Trail:
1. To prepare 1 serving, bring 1 cup water to boil early in the day.
2. Allow boiling to subside for a few seconds, then carefully pour water into 1 bag of sushi rice mixture.
3. Seal, then knead bag to further break apart remaining lumps of rice mix.
4. Insulate bag to retain heat as long as possible, and place in a safe location in your pack. By midday the rice should be fully rehydrated.

2 cups sushi rice

¼ cup granulated sugar

¼ cup rice vinegar

½ teaspoon salt

¼ cup sesame seeds

8 sheets nori seaweed

Optional: cucumber, pickled burdock, pickled radish, pickled ginger, pickled mango, dried carrot, soy sauce, powdered wasabi, miso soup powder

1 cup water per serving, added on the trail

Required Equipment on the Trail:
Cook pot

Clean, flat surface, such as a pot lid

Nutritional Information per Serving:
Calories: 424
Protein: 10 g
Fat: 5 g
Carbohydrates: 86 g
Fiber: 3 g
Sodium: 160 mg
Cholesterol: 0 mg

5. At lunchtime, lay 1 sheet of nori flat with the shiny side down on a clean surface, such as a pot lid, with the perforations in the nori running perpendicular to you.
6. Moisten nori lightly with fingers dipped in water.
7. Scoop half of the rehydrated rice onto the sheet of nori, forming a band of rice side to side across the width of the sheet about 1 inch from the end closest to you.
8. Carefully roll the nori away from you as you might a fat cigar.
9. The roll can be cut into traditional sushi slices or simply eaten like a burrito.
10. Repeat using the remaining ingredients.

Options: *To avoid home drying, prepare instant rice on the trail, adding a small amount of dried sushi seasoning, available in Oriental food stores. Any fresh ingredients in your pack at the time can also be added. And sushi doesn't necessarily need to be rolled: just place the rice and your favorite ingredients on top of nori, fold it, and pop it into your mouth!*

Tip: If you really want to impress your friends with spectacular results, a traditional bamboo mat can be used to roll the sushi. Some might frown at the additional weight of such a device (about 3½ ounces). However, once the alternate applications for such a mat are considered, the additional weight may seem less onerous: use it as a sun shade, a bug swatter, a hand fan, or a place mat for your utensils! In an emergency situation you could even burn it as kindling. Or how about this: Use it like a fig leaf in the event you're caught naked in the woods. Now that's versatility!

Christine and Tim Conners
Statesboro, Georgia

Dinner

EASTERN SUN MISO SOUP

Total Servings: 1
As Packaged for the Trail: 1 serving
Weight per Serving: 2 ounces
Preparation Time on the Trail: 15 minutes
Challenge Level: Easy

"A great lightweight recipe to warm you up before your main course."

2 dried shiitake
mushrooms, chopped

2 tablespoons dried
carrot pieces

1 (0.7-ounce) packet
Miso-Cup instant soup
with seaweed

½ ounce dried tofu,
broken into small pieces

1 sheet nori seaweed,
torn into small pieces

1½ cups water per
serving, added on the
trail

**Required Equipment on
the Trail:**
Cook pot

**Nutritional Information
per Serving:**
Calories: 135
Protein: 9 g
Fat: 2 g
Carbohydrates: 20 g
Fiber: 6 g
Sodium: 843 mg
Cholesterol: 0 mg

Preparation at Home:
Combine all dry ingredients in a pint-size
ziplock bag.

Preparation on the Trail:
1. To prepare 1 serving, bring 1½ cups water
   to boil in a cook pot.
2. Add soup mix to the hot water. Stir.
3. Immediately remove pot from heat and let
   sit for about 5 minutes before serving.

*Rachel Jolly
Burlington, Vermont*

TUEEULALA THAI SOUP

Total Servings: 3
As Packaged for the Trail: 1 serving
Weight per Serving: 3 ounces
Preparation Time on the Trail: 15 minutes
Challenge Level: Easy

"Makes for a delicious appetizer!"

Preparation at Home:
1. Thaw, chop, and dry Oriental vegetable blend in a dehydrator.
2. Divide dried vegetable mixture evenly into 3 pint-size ziplock freezer bags, about 1/3 cup for 1 serving into each.
3. Add ¼ cup TVP to each bag of dried vegetables.
4. Pack Thai noodles separately, 1 package of noodles for each serving. Include the spice packet found in Thai Kitchen noodle soup package.

Preparation on the Trail:
1. To prepare 1 serving, bring 2½ cups water to boil in a cook pot.
2. To the hot water, add contents from a bag of dried vegetable mix and a package of Thai noodles along with the contents from its spice packet.
3. Return noodles to boil for about 3 minutes.
4. Remove pot from heat, stir, cover, and let sit for an extra minute or so, giving time for the vegetables to rehydrate before serving.

Heather Burror
Martinez, California

1 (16-ounce) package frozen Oriental-blend vegetables

¾ cup unflavored textured vegetable protein (TVP)

3 (1.6-ounce) packages Thai Kitchen Garlic and Vegetable instant noodle soup

2½ cups water per serving, added on the trail

Required Equipment on the Trail:
Cook pot with lid

Nutritional Information per Serving:
Calories: 300
Protein: 17 g
Fat: 2 g
Carbohydrates: 50 g
Fiber: 8 g
Sodium: 422 mg
Cholesterol: 0 mg

BACK ROCK BAMI GORENG

Total Servings: 4
As Package for the Trail: 1 serving
Weight per Serving: 3 ounces
Preparation Time on the Trail: 15 minutes (plus 1 hour to rehydrate)
Challenge Level: Moderate

"I first witnessed the backpacking variety of bami goreng while accompanying Javanese friends on a night adventure in the jungles of South America. We were waiting for complete darkness and the moon to set, so we slung our hammocks in a clump of trees. Only trouble: I'd forgotten my hammock! For dinner, Boefie, a close friend, boiled Thai noodles, enough for the three of us. The method was very similar to that described in the recipe. Afterwards, I was off to a restless sleep. I hate sleeping on the jungle ground. Maybe it's just a basic fear of scorpions, big hairy spiders, snakes..."

1 (8-ounce) package fresh coleslaw vegetable mix

1 onion, finely chopped

2 scallions, finely chopped

1 bell pepper, finely chopped

3 ounces fresh shiitake mushrooms, finely chopped

4 (1.6-ounce) packages Thai Kitchen Spring Onion rice noodles

4 cubes vegan vegetable bouillon

4 teaspoons soy sauce

1⅓ cups water per serving, added on the trail

Required Equipment on the Trail:
Cook pot

Preparation at Home:
1. Mix coleslaw and all finely chopped vegetables and mushrooms together, then dry on a lined dehydrator tray.
2. Divide dried vegetable mix evenly between 4 pint-size ziplock bags.
3. Carry 1 noodle package, 1 bouillon cube, and 1 teaspoon soy sauce per serving separately.

Preparation on the Trail:
1. To prepare 1 serving, add ⅓ cup water to a bag of coleslaw-vegetable mix about an hour before dinner.
2. At dinnertime, bring 1 cup water to boil along with 1 bouillon cube.
3. Add contents from a pack of noodles and cook for about 3 minutes.
4. Drain broth from noodles and pour into a cup as a hot drink on the side.
5. Add oil from the Thai Kitchen noodle package to the pot and stir-fry the cooked noodles for about 1 minute.
6. Open seasoning packet from the Thai Kitchen noodle package and pour over noodles in the pot.
7. Add rehydrated veggie-mushroom mix to the pot and stir-fry once again for an additional minute.

8. Remove pot from heat and stir in 1 teaspoon soy sauce before serving.

Tip: To significantly reduce sodium content, boil the noodles without the bouillon cube.

Andreas "Marmoset" Raehmi
Zurich, Switzerland

Nutritional Information per Serving (including hot drink):
Calories: 252
Protein: 6 g
Fat: 3 g
Carbohydrates: 47 g
Fiber: 3 g
Sodium: 2,823 mg
Cholesterol: 0 mg

A Frisbee works nicely as a serving plate. You can wash it easily, pack it readily, play with it, and use it as a fan. It makes for a great, durable, multipurpose tool for eating well and having fun in the woods.

Ben "The Vegan Super Hero" Hahn
Corvallis, Oregon

BOOT-STOMPED SPUDS

Total Servings: 1
As Packaged for the Trail: 1 serving
Weight per Serving: 4 ounces
Preparation Time on the Trail: 5 minutes
Challenge Level: Easy

V-LO

"I carry this as an emergency meal. It's very light, needs little water, and doesn't have to stand to rehydrate. To take off the chill, we've eaten this on many a stormy day as soon as we got holed up in the tent."

⅔ cup instant mashed potato flakes

2 tablespoons instant dry nonfat milk

1 teaspoon Butter Buds Sprinkles

1 teaspoon dried cilantro flakes

1 teaspoon onion flakes, finely minced

2 tablespoons dry Alfredo sauce mix

2 tablespoons vegetarian imitation bacon bits

1 pinch black pepper

1 cup water per serving, added on the trail

Required Equipment on the Trail:
Cook pot

Nutritional Information per Serving:
Calories: 314
Protein: 13 g
Fat: 5 g
Carbohydrates: 56 g
Fiber: 4 g
Sodium: 1,278 mg
Cholesterol: 7 mg

Preparation at Home:
Combine all dry ingredients together in a pint-size ziplock bag.

Preparation on the Trail:
1. To prepare 1 serving, bring 1 cup water to boil in a cook pot, then remove pot from heat.
2. Add spud mix to the hot water and stir.
3. Serve immediately.

Marion "Llamalady" Davison
Apple Valley, California

PCT

BLACK MOUNTAIN POTATOES

V-LO

Total Servings: 2
As Packaged for the Trail: 2 servings
Weight per Serving: 4 ounces
Preparation Time on the Trail: 15 minutes
Challenge Level: Easy

Preparation at Home:
Combine all dry ingredients, including contents of the soup spice packet, in a quart-size ziplock bag.

Preparation on the Trail:
1. To prepare 2 servings, pour contents of ziplock bag into 3½ cups water in cook pot and bring to boil.
2. Immediately remove pot from heat, stir, cover, and let stand for 5 to 10 minutes until beans are soft.

Richard "Ranger Rick" Halbert
Traverse City, Michigan

1 cup instant mashed potato flakes

½ cup Kraft grated Parmesan cheese

½ teaspoon garlic powder

1 (3.4-ounce) package Dr. McDougall's Black Bean and Lime soup mix

3½ cups water per 2 servings, added on the trail

Required Equipment on the Trail:
Cook pot with lid

Nutritional Information per Serving:
Calories: 420
Protein: 24 g
Fat: 10 g
Carbohydrates: 60 g
Fiber: 13 g
Sodium: 888 mg
Cholesterol: 30 mg

SOUP OF MOUNT INTHANON

Total Servings: 1
As Packaged for the Trail: 1 serving
Weight per Serving: 4 ounces
Preparation Time on the Trail: 15 minutes
Challenge Level: Easy

¼ cup Fantastic World Foods instant black beans

1 (1.6-ounce) package Thai Kitchen Spring Onion rice noodles

¼ cup unflavored textured vegetable protein (TVP)

2 cups water per serving, added on the trail

Required Equipment on the Trail:
Cook pot

Nutritional Information per Serving:
Calories: 400
Protein: 22 g
Fat: 5 g
Carbohydrates: 67 g
Fiber: 16 g
Sodium: 990 mg
Cholesterol: 0 mg

Preparation at Home:
1. Combine beans, noodles, and TVP in a pint-size ziplock bag.
2. Leave spice and oil packets from rice noodles intact and include in the ziplock bag.

Preparation on the Trail:
1. To prepare 1 serving, bring 2 cups water to boil in a cook pot.
2. Add bean mixture from the ziplock bag to the pot along with contents from the spice and oil packets. Stir.
3. Immediately remove pot from heat and set aside for several minutes, allowing beans to rehydrate before serving.

Jason Rumohr
Seattle, Washington

TRAILDAD'S SPAGHETTI

Total Servings: 2
As Packaged for the Trail: 2 servings
Weight per Serving: 4 ounces
Preparation Time on the Trail: 15 minutes
Challenge Level: Easy

V-LO

"TrailDad is my father, Roy Robinson. He single-handedly packed fifty-seven resupply boxes for the Continental Divide and Pacific Crest legs of my Triple Crown hike. That required dehydrating many gallons of sauce! TrailDad's Spaghetti is my favorite recipe."

Preparation at Home:

1. If spaghetti sauce is chunky, blend it.
2. Dehydrate spaghetti sauce on lined trays until hard and brittle.
3. Place dried sauce in a pint-size ziplock bag.
4. Pack pasta, cheese, and oil separately.

Preparation on the Trail:

1. To prepare 2 servings, crumble dried spaghetti sauce into 2½ cups water in cook pot.
2. Bring pot to boiling, then add contents from bag of pasta along with 2 tablespoons olive oil.
3. Stir pasta often for several minutes, simmering if your stove permits. If a low flame is not possible with your stove, remove pot from heat to prevent scorching, but keep contents warm as long as possible by insulating pot while pasta rehydrates. In any case, the pasta will eventually soak up the liquid so there will be no need to drain the pot.
4. Add ¼ cup of Parmesan cheese to pot, then stir and serve.

Tip: Long-distance hikers may want to use this recipe as a single serving when the additional calories are needed.

1 (26-ounce) jar Classico tomato and basil spaghetti sauce (or your favorite)

4 ounces whole wheat angel-hair pasta

¼ cup Kraft grated Parmesan cheese

2 tablespoons olive oil

2½ cups water per 2 servings, added on the trail

Required Equipment on the Trail:
Cook pot

Nutritional Information per Serving:
Calories: 543
Protein: 21 g
Fat: 20 g
Carbohydrates: 64 g
Fiber: 11 g
Sodium: 1,131 mg
Cholesterol: 11 mg

*Brian "Flyin' Brian" Robinson
Mountain View, California*

SPRINGER MOUNTAIN PESTO

V-LO

Total Servings: 2
As Packaged for the Trail: 2 servings
Weight per Serving: 4 ounces
Preparation Time on the Trail: 15 minutes
Challenge Level: Easy

"Our three little ones were huddled around the cook pot on Springer Mountain one evening during a backpack trip at the AT's southern terminus. James was five years old, Michael was almost four, and Maria had just turned two. Like many kids that age, ours were pretty picky about their food, turning their little noses up at almost everything it seemed. But not that evening. It had been a long day on the trail, and they couldn't shovel that pasta in fast enough!"

¼ teaspoon garlic powder

¼ cup pine nuts

2 tablespoons chopped dried basil leaves

¼ cup Kraft grated Parmesan cheese

Optional: salt to taste

4 ounces whole wheat angel-hair pasta

¼ cup olive oil

2½ cups water per serving, added on the trail

Required Equipment on the Trail:
Cook pot

Nutritional Information per Serving:
Calories: 602
Protein: 14 g
Fat: 44 g
Carbohydrates: 38 g
Fiber: 7 g
Sodium: 202 mg
Cholesterol: 11 mg

Preparation at Home:
1. Create pesto mix by combining garlic powder, pine nuts, basil, Parmesan cheese, and optional salt in a pint-size ziplock bag.
2. Pack pasta and oil separately.

Preparation on the Trail:
1. To prepare 2 servings, bring 2½ cups water to boil in a cook pot.
2. Add pasta to pot and cook until tender, about 5 to 10 minutes. Most of the water should be absorbed by the pasta, requiring little draining.
3. Add contents from bag of pesto mix along with ¼ cup olive oil to the pasta. Toss and serve.

Christine and Tim Conners
Statesboro, Georgia

GREEK TRAIL RICE

Total Servings: 4
As Packaged for the Trail: 1 serving
Weight per Serving: 4 ounces
Preparation Time on the Trail: 15 minutes
Challenge Level: Easy

V-LO

"I love Greek cuisine, and this recipe packs all the flavors found in traditional stuffed grape leaves. It's lightweight and simple enough to take with me on all my adventures."

Preparation at Home:

1. In a medium-size cook pot, bring 1¾ cups water to boil.
2. Add rice and stir. Return rice to a boil, then reduce heat to a simmer.
3. Cover pot and continue to cook over low heat for 5 minutes or until rice is soft.
4. Add remaining ingredients, except for olive oil and water to be added on the trail. Stir.
5. Return rice to a gentle boil for several minutes, then remove pot from heat and allow to cool.
6. Evenly divide rice mixture between 4 lined dehydrator trays, about 1½ cups of rice mix onto each.
7. Once dry, package rice mixture from each tray into its own pint-size ziplock bag. Each bag provides 1 serving.
8. Carry oil separately, 1 teaspoon per serving.

Preparation on the Trail:

1. To prepare 1 serving, add contents from a bag of rice to 1½ cups water in a cook pot along with 1 teaspoon olive oil.
2. Bring pot to a boil for several minutes.
3. Stir rice, cover pot, then remove from heat. Allow pot to rest several more minutes before serving.

Curt "The Titanium Chef" White
Forks, Washington

1¾ cups water

2 cups instant brown rice

1 cup Greek yogurt

2 tablespoons lemon juice

1 teaspoon dried dill

1 teaspoon dried mint

1 teaspoon dried parsley

1 (7-ounce) jar sliced Kalamata olives, drained and rinsed

1 (12-ounce) jar marinated artichoke hearts, drained and chopped

¼ cup pine nuts

8 grape leaves, from jar, stems removed

1 cup crumbled Greek feta cheese

1 teaspoon olive oil per serving, added on the trail

1½ cups water per serving, added on the trail

Required Equipment on the Trail:
Cook pot

Nutritional Information per Serving:
Calories: 527
Protein: 17 g
Fat: 22 g
Carbohydrates: 52 g
Fiber: 4 g
Sodium: 1,383 mg
Cholesterol: 14 mg

SWEET SURF AND TURF RICE

Total Servings: 4
As Packaged for the Trail: 2 servings
Weight per Serving: 4 ounces
Preparation Time on the Trail: 15 minutes
Challenge Level: Easy

1 cup brown long grain rice

1 (13.5-ounce) can coconut milk

1 (8-ounce) can crushed pineapple

1 red bell pepper, finely chopped

1 small sweet onion, finely chopped

1 ripe mango, finely chopped

½ cup chopped pecans

1 tablespoon curry powder

2 tablespoons maple syrup

½ teaspoon salt

½ cup chopped cilantro

1 cup water

2 cups water per serving, added on the trail

Required Equipment on the Trail:
Cook pot

Nutritional Information per Serving:
Calories: 449
Protein: 8 g
Fat: 26 g
Carbohydrates: 50 g
Fiber: 5 g
Sodium: 324 mg
Cholesterol: 0 mg

Preparation at Home:
1. Combine all ingredients, including 1 cup water, in a medium-size pot. Be careful not to include water needed on the trail in this step.
2. Bring pot to boil, then simmer for about 45 minutes or until rice is fully cooked.
3. Once rice is soft, divide rice mix between 2 lined dehydrator trays, about 2 cups onto each.
4. Dry mixture, then divide evenly into each of 2 pint-size ziplock bags. Each bag will produce 2 servings.

Preparation on the Trail:
1. To prepare 2 servings, bring 2 cups water to boil in a cook pot.
2. Add contents of a ziplock bag to pot. Stir.
3. Reduce heat to a simmer and continue to cook until rice is fully rehydrated, about 10 minutes.

Christine and Tim Conners
Statesboro, Georgia

FIRE CREEK EGGPLANT MOZZARELLA

V-LO

Total Servings: 2
As Packaged for the Trail: 1 serving
Weight per Serving: 4 ounces
Preparation Time on the Trail: 15 minutes
Challenge Level: Easy

Preparation at Home:

1. Finely chop eggplants and onions in a food processor.
2. Combine chopped eggplant and onion in a pot along with garlic and diced tomatoes and chilies.
3. Bring vegetables to a low boil, then remove from heat and allow to cool.
4. Evenly divide vegetable mixture between two lined dehydrator trays, about 2½ cups onto each.
5. Spread vegetable mixture evenly and dehydrate.
6. Place dried eggplant mixture from each tray into its own pint-size ziplock bag. Each bag will provide 1 serving.
7. Carry cheese in original packaging, 1 stick per serving, and pack oil separately, using 2 tablespoons per serving.

Preparation on the Trail:

1. To prepare 1 serving, add 2 cups water to a pot along with contents from a bag of eggplant mix.
2. Cut 1 mozzarella stick into pieces and add to pot along with 2 tablespoons olive oil.
3. Stir well and bring all to a boil, then immediately remove from heat.
4. Cover pot and set aside for 5 to 10 minutes while contents rehydrate.

2 medium eggplants

2 medium onions

4 cloves garlic, minced

2 (10-ounce) cans diced tomatoes and green chilies, undrained

2 sticks mozzarella string cheese

4 tablespoons olive oil

2 cups water per serving, added on the trail

Required Equipment on the Trail:
Cook pot with lid

Nutritional Information per Serving:
Calories: 565
Protein: 17 g
Fat: 35 g
Carbohydrates: 57 g
Fiber: 24 g
Sodium: 1,178 mg
Cholesterol: 15 mg

Christine and Tim Conners
Statesboro, Georgia

OLANCHA SWEET PEPPER PASTA

Total Servings: 2
As Packaged for the Trail: 1 serving
Weight per Serving: 5 ounces
Preparation Time on the Trail: 20 minutes
Challenge Level: Easy

1 red onion, finely chopped

2 sweet red peppers, finely chopped

3 cloves garlic, minced

1 tablespoon finely chopped fresh basil

1 tablespoon finely chopped fresh oregano

Optional: garlic salt to taste

8 ounces capellini noodles

2 tablespoons olive oil

1 cook pot full of water, added on the trail

Required Equipment on the Trail:
Cook pot with lid

Nutritional Information per Serving:
Calories: 602
Protein: 15 g
Fat: 16 g
Carbohydrates: 92 g
Fiber: 3 g
Sodium: 6 mg
Cholesterol: 0 mg

Preparation at Home:
1. In a bowl, combine vegetables, garlic, and herbs. Stir well.
2. Evenly divide vegetable mixture over each of 2 lined dehydrator trays, about 1 cup of mixture onto each. Each tray will produce 1 serving of dried vegetable mix.
3. Place each serving of dried vegetable mix into a pint-size ziplock bag. Add optional garlic salt at this time.
4. Pack noodles and olive oil (1 tablespoon per serving) separately.

Preparation on the Trail:
1. Fill cook pot with water.
2. Pour ½ cup of water from pot into bag of dried vegetable mix and set aside to rehydrate.
3. Bring remaining of water in pot to boil, then add contents from bag of noodles.
4. Cook until noodles are tender, about 5 to 10 minutes.
5. Drain noodles, then add vegetable mix along with 1 tablespoon olive oil. Stir well.
6. Cover pot and set aside for a few minutes while vegetables finish rehydrating.

Mara Naber
Mountain Ranch, California

RANGE ROVIN' RAMEN

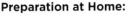

Total Servings: 1
As Packaged for the Trail: 1 serving
Weight per Serving: 5 ounces
Preparation Time on the Trail: 15 minutes
Challenge Level: Easy

V-LO

"Authors' Note: Brian Robinson said this was his first course every night during his record-breaking Triple Crown hike. What he calls an appetizer might be a meal for folks out on a weekend jaunt. The raging dietary furnace of the long-distance hiker is one of the wonders of the natural world. Brian states, 'I consumed, on average, 6,000 calories each day and didn't gain or lose a pound all year.'"

Preparation at Home:
1. Keep ramen noodles and spice packet in their package.
2. Pack dried vegetables in a small ziplock bag.

Preparation on the Trail:
1. To prepare 1 serving, crush ramen noodles and pour them, along with dried vegetables, into 2½ cups water in a cook pot.
2. Add contents of ramen spice packet to water, then bring to boil.
3. Cook for several minutes, being careful not to allow noodles to become mushy.
4. Remove from heat and serve once vegetables are rehydrated.

Brian "Flyin' Brian" Robinson
Mountain View, California

1 (3-ounce) package mushroom flavored ramen

½ cup dried mixed vegetables (such as Just Tomatoes, Etc! brand)

2½ cups water per serving, added on the trail

Required Equipment on the Trail:
Cook pot

Nutritional Information per Serving:
Calories: 505
Protein: 15 g
Fat: 16 g
Carbohydrates: 77 g
Fiber: 7 g
Sodium: 1,920 mg
Cholesterol: < 1 mg

DETERMINATION PAD THAI

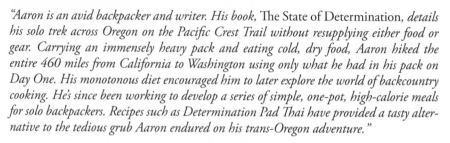

V-LO

Total Servings: 2
As Packaged for the Trail: 2 servings
Weight per Serving: 5 ounces
Preparation Time on the Trail: 15 minutes
Challenge Level: Easy

"Aaron is an avid backpacker and writer. His book, The State of Determination, *details his solo trek across Oregon on the Pacific Crest Trail without resupplying either food or gear. Carrying an immensely heavy pack and eating cold, dry food, Aaron hiked the entire 460 miles from California to Washington using only what he had in his pack on Day One. His monotonous diet encouraged him to later explore the world of backcountry cooking. He's since been working to develop a series of simple, one-pot, high-calorie meals for solo backpackers. Recipes such as Determination Pad Thai have provided a tasty alternative to the tedious grub Aaron endured on his trans-Oregon adventure."*

¼ cup instant dry nonfat milk

½ cup dried wasabi peas

½ cup shredded sweetened coconut

1 dried pineapple ring, chopped

Optional: 1 teaspoon red pepper flakes

¼ cup crunchy peanut butter

2 tablespoons soy sauce

2 ounces thin rice noodles, broken

1½ cups water per 2 servings, added on the trail

Required Equipment on the Trail:
Cook pot with lid

Nutritional Information per Serving:
Calories: 520
Protein: 15 g
Fat: 24 g
Carbohydrates: 66 g
Fiber: 6 g
Sodium: 1,244 mg
Cholesterol: 2 mg

Preparation at Home:
1. Combine dry milk, peas, coconut, pineapple, and optional red pepper flakes in a pint-size ziplock bag.
2. Package peanut butter, soy sauce, and noodles separately for the trail.

Preparation on the Trail:
1. To prepare 2 servings, pour contents of ziplock bag into a cook pot containing 1½ cups water.
2. Add ¼ cup crunchy peanut butter and 2 tablespoons soy sauce to the pot.
3. Cover pot and bring to a boil. Stir.
4. Add broken rice noodles to the pot and stir.
5. Reduce heat and simmer, uncovered, for 3 minutes, stirring occasionally.
6. Remove pot from heat.
7. Cover pot and let stand for about 5 minutes before stirring and serving.

Aaron J. Nicholson
Eugene, Oregon

THUNDER & LIGHTNING STIR-FRY

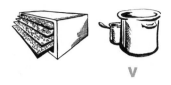

Total Servings: 10
As Packaged for the Trail: 1 serving
Weight per Serving: 5 ounces
Preparation Time on the Trail: 20 minutes
Challenge Level: Easy

Preparation at Home:

1. Cook brown rice according to package directions.
2. Lightly steam chopped vegetables.
3. Return veggies to cutting board and chop further, reducing size of pieces as much as practical to improve dehydration and rehydration.
4. Combine rice and chopped vegetables in a large bowl.
5. In a separate bowl, mix teriyaki sauce with brown sugar, ginger, and garlic powder.
6. Pour sauce mix over rice and vegetables. Stir well, coating everything with the sauce.
7. Spread 2 cups rice and vegetable mixture over a lined dehydrator tray, then dry. Each tray provides 1 serving, and 10 servings are produced by this recipe. So repeat this step using as many trays as are available, and plan to dry in batches.
8. Pour dried stir-fry mix from each tray into its own pint-size ziplock bag, for a total of 10 separate bags. Each bag provides 1 serving.

Preparation on the Trail:

1. To prepare 1 serving, bring 1½ cups water to boil in a pot.
2. Pour contents from a bag of stir-fry mix into pot. Stir, then remove pot from heat.
3. Wait 10 to 15 minutes for the mixture to rehydrate before serving.

Option: A less-sodium teriyaki sauce can be substituted to reduce sodium content.

*Chris "Flatfoot" Ibbeson
Hemet, California*

5 cups brown rice (about 2 pounds)

1 bunch (about 4 stalks) broccoli, chopped

2 medium zucchini squash, chopped

2 pounds carrots, peeled and chopped

1 head cauliflower, chopped

2 medium onions, chopped

1 (15-ounce) bottle Kikkoman Teriyaki Marinade & Sauce

¼ cup brown sugar

1 teaspoon ground ginger

1 teaspoon garlic powder

1½ cups water per serving, added on the trail

Required Equipment on the Trail:
Cook pot

Nutritional Information per Serving:
Calories: 480
Protein: 15 g
Fat: 4 g
Carbohydrates: 96 g
Fiber: 8 g
Sodium: 1,919 mg
Cholesterol: 0 mg

MEXICAN VOLCANO

Total Servings: 1
As Packaged for the Trail: 1 serving
Weight per Serving: 5 ounces
Preparation Time on the Trail: 30 minutes
Challenge Level: Easy

½ cup polenta (corn grits)

½ cup Fantastic World Foods instant refried beans

2 cups water per serving, added on the trail

Required Equipment on the Trail:
Cook pot with lid

Nutritional Information per Serving:
Calories: 520
Protein: 20 g
Fat: 5 g
Carbohydrates: 96 g
Fiber: 18 g
Sodium: 620 mg
Cholesterol: 0 mg

Preparation at Home:
Place each item into its own small ziplock bag.

Preparation on the Trail:
1. To prepare 1 serving, warm 2 cups of water.
2. Pour ½ cup of heated water into bag of bean mix and set aside to rehydrate.
3. Bring remaining water in pot to boil and add polenta.
4. Reduce heat, cover pot, and simmer for about 10 minutes.
5. Remove pot from heat, cover, and set aside for about 15 minutes while polenta rehydrates.
6. Pour rehydrated bean mix over polenta and serve.

Option: Instant polenta is more challenging to find, but eliminates the simmering time required for non-instant versions, such as the one in this recipe. Be advised that a change in water required to rehydrate may be necessary for instant polenta. Read package directions carefully.

*Ramona Hammerly
Anacortes, Washington*

TIME-TRAVELER'S TAMALE CHILI

Total Servings: 2
As Packaged for the Trail: 1 serving
Weight per Serving: 5 ounces
Preparation Time on the Trail: 15 minutes
Challenge Level: Easy

Preparation at Home:

1. Pour about ¾ cup chili mix into each of 2 pint-size ziplock bags.
2. To each bag, add ¼ cup cornmeal, ½ teaspoon chili powder, ¼ cup dried corn, ¼ teaspoon garlic powder, and optional chopped tomatoes. Each bag provides 1 serving.

Preparation on the Trail:

1. To prepare 1 serving, bring 2 cups water to boil in a pot.
2. Pour contents from a bag of chili mix into the pot. Stir.
3. Immediately remove pot from heat and allow chili to rehydrate 8 to 10 minutes before serving.

Brandon "Uluheman" Stone
Honolulu, Hawaii

1 (6.4-ounce) package Fantastic World Foods vegetarian chili

½ cup cornmeal

1 teaspoon chili powder

½ cup dried corn (such as Just Tomatoes, Etc! brand)

½ teaspoon garlic powder

Optional: 3 ounces chopped sun-dried tomatoes

2 cups water per serving, added on the trail

Required Equipment on the Trail:
Cook pot

Nutritional Information per Serving:
Calories: 430
Protein: 28 g
Fat: 4 g
Carbohydrates: 84 g
Fiber: 13 g
Sodium: 1,787 mg
Cholesterol: 0 mg

KILAUEA CHILI

Total Servings: 1
As Packaged for the Trail: 1 serving
Weight per Serving: 5 ounces
Preparation Time on the Trail: 15 minutes
Challenge Level: Easy

½ cup instant brown rice

½ cup Fantastic World Foods vegetarian chili

¼ cup dried corn

1 teaspoon chili powder

¼ teaspoon lemon peel powder

1 clove garlic or ⅛ teaspoon garlic powder

1¾ cups water per serving, added on the trail

Required Equipment on the Trail:
Cook pot with lid

Nutritional Information per Serving:
Calories: 472
Protein: 23 g
Fat: 4 g
Carbohydrates: 89 g
Fiber: 16 g
Sodium: 630 mg
Cholesterol: 0 mg

Preparation at Home:
Place all dry ingredients and the garlic clove or garlic powder into a pint-size ziplock bag.

Preparation on the Trail:
1. To prepare 1 serving, bring 1¾ cups water to boil in a cook pot.
2. If using a garlic clove, chop into small pieces and toss into pot.
3. Pour contents of the bag of chili mix into cook pot and stir.
4. Immediately remove pot from heat, cover, and allow to stand 8 to 10 minutes.

Brandon "Uluheman" Stone
Honolulu, Hawaii

SOUL FOOD

V-LO

Total Servings: 1
As Packaged for the Trail: 1 serving
Weight per Serving: 5 ounces
Preparation Time on the Trail: 30 minutes
Challenge Level: Easy

Preparation at Home:
Combine all dry ingredients together in a pint-size ziplock bag.

Preparation on the Trail:
1. To prepare 1 serving, bring 2 cups water to boil in a pot.
2. Add contents from ziplock bag to pot and stir well.
3. Cover pot. Remove from heat and let stand for 20 minutes before serving.

Marion "Llamalady" Davison
Apple Valley, California

1 cup instant brown rice

⅓ cup beans, cooked and dried

2 tablespoons Lipton Recipe Secrets onion soup mix

1 teaspoon dried minced onion

1 pinch ground black pepper

¼ teaspoon garlic powder

½ teaspoon parsley flakes

2 tablespoons imitation bacon bits

¼ teaspoon soul seasoning (Cajun or Creole seasoning will substitute)

Optional: 1 dash ground cayenne pepper

2 cups water per serving, added on the trail

Required Equipment on the Trail:
Cook pot with lid

Nutritional Information per Serving:
Calories: 623
Protein: 21 g
Fat: 4 g
Carbohydrates: 123 g
Fiber: 9 g
Sodium: 1,869 mg
Cholesterol: < 1 mg

CHAINSAW'S PUMPKIN PLEASER

Total Servings: 3
As Packaged for the Trail: 1 serving
Weight per Serving: 5 ounces
Preparation Time on the Trail: 15 minutes
Challenge Level: Easy

1 (29-ounce) can pure pumpkin

½ cup dry sherry

¾ teaspoon ground black pepper

1 red bell pepper, finely chopped

2 tablespoons dried onion flakes

1 tablespoon brown sugar

2 teaspoons ground coriander seed

2 teaspoons dried mustard

1 teaspoon dried lemon peel

1 teaspoon garlic powder

¼ teaspoon ground cayenne pepper

¼ teaspoon ground turmeric

2 tablespoons chopped dry-roasted peanuts

½ cup flaked sweetened coconut

1½ cups instant brown rice

Optional: olive oil to taste

2 cups water per serving, added on the trail

Preparation at Home:

1. Combine pumpkin, sherry, and black pepper in a bowl. Mix well.
2. Thinly spread pumpkin mixture on a lined dehydrator tray.
3. Spread chopped bell pepper on a separate dehydrator tray.
4. Dry both the pumpkin blend and bell pepper.
5. Tear dried pumpkin leather into small pieces and combine in a large bowl with the dried bell pepper, sugar, all the seasonings, peanuts, and coconut flakes. Mix well.
6. Pour ½ cup brown rice into each of 3 pint-size ziplock freezer bags. Each bag will provide a single serving.
7. Divide dried pumpkin mix into the 3 ziplock bags containing the rice, about 1 cup into each.
8. Pack optional olive oil separately for the trail.

Preparation on the Trail:

1. To prepare 1 serving, bring 2 cups water to boil in a cook pot.
2. Add contents from a bag of pumpkin-rice mix. Optional olive oil can be added to taste at this time.
3. Reduce heat to a simmer, stirring occasionally. Serve once ingredients have fully rehydrated, about 10 minutes.

Dave "Chainsaw" Hicks
Dublin, Virginia

Required Equipment on the Trail:
Cook pot

Nutritional Information per Serving:
Calories: 414
Protein: 12 g
Fat: 10 g
Carbohydrates: 70 g
Fiber: 17 g
Sodium: 315 mg
Cholesterol: 0 mg

PROCRASTINATOR'S DELIVERANCE

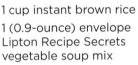

Total Servings: 1
As Packaged for the Trail: 1 serving
Weight per Serving: 5 ounces
Preparation Time on the Trail: 15 minutes
Challenge Level: Easy

"If you've found yourself procrastinating in preparation for your next backpacking trip, consider this recipe. It's very easy to throw together and takes only a few minutes to prepare out of the backpack . . . or canoe."

1 cup instant brown rice

1 (0.9-ounce) envelope Lipton Recipe Secrets vegetable soup mix

¼ teaspoon dried basil

¼ teaspoon dried oregano

¼ teaspoon ground cumin

1½ cups water per serving, added on the trail

Required Equipment on the Trail:
Cook pot

Nutritional Information per Serving:
Calories: 460
Protein: 12 g
Fat: 3 g
Carbohydrates: 100 g
Fiber: 7 g
Sodium: 1,541 mg
Cholesterol: 0 mg

Preparation at Home:
Combine all dry ingredients in a pint-size ziplock bag.

Preparation on the Trail:
1. To prepare 1 serving, bring 1½ cups water to boil in a cook pot.
2. Pour contents of ziplock bag into pot. Stir.
3. Remove pot from heat and set aside for about 10 minutes while rice rehydrates.

Mara Naber
Mountain Ranch, California

KINCORA RICE

Total Servings: 4
As Packaged for the Trail: 1 serving
Weight per Serving: 5 ounces
Preparation Time on the Trail: 15 minutes
Challenge Level: Easy

Preparation at Home:

1. Thaw, drain, and dehydrate spinach.
2. Crumble dried spinach and combine with remaining dry ingredients in a large bowl.
3. Divide dry mixture evenly between 4 pint-size ziplock bags, 1 heaping cup into each. Each bag provides a single serving.

Preparation on the Trail:

1. To prepare 1 serving, bring 1¼ cups water to boil in a cook pot.
2. Add contents of a ziplock bag to the pot. Stir.
3. Immediately remove pot from heat and set aside while rice rehydrates, about 10 minutes.

Dave "Chainsaw" Hicks
Dublin, Virginia

1 (10-ounce) package frozen spinach

3 cups instant brown rice

⅔ cup raisins

⅔ cup pine nuts

1 teaspoon ground nutmeg

1 teaspoon salt

2 teaspoons ground ginger

1¼ cups water per serving, added on the trail

Required Equipment on the Trail:
Cook pot

Nutritional Information per Serving:
Calories: 521
Protein: 19 g
Fat: 13 g
Carbohydrates: 93 g
Fiber: 9 g
Sodium: 680 mg
Cholesterol: 0 mg

PEAKS OF DOLOMITI RICE AND BEANS

Total Servings: 4
As Packaged for the Trail: 1 serving
Weight per Serving: 5 ounces
Preparation Time on the Trail: 20 minutes
Challenge Level: Easy

"I often crave Italian flavors on the trail and this recipe helps satisfy the desire."

1 (15-ounce) can low sodium black beans, rinsed

1 (12-ounce) can tomato paste

½ teaspoon salt

2 cups instant brown rice

1 cup unflavored textured vegetable protein (TVP)

½ cup dried vegetable flakes

1 tablespoon salt-free Italian seasoning

1 tablespoon minced onion flakes

1 tablespoon Mrs. Dash Garlic and Herb Seasoning

2 cups water per serving, added on the trail

Required Equipment on the Trail:
Cook pot with lid

Nutritional Information per Serving:
Calories: 453
Protein: 24 g
Fat: 2 g
Carbohydrates: 87 g
Fiber: 16 g
Sodium: 949 mg
Cholesterol: 0 mg

Preparation at Home:
1. Dry black beans in a dehydrator.
2. Evenly spread tomato paste over lined dehydrator tray.
3. Dry paste, then tear resulting tomato leather into 4 pieces of roughly equal size.
4. Place each piece of leather into its own quart-size ziplock bag for 4 bags total.
5. Place 1 dash of salt (about ⅛ teaspoon) into each of the 4 bags.
6. Combine remaining dry ingredients in a large bowl along with previously dried black beans. Mix well.
7. Evenly divide rice and bean mixture into each of the 4 bags containing the tomato leather, about 1 heaping cup into each. Each bag will provide 1 serving.

Preparation on the Trail:
1. To prepare 1 serving, bring 2 cups water to boil in a cook pot, then add contents from a bag of rice and bean mix.
2. Stir well, cover, and simmer over low heat for 5 minutes.
3. Remove pot from heat, stir, and allow to rest, with lid on, for about 10 minutes before serving.

Marion "Llamalady" Davison
Apple Valley, California

SHORE PINE SWEET POTATOES

V

Total Servings: 6
As Packaged for the Trail: 1 serving
Weight per Serving: 5 ounces
Preparation Time on the Trail: 20 minutes
Challenge Level: Easy

Preparation at Home:
1. Fill a large pot with water, add sweet potatoes, and bring to boil.
2. Cook sweet potatoes until tender.
3. Drain pot, allow potatoes to cool, then remove potato skins.
4. To a large bowl, add potatoes along with coconut milk, coconut oil, maple syrup, cinnamon, nutmeg, orange juice, and salt.
5. Blend potatoes and other ingredients using a mixer until smooth, then add pecans. Briefly blend once more.
6. Evenly spread about 2 cups sweet potato mixture onto each of 6 separate trays. Note that the actual amount required to evenly divide among the trays will depend on the size of the sweet potatoes.
7. Dry, then crumble contents from each tray into a pint-size ziplock bag, for 6 bags total. Each bag will provide 1 serving.

Preparation on the Trail:
1. To prepare 1 serving, add contents from a bag of dried sweet potato mix to 1½ cups water.
2. Bring to boil while stirring and breaking up pieces of dried sweet potato with a spoon. Once boiling, remove pot from heat.
3. Cover pot and allow potatoes to rehydrate for about 15 minutes, stirring periodically. Add a little more water if potatoes seem overly thick.

8 large sweet potatoes

1 (13.5-ounce) can coconut milk

2 tablespoon coconut oil

⅔ cup maple syrup

1 tablespoon ground cinnamon

1 teaspoon ground nutmeg

1 orange, juiced

½ teaspoon salt

2 cups chopped raw pecans

1½ cups water per serving, added on the trail

Required Equipment on the Trail:
Cook pot with lid

Nutritional Information per Serving:
Calories: 650
Protein: 10 g
Fat: 35 g
Carbohydrates: 83 g
Fiber: 11 g
Sodium: 990 mg
Cholesterol: 0 mg

Christine and Tim Conners
Statesboro, Georgia

TAEBAEK COUSCOUS

Total Servings: 2
As Packaged for the Trail: 2 servings
Weight per Serving: 5 ounces
Preparation Time on the Trail: 15 minutes
Challenge Level: Easy

1 (5.7-ounce) package Near East Mediterranean Curry couscous

1/3 cup slivered roasted almonds

1/3 cup dried cranberries

¼ teaspoon paprika

1 pinch garlic powder

1 pinch ground black pepper

1 pinch ground basil

2 teaspoons olive oil

1½ cups water per 2 servings, added on the trail

Required Equipment on the Trail:
Cook pot with lid

Nutritional Information per Serving:
Calories: 493
Protein: 15 g
Fat: 15 g
Carbohydrates: 79 g
Fiber: 7 g
Sodium: 897 mg
Cholesterol: 0 mg

Preparation at Home:
1. Combine contents from package of couscous with remainder of dry ingredients in a quart-size ziplock bag.
2. Package oil separately for the trail.

Preparation on the Trail:
1. To prepare 2 servings, bring 1½ cups water to boil in a cook pot.
2. Add contents from bag of couscous mix to pot along with 2 teaspoons olive oil. Stir well.
3. Cover pot, remove from heat, and allow to rest about 5 minutes before serving.

Peter Kim
Durham, North Carolina

PINE VALLEY COUSCOUS

Total Servings: 3
As Packaged for the Trail: 1 serving
Weight per Serving: 5 ounces
Preparation Time on the Trail: 15 minutes
Challenge Level: Easy

Preparation at Home:
1. Combine and thoroughly mix all dry ingredients in a bowl.
2. Evenly divide couscous mixture between 3 pint-size ziplock bags, 1 heaping cup into each. Each bag produces 1 serving.

Preparation on the Trail:
1. To prepare 1 serving, bring 1 cup water to boil.
2. Remove pot from heat and add contents from a bag of couscous mixture. Stir well.
3. Allow couscous to rehydrate for about 10 minutes before serving.

Carolyn Hiestand
Seattle, Washington

10 ounces plain couscous

1 cup sun-dried tomatoes, chopped

½ cup dried shiitake mushrooms

½ cup pine nuts

1 teaspoon dried parsley flakes

1 teaspoon dried oregano

1 teaspoon dried basil

1 teaspoon turmeric

1 teaspoon garlic salt

1 cup water per serving, added on the trail

Required Equipment on the Trail:
Cook pot

Nutritional Information per Serving:
Calories: 545
Protein: 19 g
Fat: 18 g
Carbohydrates: 85 g
Fiber: 8 g
Sodium: 1,039 mg
Cholesterol: 0 mg

WIND SONG GINGER NOODLES

Total Servings: 3
As Packaged for the Trail: 1 serving
Weight per Serving: 5 ounces
Preparation Time on the Trail: 30 minutes
Challenge Level: Moderate

4 ounces maifun (rice stick noodles)

2 portabella mushroom caps, finely chopped

10 ounces match stick cut carrots

3 tablespoons finely chopped fresh ginger

1 cup frozen peas

1 cup raw cashews

3 cups water

6 tablespoons less-sodium soy sauce

¼ cup toasted sesame seeds

1 tablespoon sesame seed oil

1 ¼ cups water per serving, added on the trail

Required Equipment on the Trail:
Cook pot with lid

Nutritional Information per Serving:
Calories: 554
Protein: 16 g
Fat: 26 g
Carbohydrates: 68 g
Fiber: 10 g
Sodium: 1,343 mg
Cholesterol: 0 mg

Preparation at Home:

1. Combine noodles, mushrooms, carrots, ginger, peas, cashews, and 3 cups water in a medium-size pot.

2. Cook over high heat until noodles and carrots are tender, about 10 minutes.

3. Thoroughly drain excess water, then add soy sauce and sesame seeds. Stir well.

4. Evenly spread about 2 cups noodle mix onto each of 3 lined dehydrator trays.

5. Dry, then place contents from each tray into a pint-size ziplock bag, for 3 bags total. Each bag will provide 1 serving.

6. Pack sesame seed oil separately, using 1 teaspoon per serving.

Preparation on the Trail:

1. In a cook pot, combine 1 ¼ cups water, the contents from a bag of ginger noodle mixture, and 1 teaspoon sesame seed oil.

2. Bring to a low boil, then continue to cook for about 15 minutes, stirring frequently.

3. Cover pot, then remove from heat. Allow to rest for about 10 minutes or until peas have softened.

Brian Mettler
Spearfish, South Dakota

VEGAN SUPER HERO BURRITOS

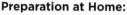

Total Servings: 4
As Packaged for the Trail: 4 servings
Weight per Serving: 5 ounces
Preparation Time on the Trail: 30 minutes
Challenge Level: Moderate

"I prepared this meal on the Low Divide Trail one evening. I was very hungry. When I took a bite, I leaned back from my sitting position in contentment but accidentally fell off an embankment into a creek."

Preparation at Home:
For 4 servings, package all ingredients separately for the trail.

Preparation on the Trail:
1. To prepare 4 servings, add 2 cups dried corn, the contents from the package of bean and rice mix, 1 tablespoon vegetable oil, and 3¼ cups water to cook pot.
2. Bring contents to a boil and cook for 5 minutes.
3. Reduce heat, cover pot, then simmer for about 20 minutes until rice is fully cooked.
4. Scoop bean and rice mixture onto 4 tortillas, then fold and serve.

Ben "The Vegan Super Hero" Hahn
Corvallis, Oregon

2 cups dried corn

1 (8-ounce) package Zatarain's Red Beans and Rice mix

1 tablespoon vegetable oil

4 burrito-size whole wheat tortillas

3¼ cups water per 4 servings, added on the trail

Required Equipment on the Trail:
Cook pot with lid

Nutritional Information per Serving:
Calories: 551
Protein: 18 g
Fat: 10 g
Carbohydrates: 99 g
Fiber: 9 g
Sodium: 1,283 mg
Cholesterol: 0 mg

SECRET LAKE GARLIC LENTILS

Total Servings: 1
As Packaged for the Trail: 1 serving
Weight per Serving: 5 ounces
Preparation Time on the Trail: 30 minutes
Challenge Level: Moderate

½ cup dried lentils

1½ tablespoons granulated garlic

2 tablespoons chopped dried tomatoes

1 teaspoon Italian herb seasoning

¼ teaspoon salt

2 tablespoons vegetable oil

1¼ cups water per serving, added on the trail

Required Equipment on the Trail:
Cook pot with lid

Nutritional Information per Serving:
Calories: 597
Protein: 23 g
Fat: 30 g
Carbohydrates: 64 g
Fiber: 25 g
Sodium: 742 mg
Cholesterol: 0 mg

Preparation at Home:
1. Combine all dry ingredients in a pint-size ziplock bag.
2. Pack oil separately.

Preparation on the Trail:
1. To prepare 1 serving, warm 2 tablespoons vegetable oil in cook pot over low flame.
2. Add lentil mixture to pot and stir to coat with oil.
3. Add 1¼ cups water to pot and bring to boil for a few minutes.
4. Cover pot and reduce heat.
5. Simmer for about 25 to 30 minutes before serving.

Tip: Because of the long simmer time, this recipe works best when using a stove that can produce a low flame.

Traci Marcroft
Arcata, California

TRIPLE CROWN CURRY COUSCOUS

V-LO

Total Servings: 1
As Packaged for the Trail: 1 serving
Weight per Serving: 6 ounces
Preparation Time on the Trail: 15 minutes
Challenge Level: Easy

Authors' Note: While many of us dream about hiking a single long trail end to end in one season, Flyin' Brian knocked off all three of the Pacific Crest, Appalachian, and the Continental Divide Trails in 2001, becoming the first person to hike in a single year what has come to be known as the 'Triple Crown.' In this section you'll find several of Brian's favorite recipes that helped power him into history.

Preparation at Home:
1. Combine all dry ingredients together in a pint-size ziplock bag.
2. Carry olive oil separately.

Preparation on the Trail:
1. To prepare 1 serving, bring 1½ cups water to boil in a cook pot.
2. Stir in contents from the ziplock bag along with 2 tablespoons olive oil.
3. Remove pot from heat, cover, and let stand until liquid is absorbed, about 10 minutes.
4. Fluff the dish before serving.

Brian "Flyin' Brian" Robinson
Mountain View, California

½ cup plain couscous

¼ cup cashew halves

¼ teaspoon curry powder

2 tablespoons Mayacamas chicken-flavored vegetarian gravy mix

2 tablespoons olive oil

1½ cups water per serving, added on the trail

Required Equipment on the Trail:
Cook pot with lid

Nutritional Information per Serving:
Calories: 787
Protein: 18 g
Fat: 45 g
Carbohydrates: 82 g
Fiber: 5 g
Sodium: 420 mg
Cholesterol: < 1 mg

On my Triple Crown trip, I used a homemade alcohol stove and ate straight out of the pot. I carried just the stove, one pot, and a spoon.
Brian "Flyin' Brian" Robinson
Mountain View, California

CHIWAUKUM QUINOA

Total Servings: 8
As Packaged for the Trail: 2 servings
Weight per Serving: 6 ounces
Preparation Time on the Trail: 15 minutes
Challenge Level: Easy

1 pound dried black beans

12 ounces quinoa

2 (26-ounce) jars spaghetti sauce (blend if chunky)

1 cup chopped pecans or nuts of your choice

4 cloves garlic (or ½ teaspoon garlic powder)

½ cup olive oil

2½ cups water per 2 servings, added on the trail

Required Equipment on the Trail:
Cook pot

Nutritional Information per Serving:
Calories: 462
Protein: 20 g
Fat: 18 g
Carbohydrates: 63 g
Fiber: 15 g
Sodium: 920 mg
Cholesterol: 0 mg

Preparation at Home:
1. Thoroughly cook beans and quinoa.
2. Dry beans and quinoa in a dehydrator.
3. Place dried beans and quinoa in a bowl. Add pecans and stir well.
4. Dry spaghetti sauce on lined dehydrator trays, 1 jar of sauce per tray.
5. Tear each sheet of dried spaghetti sauce evenly in half, for 4 pieces total.
6. Crumble each piece of sauce leather into a pint-size ziplock bag.
7. Add about 1½ cups of bean-quinoa-nut mix along with 1 clove of garlic (or a pinch of garlic powder) to each of the 4 bags of sauce leather. Each bag provides 2 servings.
8. Pack oil separately for the trail, 2 tablespoons per 2 servings.

Preparation on the Trail:
1. To prepare 2 servings, bring 2½ cups water to boil in a cook pot.
2. If using a garlic clove, chop and add to the pot.
3. Pour contents from a bag of quinoa mix into boiling water along with 2 tablespoons oil. Stir.
4. Reduce heat to a simmer, stirring occasionally, until beans rehydrate, about 10 minutes.

Jason Rumohr
Seattle, Washington

MISO MADNESS

Total Servings: 1
As Packaged for the Trail: 1 serving
Weight per Serving: 6 ounces
Preparation Time on the Trail: 15 minutes
Challenge Level: Easy

Preparation at Home:
Place all dry ingredients and the garlic clove or garlic powder into a quart-size ziplock bag.

Preparation on the Trail:
1. To prepare 1 serving, bring 2½ cups water to boil in a pot.
2. If using a garlic clove, cut into small pieces and add to pot.
3. Add contents from the bag of ingredients.
4. Stir, cover pot, and allow to rest for 8 to 10 minutes before serving.

Brandon "Uluheman" Stone
Honolulu, Hawaii

1¼ cups instant brown rice

1 (0.7-ounce) packet Miso-Cup instant soup with seaweed

½ cup chopped dried shiitake mushrooms

¼ cup hijiki or wakame seaweed

¼ cup dried carrots and peas

1 teaspoon sesame seeds

1 garlic clove or ⅛ teaspoon garlic powder

2½ cups water per serving, added on the trail

Required Equipment on the Trail:
Cook pot with lid

Nutritional Information per Serving:
Calories: 729
Protein: 20 g
Fat: 8 g
Carbohydrates: 150 g
Fiber: 15 g
Sodium: 1,675 mg
Cholesterol: 0 mg

PACIFIC CREST TORTILLAS

Total Servings: 3
As Packaged for the Trail: 1 serving
Weight per Serving: 6 ounces
Preparation Time on the Trail: 20 minutes
Challenge Level: Easy

1 (4.4-ounce) package Fantastic World Foods taco filling

1 (7-ounce) package Fantastic World Foods instant refried beans

6 medium-size flour tortillas

1 cup water per serving, added on the trail

Required Equipment on the Trail:
Cook pot

Nutritional Information per Serving:
Calories: 580
Protein: 33 g
Fat: 12 g
Carbohydrates: 79 g
Fiber: 14 g
Sodium: 1,899 mg
Cholesterol: 0 mg

Preparation at Home:
1. Combine taco filling and instant refried beans in a bowl.
2. Stir well, then divide mixture evenly between 3 pint-size ziplock bags. Each bag produces 1 serving.
3. Carry tortillas separately, 2 tortillas per serving.

Preparation on the Trail:
1. To prepare 1 serving, bring 1 cup water to boil in a pot.
2. Pour contents from a bag of taco filling and refried bean mix into the pot. Stir.
3. Immediately remove pot from heat and allow tortilla filling to rehydrate for about 10 minutes.
4. Spoon filling onto 2 tortillas, then roll and serve.

Liz Bergeron
Sacramento, California

PCT

BLUE BLAZER'S SOUP

V-LO

Total Servings: 4
As Packaged for the Trail: 1 serving
Weight per Serving: 6 ounces
Preparation Time on the Trail: 15 minutes
Challenge Level: Easy

Preparation at Home:

1. Evenly spread tomato paste over lined dehydrator tray.
2. Dry paste, then tear resulting tomato leather into 4 pieces of roughly equal size.
3. Place each piece of leather into its own quart-size ziplock bag for 4 bags total.
4. Drain, chop, and dry spinach in dehydrator.
5. In a bowl, crumble dehydrated spinach and add remainder of dry ingredients. Stir well to ensure seasonings are evenly distributed.
6. Divide spinach-pasta mixture evenly into each of the 4 ziplock bags containing the tomato leather, about ¾ cup mixture into each. Each bag provides 1 serving.

Preparation on the Trail:

1. To prepare 1 serving, bring 3½ cups water to boil in a pot.
2. Add contents from a bag of soup mix to the pot.
3. Return soup to gentle boil for about 7 to 10 minutes, stirring occasionally. Soup is ready to serve once pasta becomes tender and tomato leather is fully dissolved.

Heather Burror
Martinez, California

1 (12-ounce) can tomato paste

1 (10-ounce) package frozen spinach

½ teaspoon salt

1 (1.5-ounce) package Knorr Four Cheese sauce mix

16 ounces orzo or other small pasta

3½ cups water per serving, added on the trail

Required Equipment on the Trail:
Cook pot

Nutritional Information per Serving:
Calories: 542
Protein: 18 g
Fat: 4 g
Carbohydrates: 110 g
Fiber: 10 g
Sodium: 1,282 mg
Cholesterol: 5 mg

DANCING MOOSE BLACK BEAN SOUP

V

Total Servings: 3
As Packaged for the Trail: 1 serving
Weight per Serving: 6 ounces
Preparation Time on the Trail: 15 minutes
Challenge Level: Easy

3 (15-ounce) cans low-sodium black beans, rinsed and drained

1 (16-ounce) jar mild salsa

½ cup fresh cilantro, chopped

2 cups water

2 cups instant brown rice

2½ cups water, per serving, added on the trail

Required Equipment on the Trail:
Cook pot

Nutritional Information per Serving:
Calories: 643
Protein: 26 g
Fat: 4 g
Carbohydrates: 130 g
Fiber: 22 g
Sodium: 1,211 mg
Cholesterol: 0 mg

Preparation at Home:
1. Pour about half of the beans into a pot and the remainder into a blender.
2. Add salsa, cilantro, and 2 cups water to the blender. Blend until smooth.
3. Add blended bean mixture to the whole beans in the pot along with 2 cups rice.
4. Cover pot and cook over medium heat until rice is soft, about 20 minutes. Stir frequently to avoid burning.
5. Allow soup to cool, then place about 2 cups bean soup mixture onto each of 3 lined dehydrator trays. Each tray will produce 1 serving.
6. Dry, then crumble contents from each tray into a pint-size ziplock bag, for 3 bags total.

Preparation on the Trail:
1. To prepare 1 serving, bring 2½ cups water to boil in a cook pot.
2. Add contents from a bag of bean soup mix to the pot.
3. Cook over medium heat for a few minutes, stirring often.
4. Remove pot from heat and allow to rest for about 5 minutes or until beans and rice fully rehydrate.

Brian Mettler
Spearfish, South Dakota

THANKSGIVING FROM THE PACK

Total Servings: 4
As Packaged for the Trail: 1 serving
Weight per Serving: 6 ounces
Preparation Time on the Trail: 15 minutes
Challenge Level: Easy

V-LO

"Thanks to my good friend Spencer Newman, who provided the inspiration for the original recipe. Spencer and I have shared many good and not-so-good meals on the trail."

Preparation at Home:

1. Cook cutlets for about 4 minutes at high power in microwave.
2. Chop cooked cutlets into small pieces.
3. Dry chopped cutlets in dehydrator.
4. Divide dried cutlets evenly between 4 pint-size ziplock bags.
5. Add ½ cup dried corn, 1/3 cup mashed potato flakes, ½ cup stuffing mix, ½ cup dried cranberries, and about 1 tablespoon gravy mix to each of the 4 bags. Each bag will produce 1 serving.
6. Pack ghee separately for the trail, using 1 teaspoon per serving (see Tip).

Preparation on the Trail:

1. To prepare 1 serving, bring 2¼ cups water to boil in a cook pot.
2. Add thanksgiving mix from a ziplock bag to the pot along with 1 teaspoon ghee. Stir well.
3. Remove pot from stove, cover, and allow contents to rehydrate for 5 to 10 minutes. Stir before serving.

Tip: Ghee is a form of clarified butter. Provided it is stored in a clean container, it can have an unrefrigerated life of several months or more, making it a suitable option for the trail, especially in cooler weather. Butter Buds Sprinkles can be substituted for the ghee, if desired, by adding about ½ teaspoon Sprinkles to each of the single-serving ziplock bags along with the other dry ingredients.

Alex Messinger
Burlington, Vermont

1 (9.7-ounce) package Quorn meat-free Chik'n Cutlets

2 cups dried corn (such as Just Tomatoes, Etc! brand)

1 1/3 cups instant mashed potato flakes

2 cups Arrowhead Mills Organic Savory Herb stuffing

2 cups dried cranberries

1 (1-ounce) package Road's End Organics Savory Herb Quick Gravy mix

4 teaspoons ghee

2¼ cups water per serving, added on the trail

Required Equipment on the Trail:
Cook pot with lid

Nutritional Information per Serving:
Calories: 730
Protein: 21 g
Fat: 13 g
Carbohydrates: 137 g
Fiber: 11 g
Sodium: 940 mg
Cholesterol: 13 mg

DIRT BAGGER'S PASTA PARMESAN

V-LO

Total Servings: 1
As Packaged for the Trail: 1 serving
Weight per Serving: 6 ounces
Preparation Time on the Trail: 15 minutes
Challenge Level: Easy

4 ounces thin pasta noodles

3 tablespoons parsley flakes

3 tablespoons olive oil

¼ cup Kraft grated Parmesan cheese

Optional: salt and ground black pepper to taste

2½ cups water per serving, added on the trail

Required Equipment on the Trail:
Cook pot

Nutritional Information per Serving:
Calories: 841
Protein: 22 g
Fat: 48 g
Carbohydrates: 84 g
Fiber: 4 g
Sodium: 340 mg
Cholesterol: 16 mg

Preparation at Home:
Pack each item separately. (Combining the parsley with the cheese can result in undesirable clumping when cooking.)

Preparation on the Trail:
1. To prepare 1 serving, cook pasta in 2½ cups boiling water until tender, about 10 minutes. Most of the water should be absorbed once pasta becomes soft. Reduce heat toward end of cooking time to avoid scorching pasta.
2. Remove pot from heat and stir in 3 tablespoons each of parsley flakes and olive oil.
3. Top with ¼ cup Parmesan cheese. Add optional salt and black pepper, if desired.

Craig "Nigal" Turner
Piqua, Ohio

On making spaghetti sauce leather in the oven: Pour contents from a large jar of your favorite spaghetti sauce into a nonstick baking sheet with a high rim. (If sauce is chunky, first puree it in a blender.) Tap baking sheet on the counter, tilting it to and fro, whatever it takes to distribute the sauce evenly on the sheet. Set sheet on middle rack in oven at 200°F or lower with the door slightly ajar. Heat the sauce until it loses all moisture. Cool, then remove leather from sheet with a spatula. Store in tightly sealed baggies in freezer until sauce leather is needed.

Barbara "Mule 2" Hodgin
Sacramento, California

RIB-STICKIN' RAMEN

V-LO

Total Servings: 1
As Packaged for the Trail: 1 serving
Weight per Serving: 6 ounces
Preparation Time on the Trail: 15 minutes
Challenge Level: Easy

"This simple dish is one I often ate while thru-hiking the Appalachian Trail. It began as my so-called 'extra meal,' a spare dinner in case I was on the trail longer than expected between resupplies or if I was just really hungry. It turned out to be my favorite recipe!"

Preparation at Home:
1. Combine flour with Mrs. Dash, garlic salt, cayenne pepper, and Butter Buds in a small ziplock bag.
2. Carry ramen noodles and cheese separately.

Preparation on the Trail:
1. To prepare 1 serving, bring 2 cups water to boil in a cook pot, then add noodles.
2. Once noodles are soft, after a minute or so, remove pot from heat.
3. Cut 2 ounces block cheese into cubes.
4. Add flour-seasoning mix from ziplock bag to pot along with cheese cubes.
5. Stir until cheese melts.

Will "Hayduke" Jaynes
Three Rivers, California

2 tablespoons all-purpose wheat flour

1 tablespoon Mrs. Dash Garlic and Herb seasoning blend

¼ teaspoon garlic salt

1 dash ground cayenne pepper

1 teaspoon Butter Buds Sprinkles

1 (3-ounce) package ramen noodles, seasoning packet removed

2 ounces sharp cheddar cheese, from block

2 cups water per serving, added on the trail

Required Equipment on the Trail:
Cook pot

Nutritional Information per Serving:
Calories: 420
Protein: 18 g
Fat: 26 g
Carbohydrates: 30 g
Fiber: 1 g
Sodium: 1,444 mg
Cholesterol: 60 mg

GOLDEN BEAR GADO-GADO

Total Servings: 2
As Packaged for the Trail: 2 servings
Weight per Serving: 6 ounces
Preparation Time on the Trail: 15 minutes
Challenge Level: Easy

2 tablespoons crushed roasted peanuts

2 tablespoons dried onion flakes

¼ cup brown sugar

⅛ teaspoon ground cayenne pepper

1 teaspoon garlic powder

4 ounces orzo pasta

2 tablespoons less-sodium soy sauce

3 tablespoons olive oil

3 tablespoons rice vinegar

1 cook pot full of water, added on the trail

Required Equipment on the Trail:
Cook pot

Nutritional Information per Serving:
Calories: 552
Protein: 10 g
Fat: 19 g
Carbohydrates: 88 g
Fiber: 2 g
Sodium: 1,628 mg
Cholesterol: 0 mg

Preparation at Home:
1. Combine all dry ingredients, except pasta, in a pint-size ziplock bag.
2. In a 4-ounce plastic bottle, combine soy sauce, olive oil, and vinegar.
3. Package pasta separately in a small ziplock bag.

Preparation on the Trail:
1. To prepare 2 servings, add oil and vinegar from 4-ounce bottle to the bag of dry ingredients, reseal, and knead bag to mix contents.
2. Bring cook pot filled with water to boil and add contents from bag of pasta.
3. Heat pasta until tender, about 10 minutes, then drain excess water.
4. Add sauce mix to pasta and stir.

Rachel Jolly
Burlington, Vermont

LOST COWBOY CHILI
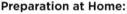

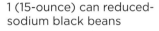

Total servings: 2
As Packaged for the Trail: 1 serving
Weight per Serving: 6 ounces
Preparation Time on the Trail: 15 minutes
Challenge Level: Easy

"Legend has it that late one morning, after a long night of festivities, a cowboy awoke to find that his herd and buddies had hit the trail without him. Cattle and companions gone, Lost Cowboy was forced to invent the very first vegan chili recipe!"

Preparation at Home:

1. Drain, rinse, and chop beans, then pour into a large pot.
2. Drain juice from can of tomatoes into pot, then chop tomatoes and add to the pot as well.
3. Combine remainder of ingredients in pot. Don't mistakenly add water.
4. Simmer over low heat until onions are thoroughly cooked.
5. Divide mixture evenly between each of 2 lined dehydrator trays, about 3 cups of mixture onto each. Spread thinly. Each tray will produce 1 serving.
6. Thoroughly dry mixture in dehydrator.
7. Crumble each sheet of dried chili leather into its own pint-size ziplock bag.

Preparation on the Trail:

1. To prepare 1 serving, bring 2¼ cups water to boil in a cook pot.
2. Pour crumbled chili leather from a ziplock bag into boiling water. Reduce heat.
3. Occasionally stir chili until fully rehydrated, about 5 to 10 minutes.

*Christine and Tim Conners
Statesboro, Georgia*

1 (15-ounce) can reduced-sodium black beans

1 (15-ounce) can reduced-sodium kidney beans

1 (14.5-ounce) can no-salt-added stewed tomatoes

1 (10.75-ounce) can condensed tomato soup

1 medium onion, finely chopped

1 green bell pepper, finely chopped

1 clove garlic, minced

1 cup frozen white corn

¼ teaspoon ground cayenne pepper

¼ cup maple syrup

2¼ cups water per serving, added on the trail

Required Equipment on the Trail:
Cook pot

Nutritional Information per Serving:
Calories: 780
Protein: 31 g
Fat: 1 g
Carbohydrates: 162 g
Fiber: 30 g
Sodium: 1,248 mg
Cholesterol: 0 mg

TACONIC MOUNTAIN CHEESY RICE

Total Servings: 1
As Packaged for the Trail: 1 serving
Weight per Serving: 6 ounces
Preparation Time on the Trail: 15 minutes
Challenge Level: Easy

V-LO

½ cup instant brown rice

1 tablespoon dried onion flakes

1 teaspoon garlic salt

¼ teaspoon ground black pepper

1 teaspoon dried oregano

1 teaspoon Butter Buds Sprinkles

2 (1-ounce) sticks string cheese, your choice

1¼ cups water per serving, added on the trail

Preparation at Home:
1. Combine rice, seasonings, and Butter Buds in a pint-size ziplock bag.
2. Carry cheese separately in its original packaging.

Preparation on the Trail:
1. Bring 1¼ cups water to boil in a cook pot.
2. Pour contents of ziplock bag into pot along with 2 ounces (2 sticks) string cheese.
3. Reduce heat to simmer and occasionally stir until rice is rehydrated and cheese is melted, about 5 to 10 minutes.

Rachel Jolly / Chewonki Foundation
Burlington, Vermont

Required Equipment on the Trail:
Cook pot

Nutritional Information per Serving:
Calories: 367
Protein: 20 g
Fat: 14 g
Carbohydrates: 45 g
Fiber: 2 g
Sodium: 948 mg
Cholesterol: 30 mg

Frozen vegetables (such as peas and corn) or peeled potatoes (thinly sliced and blanched) can be dried to add the final touch to soups, stews, or pastas.

Matthew Farnell
Woodland, Washington

LEAHI TRAIL RICE

Total Servings: 1
As Packaged for the Trail: 1 serving
Weight per Serving: 6 ounces
Preparation Time on the Trail: 15 minutes
Challenge Level: Easy

Preparation at Home:
Combine dry ingredients and the garlic clove or garlic powder in a pint-size ziplock bag.

Preparation on the Trail:
1. To prepare 1 serving, bring ¾ cup water to boil in a cook pot.
2. If using a garlic clove, chop into small pieces and toss into pot.
3. Pour contents of ziplock bag into pot. Stir.
4. Remove pot from heat and allow to stand 8 to 10 minutes, stirring occasionally to help ensure all ingredients are evenly hydrated.

Brandon "Uluheman" Stone
Honolulu, Hawaii

¾ cup instant brown rice

¼ cup chopped walnuts

¼ cup dried cranberries

½ cube vegan vegetable bouillon

¼ teaspoon lemon pepper seasoning

1 clove garlic or 1 dash garlic powder

¾ cup water per serving, added on the trail

Required Equipment on the Trail:
Cook pot

Nutritional Information per Serving:
Calories: 564
Protein: 11 g
Fat: 23 g
Carbohydrates: 87 g
Fiber: 7 g
Sodium: 1,050 mg
Cholesterol: 0 mg

EVIL LIME RICE

Total Servings: 4
As Packaged for the Trail: 2 servings
Weight per Serving: 6 ounces
Preparation Time on the Trail: 15 minutes
Challenge Level: Easy

"I credit the name of this recipe to my wife. She dubbed it 'evil' because she couldn't stop eating it."

1 (14-ounce) package instant brown rice

¼ cup coconut cream powder

1 cup roasted and salted cashews

1 tablespoon dried cilantro

1 tablespoon dried chives

¼ teaspoon salt

2 tablespoons vegetable oil

3 tablespoons Thai Kitchen green curry paste

6 tablespoons lime juice

2¼ cups water per 2 servings, added on the trail

Required Equipment on the Trail:
Cook pot

Nutritional Information per Serving:
Calories: 672
Protein: 15 g
Fat: 24 g
Carbohydrates: 87 g
Fiber: 6 g
Sodium: 570 mg
Cholesterol: 0 mg

Preparation at Home:
1. Combine rice, coconut cream powder, cashews, cilantro, chives, and salt in a bowl. Mix well.
2. Evenly divide rice mix between 2 pint-size ziplock bags, about 1½ cups into each. One bag provides 2 servings.
3. For 2 servings, combine 1 tablespoon vegetable oil, 1½ tablespoons curry paste, and 3 tablespoons lime juice in a small, drip-proof container.

Preparation on the Trail:
1. To prepare 2 servings, combine dry mix from a ziplock bag, a container of liquid ingredients, and 2¼ cups water in a cook pot.
2. Bring liquid to a boil, then reduce heat and continue to simmer for about 10 minutes, stirring occasionally. Dish is ready to serve once rice is tender.

*Curt "The Titanium Chef" White
Forks, Washington*

TRAIL-ANGEL CHEESE SOUP

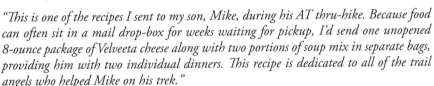

Total Servings: 1
As Packaged for the Trail: 1 serving
Weight per Serving: 7 ounces
Preparation Time on the Trail: 15 minutes
Challenge Level: Easy

V-LO

"This is one of the recipes I sent to my son, Mike, during his AT thru-hike. Because food can often sit in a mail drop-box for weeks waiting for pickup, I'd send one unopened 8-ounce package of Velveeta cheese along with two portions of soup mix in separate bags, providing him with two individual dinners. This recipe is dedicated to all of the trail angels who helped Mike on his trek."

Preparation at Home:

1. Remove Velveeta from its box, but keep the cheese *unopened* in its original foil wrapper. Only half of the cheese block is needed per serving, so plan on using the remaining cheese for a second serving, or later in the trip for a second pot of soup, or even served with crackers for lunch.
2. Place potato flakes, flour, parsley flakes, and Butter Buds in a pint-size ziplock bag.
3. Package oyster crackers separately.

Preparation on the Trail:

1. To prepare 1 serving, bring 2 cups water to boil in a cook pot.
2. While water heats, slice half of the Velveeta cheese block into small cubes and add to pot.
3. Remove pot from heat once water begins to boil.
4. Add potato mixture to the pot a little at a time while stirring.
5. Allow soup to rest for about 5 minutes.
6. Serve soup with crackers.

½ (8-ounce) package Velveeta cheese (see preparation steps for important note)

¼ cup instant mashed potato flakes

2 tablespoons all-purpose wheat flour

½ teaspoon parsley flakes

1 teaspoon Butter Buds Sprinkles

1 cup oyster crackers

2 cups water per serving, added on the trail

Required Equipment on the Trail:
Cook pot

Nutritional Information per Serving:
Calories: 548
Protein: 27 g
Fat: 25 g
Carbohydrates: 60 g
Fiber: 1 g
Sodium: 2,129 mg
Cholesterol: 100 mg

*Mike "Spiderman" and
Sue "Ground Control" Reynolds
Columbus, Indiana*

BRUNSWICK STEW

Total Servings: 4
As Packaged for the Trail: 1 serving
Weight per Serving: 7 ounces
Preparation Time on the Trail: 30 minutes
Challenge Level: Easy

V-LO

"This recipe won first-place in the REI 'Back-Country One-Pot Cook-Off' competition."

1 pound frozen baby lima beans

1 pound frozen cut corn

1 pound frozen southern-style hash-browned potatoes

½ cup finely chopped dried tomatoes

2 cubes vegan vegetable bouillon

½ cup dried onion flakes

1½ cups unflavored textured vegetable protein (TVP)

4 teaspoons tomato powder

½ cup instant mashed potato flakes

¼ teaspoon ground black pepper

4 tablespoons ghee or light-flavored vegetable oil

2½ cups water per serving, added on the trail

Required Equipment on the Trail:
Cook pot with lid

Nutritional Information per Serving:
Calories: 835
Protein: 34 g
Fat: 30 g
Carbohydrates: 108 g
Fiber: 18 g
Sodium: 1,139 mg
Cholesterol: 36 mg

Preparation at Home:
1. Thaw and dehydrate all frozen vegetables.
2. In a large bowl, combine dried lima beans, corn, potatoes, and tomatoes.
3. Divide dried vegetables evenly into 4 pint-size ziplock freezer bags, 1 heaping cup into each. Label each bag "Brunswick Stew A."
4. Into each of 4 separate pint-size ziplock freezer bags, place ½ of a crushed bouillon cube, 2 tablespoons dried onion flakes, 6 tablespoons textured vegetable protein, 1 teaspoon tomato powder, 2 tablespoons potato flakes, and a pinch of black pepper. Label each of these bags "Brunswick Stew B."
5. Pack ghee or oil separately, 1 tablespoon per serving.
6. When packing for the trail, 1 bag of "Brunswick Stew A" combined with 1 bag of "Brunswick Stew B" provides 1 serving.

Preparation on the Trail:
1. To prepare 1 serving, bring 2½ cups water to boil in a cook pot.
2. Pour contents from a bag of "Brunswick Stew A" into the boiling water and continue to cook until vegetables soften.
3. Remove pot from heat and add contents from a bag of "Brunswick Stew B" along with 1 tablespoon ghee or vegetable oil. Stir. Note that if bag "B" is added prior to removing from heat, the mix may scorch.
4. Cover pot and allow to stand until vegetables fully soften and flavor develops.

Dave "Chainsaw" Hicks
Dublin, Virginia

SOUTH SISTER STROGANOFF

V-LO

Total Servings: 2
As Packaged for the Trail: 1 serving
Weight per Serving: 7 ounces
Preparation Time on the Trail: 20 minutes (plus 1 hour to rehydrate)
Challenge Level: Easy

Preparation at Home:
1. In a frying pan, sauté onions, garlic, and mushrooms in the butter.
2. Add seasonings along with sherry to the pan and stir. Reduce heat.
3. In a bowl, combine vegetable broth with flour and stir.
4. Pour broth mix into pan and cook an additional 5 minutes or so.
5. Stir sour cream into pan and let simmer momentarily.
6. Remove pan from heat, allow to cool, then spread sauce mixture thinly over 1 or 2 lined dehydrator trays.
7. Dry, then crumble sauce leather into small pieces or chop in a food processor.
8. Divide sauce leather pieces evenly into 2 pint-size ziplock bags.
9. Divide pasta evenly into 2 separate pint-size ziplock bags.
10. When packing for the trail, 1 bag of sauce leather combined with 1 bag of pasta provides 1 serving.

Preparation on the Trail:
1. To prepare 1 serving, pour a little water into a bag of dried sauce leather, enough to barely cover contents, about 1 hour prior to dinner.
2. At dinnertime, bring 2 cups water to boil in a cook pot.
3. Add contents from a bag of pasta to pot.
4. Once pasta is fully cooked, about 5 to 10 minutes, drain pot and remove from heat.
5. Add rehydrated sauce mix to pot and stir.
6. Allow pot to rest, covered, for a few minutes before serving.

1 small onion, minced

3 cloves garlic, minced

1 pound fresh mushrooms, chopped

2 tablespoons butter

½ teaspoon salt

½ teaspoon ground black pepper

2 tablespoons dry sherry

¾ cup vegetable broth

2 tablespoons all-purpose wheat flour

½ cup sour cream

8 ounces angel-hair pasta

Slightly more than 2 cups water per serving, added on the trail

Required Equipment on the Trail:
Cook pot with lid

Nutritional Information per Serving:
Calories: 791
Protein: 24 g
Fat: 25 g
Carbohydrates: 110 g
Fiber: 5 g
Sodium: 1,006 mg
Cholesterol: 55 mg

Beth Murdock
Portland, Oregon

WASATCH TOMATO PARMESAN

Total Servings: 2
As Packaged for the Trail: 1 serving
Weight per Serving: 7 ounces
Preparation Time on the Trail: 20 minutes (plus 1 hour to rehydrate)
Challenge Level: Easy

V-LO

2½ tablespoons butter

3 tablespoons all-purpose wheat flour

1 cup milk

1 cup tomato-based pasta sauce

¼ cup Kraft grated Parmesan cheese

2 tablespoons dry red wine

8 ounces angel-hair pasta

Slightly more than 2 cups water per serving, added on the trail

Required Equipment on the Trail:
Cook pot with lid

Nutritional Information per Serving:
Calories: 714
Protein: 24 g
Fat: 22 g
Carbohydrates: 99 g
Fiber: 1 g
Sodium: 1,618 mg
Cholesterol: 60 mg

Preparation at Home:
1. Over medium heat, melt butter in a saucepan, stir in flour, and cook for about 1 minute.
2. Add milk and pasta sauce to the saucepan.
3. Continue to cook, stirring often until sauce thickens.
4. Add cheese and wine to the saucepan. Stir.
5. Simmer until cheese melts.
6. Allow sauce to cook, then spread thinly over 1 or 2 lined dehydrator trays. Dry.
7. Crumble dried sauce leather into small pieces or chop in a food processor.
8. Divide dried sauce evenly between 2 pint-size ziplock bags.
9. Into 2 separate pint-size ziplock bags, evenly divide the pasta.
10. When packing for the trail, 1 bag of dried sauce combined with 1 bag of pasta provides 1 serving.

Preparation on the Trail:
1. To prepare 1 serving, pour a little water into 1 bag of dried sauce, enough to barely cover contents, about 1 hour before dinner.
2. At dinnertime, bring 2 cups water to boil in a cook pot.
3. Add contents from a bag of pasta to boiling water.
4. Once pasta is fully cooked, about 5 to 10 minutes, drain pot and remove from heat.
5. Add rehydrated sauce mix to pot and stir.
6. Allow pot to sit, covered, for a few minutes before serving.

Beth Murdock
Portland, Oregon

DEATH VALLEY CHILI

Total Servings: 5
As Packaged for the Trail: 1 serving
Weight per Serving: 7 ounces
Preparation Time on the Trail: 30 minutes
Challenge Level: Easy

V-LO

"Every August, a motley group of employees from NASA's Dryden Flight Research Center in the Mojave Desert would make a pilgrimage to Death Valley to revel in the incredibly oppressive heat. A ban on the use of auto air conditioning. High-noon foot racing at Badwater. Cooking eggs on a searing hot car hood. Cheap wine and beer followed by an impossible attempt to sleep in the 100-degree nighttime air. You know, the usual traditions. This chili recipe is an adaptation from one of the expedition's eccentricities: for dinner, a deep pan into which all participants combined their favorite ingredients."

Preparation at Home:

1. In a large pot, add all ingredients except the chocolate and cheese. Don't mistakenly add water.
2. Cook over medium heat. Once onions are soft, add chocolate and cheese and stir until melted.
3. Pour chili into a blender and puree.
4. Pour 2 heaping cups of blended chili onto each of 5 lined dehydrator trays. If any excess chili remains, divide the remainder among the trays. Ensure that the chili mixture is spread evenly and thinly. Each tray will produce 1 serving.
5. Dry, then crumble the sheet of chili leather from each tray into its own pint-size ziplock bag.

Preparation on the Trail:

1. To prepare 1 serving, pour 1½ cups water into a bag containing chili.
2. Allow chili to rehydrate for about 15 minutes, occasionally kneading bag to help accelerate the process.
3. Pour chili mixture into a cook pot or pan and bring to a simmer. Heat until the chili finishes rehydrating, about 10 minutes, stirring occasionally to prevent burning.

Dean "El Lobo" Webb
Lancaster, California

5 (15-ounce) cans Hormel vegetarian chili

⅓ cup raisins

1 (8-ounce) can crushed pineapple

1 red onion, chopped

1 white onion, chopped

3 fresh jalapeño peppers, chopped

3 bread-and-butter pickles, diced

3 cloves fresh garlic, minced

1 tablespoon prepared mustard

1 teaspoon catsup

¼ cup honey

2 Baker's chocolate squares

8 ounces Monterey Jack, cubed

8 ounces longhorn cheddar, cubed

1½ cups water per serving, added on the trail

Required Equipment on the Trail:
Cook pot

Nutritional Information per Serving:
Calories: 970
Protein: 45 g
Fat: 35 g
Carbohydrates: 140 g
Fiber: 17 g
Sodium: 2,419 mg
Cholesterol: 96 mg

DINNER IN DENALI

V-LO

Total Servings: 2
As Packaged for the Trail: 1 serving
Weight per Serving: 7 ounces
Preparation Time on the Trail: 15 minutes
Challenge Level: Easy

1 (14-ounce) package frozen baby lima beans

1 (10-ounce) package frozen spinach

1½ cups instant brown rice

⅓ cup dried onion flakes

1 tablespoon dried dill weed

2 teaspoons instant dry whole milk

2 teaspoons whole egg powder

¼ teaspoon salt

2 teaspoons lemon pepper seasoning

1½ cups water per serving, added on the trail

Required Equipment on the Trail:
Cook pot with lid

Nutritional Information per Serving:
Calories: 661
Protein: 27 g
Fat: 5 g
Carbohydrates: 134 g
Fiber: 21 g
Sodium: 1,517 mg
Cholesterol: 34 mg

Preparation at Home:
1. Dry lima beans and spinach separately in a food dehydrator.
2. Pulverize lima beans in a food grinder or processor.
3. Combine dried lima beans and spinach, rice, and onion flakes in a bowl. Stir well.
4. Divide mixture evenly into each of 2 pint-size ziplock bags. Each bag will produce 1 serving.
5. To each bag add ½ tablespoon dill weed, 1 teaspoon dried milk, 1 teaspoon egg powder, 1 pinch salt, and 1 teaspoon lemon pepper.

Preparation on the Trail:
1. To prepare 1 serving, bring 1½ cups water to boil in a cook pot.
2. Pour contents from a ziplock bag into pot. Stir.
3. Remove pot from heat. Cover, set aside, and insulate, if possible, to preserve heat.
4. Allow pot to rest for about 10 minutes before serving.

Dave "Chainsaw" Hicks
Dublin, Virginia

ABSAROKA SWEET & SOUR

Total Servings: 1
As Packaged for the Trail: 1 serving
Weight per Serving: 7 ounces
Preparation Time on the Trail: 15 minutes
Challenge Level: Easy

Preparation at Home:
Combine all dry ingredients in a pint-size ziplock bag.

Preparation on the Trail:
1. To prepare 1 serving, bring 1½ cups water to boil in a pot.
2. Add contents of ziplock bag to the pot.
3. Cook for about 5 minutes, stirring occasionally, before serving.

Tip: Some instant rice–based recipes are sensitive to the rice used. If you have poor results, try another brand. We've had consistently good results with Uncle Ben's Instant.

Ken Harbison
Rochester, New York

¾ cup instant white rice

¼ cup dried carrots

¼ cup chopped candied pineapple pieces

2 tablespoons dried bell pepper flakes

1 tablespoon dried minced onion

2 tablespoons chopped sun-dried tomato

1 tablespoon brown sugar

½ (0.875-ounce) packet Sun Bird sweet and sour dry seasoning mix

1½ cups water per serving, added on the trail

Required Equipment on the Trail:
Cook pot

Nutritional Information per Serving:
Calories: 760
Protein: 15 g
Fat: 14 g
Carbohydrates: 140 g
Fiber: 11 g
Sodium: 704 mg
Cholesterol: 0 mg

A great addition to Italian or Mexican recipes are dried tomato chunks. Drain a number-ten can of tomato chunks, then dump them onto a lined dehydrator tray. Dry for 5 to 8 hours. They are reduced to large flakes that will rehydrate back into chunks very easily. They taste delicious. I add about a tablespoon of them per serving.

Marion "Llamalady" Davison
Apple Valley, California

BURRITO OLÉ FOR TWO

V-LO

Total Servings: 4
As Packaged for the Trail: 2 servings
Weight per Serving: 7 ounces
Preparation Time on the Trail: 15 minutes
Challenge Level: Easy

1 (5.6-ounce) package
Knorr Fiesta Sides
Spanish rice

1 (7-ounce) package
Fantastic World Foods
instant refried beans

1 (8-ounce) block sharp
cheddar cheese

4 burrito-size flour
tortillas

Optional: hot sauce
condiment packs

2 cups water per 2
servings, added on the
trail

**Required Equipment on
the Trail:**
Cook pot with lid

**Nutritional Information
per Serving:**
Calories: 785
Protein: 31 g
Fat: 27 g
Carbohydrates: 96 g
Fiber: 25 g
Sodium: 1,836 mg
Cholesterol: 60 mg

Preparation at Home:

1. Evenly divide Spanish rice between 2 pint-size ziplock bags, a little more than ½ cup into each. Each bag will produce 2 servings.

2. Evenly divide refried bean mix between the 2 bags containing the rice, about ¾ cup into each.

3. Pack block cheese and tortillas separately, 4 ounces of cheese and 2 tortillas for each 2-serving bag of rice and bean mix.

4. Carry optional hot sauce packs separately.

Preparation on the Trail:

1. To prepare 2 servings, bring 2 cups water to boil in a pot.

2. Pour contents from a bag of rice and bean mix into pot. Stir.

3. Remove pot from heat. Cover pot and allow to rest for about 5 minutes, until rice and bean mix is rehydrated.

4. Fill 2 tortillas with rehydrated rice and bean mix.

5. Cut block cheese into slices, covering beans and rice, then top with optional hot sauce.

6. Roll burritos and serve.

Option: *To reduce weight, cheese powder may be substituted for the cheddar cheese.*

Rich "Richman-Poorman" Simmons
Plymouth, Michigan

AT

EZ ED'S BURRITOS

Total Servings: 4
As Packaged for the Trail: 1 serving
Weight per Serving: 7 ounces
Preparation Time on the Trail: 30 minutes
Challenge Level: Moderate

V-LO

"This recipe was a favorite on my PCT thru-hike attempt in 2002. I had it every fifth trail day. It's tasty, provides ample energy, and isn't difficult to prepare. It has a good mix of carbs. The recipe generally makes enough so that I can save one burrito for breakfast the next day. Typically, I would just stay inside my sleeping bag in the morning while noshing on the leftover burrito."

Preparation at Home:

1. Except for the tortillas, combine all dry ingredients in a bowl and stir. Include contents of the spice packet from the package of black bean and lime soup.
2. Divide burrito mixture evenly into 4 pint-size ziplock bags, a little less than 1 cup into each. Each bag produces 1 serving.
3. Carry tortillas, 2 per serving, and optional hot sauce separately.

Preparation on the Trail:

1. To prepare 1 serving, bring 1¼ cups water to boil in a cook pot.
2. Add contents from a bag of burrito mixture to cook pot. Stir well.
3. Immediately remove pot from heat. Cover, then insulate pot, if possible.
4. Set pot aside for at least 10 minutes, stirring contents periodically.
5. Spoon rehydrated contents into each of 2 tortillas. Add optional hot sauce.
6. Roll to form burritos and serve.

Ed "EZ Ed" Molash
Olympia, Washington

1 (5.6-ounce) package Knorr Fiesta Sides Spanish rice

¼ cup Fantastic World Foods instant refried beans

1 (3.4-ounce) package Dr. McDougall's Black Bean and Lime soup mix

½ cup dried corn (such as Just Tomatoes, Etc! brand)

¼ cup dried minced onion

3 tablespoons unflavored textured vegetable protein (TVP)

2 tablespoons dried cilantro

1 teaspoon red pepper flakes

1 (1.5-ounce) package Knorr Four Cheese sauce mix

8 medium-size flour tortillas

Optional: hot sauce condiment packets

1¼ cups water per serving, added on the trail

Required Equipment on the Trail:
Cook pot with lid

Nutritional Information per Serving:
Calories: 670
Protein: 23 g
Fat: 11 g
Carbohydrates: 117 g
Fiber: 12 g
Sodium: 2,051 mg
Cholesterol: 3 mg

GREEN DRAGON PAD THAI

V-LO

Total Servings: 1
As Packaged for the Trail: 1 serving
Weight per Serving: 7 ounces
Preparation Time on the Trail: 20 minutes
Challenge Level: Moderate

"Be prepared for a visual surprise when you add water to the sauce mix. It will quickly become obvious how this dish came by its name!"

1 teaspoon garlic flakes

1 tablespoon granulated sugar

¼ cup crushed raw peanuts

1 dash ground cayenne pepper

1 teaspoon dried cilantro

3 tablespoons shredded unsweetened coconut

1 (0.13-ounce) packet unsweetened lime-flavored Kool-Aid powder

1 tablespoon dried chives

¼ cup dried vegetables (such as Just Tomatoes, Etc! brand)

¼ cup whole egg powder

½ (8.8-ounce) package Thai Kitchen thin rice noodles

1 cook pot full of water, added on the trail

Required Equipment on the Trail:
Cook pot with lid

Nutritional Information per Serving:
Calories: 860
Protein: 36 g
Fat: 28 g
Carbohydrates: 122 g
Fiber: 6 g
Sodium: 432 mg
Cholesterol: 410 mg

Preparation at Home:
1. Place all dry ingredients, except egg powder and noodles, in a pint-size ziplock bag. Label the bag "Green Dragon Sauce Mix."
2. Carry egg powder in a ziplock sandwich bag and noodles in a separate pint-size ziplock bag.

Preparation on the Trail:
1. Fill cook pot with water.
2. To prepare 1 serving, add ¼ cup of the water to bag labeled "Green Dragon Sauce Mix" and knead until all large lumps are eliminated.
3. Add ¼ cup of the water to the bag of egg powder and knead into a batter.
4. Bring remaining water in the cook pot to boil.
5. Add Thai noodles to the boiling water and cook for 2 minutes.
6. Remove pot from heat and drain noodles.
7. Pour both the reconstituted sauce and egg batter into noodle pot. Stir well.
8. Cover pot and allow to rest for a few minutes before serving.

Barbara "Mule 2" Hodgin
Sacramento, California

FUJI FEAST

Total Servings: 2
As Packaged for the Trail: 1 serving
Weight per Serving: 7 ounces
Preparation Time on the Trail: 20 minutes
Challenge Level: Moderate

Preparation at Home:
1. Chop eggplant and onion into small pieces using a food processor.
2. In a large bowl, mix together chopped eggplant and onions, mushrooms, garlic, and ginger.
3. Add soy sauce to the bowl, then mix, allowing sauce to saturate all ingredients.
4. Set aside to soak for about 20 minutes, then drain excess liquid.
5. Divide mixture between 2 lined dehydrator trays, about 2 cups onto each.
6. When mixture is dry, divide between 2 pint-size ziplock bags.
7. Evenly divide noodles between 2 separate pint-size ziplock bags.
8. Carry 1 bag of vegetable mixture and 1 bag of noodles to provide 1 serving.

Preparation on the Trail:
1. Fill cook pot with water.
2. To prepare 1 serving, pour 1 cup of the water into a bag of eggplant mixture to allow contents to begin rehydrating.
3. Bring pot of water to boil, then add contents from a bag of noodles.
4. Cook noodles for a couple of minutes, then drain water.
5. Add eggplant mixture to the pot. Stir.
6. Cover pot and allow to rest for 5 to 10 minutes before serving.

1 medium eggplant, peeled

1 onion

4 ounces fresh mushrooms, finely chopped

3 cloves garlic, minced

1 ounce fresh ginger, grated

⅓ cup less-sodium soy sauce

8 ounces somen noodles

1 cook pot full of water, added on the trail

Required Equipment on the Trail:
Cook pot with lid

Nutritional Information per Serving:
Calories: 585
Protein: 21 g
Fat: 3 g
Carbohydrates: 121 g
Fiber: 14 g
Sodium: 1,671 mg
Cholesterol: 0 mg

Option: *If in need of a dinner with more calories, olive oil can be added to taste on the trail.*

Mara Naber
Mountain Ranch, California

UPSIDEDOWN SHEPHERDLESS PIE

V-LO

Total Servings: 2
As Packaged for the Trail: 2 servings
Weight per Serving: 7 ounces
Preparation Time on the Trail: 30 minutes
Challenge Level: Moderate

6 ounces Morningstar Farms Meal Starter Grillers Recipe Crumbles

1 cup dried peas

1 pinch ground cayenne pepper

1 (0.7-ounce) package Hain vegetarian brown gravy mix

1⅓ cups instant mashed potatoes

¼ teaspoon garlic powder

¼ cup instant dry whole milk

2 (1.25-ounce) packages regular Philadelphia cream cheese minis

4 cups water per 2 servings, added on the trail

Required Equipment on the Trail:
Cook pot with lid

Medium-size serving bowl

Nutritional Information per Serving:
Calories: 645
Protein: 36 g
Fat: 20 g
Carbohydrates: 83 g
Fiber: 11 g
Sodium: 1,260 mg
Cholesterol: 52 mg

Preparation at Home:
1. Dry Morning Star Crumbles on a lined dehydrator tray.
2. Combine dried Crumbles, dried peas, cayenne pepper, and gravy mix in a quart-size ziplock bag.
3. In another quart-size bag, combine instant potatoes, garlic powder, and dry milk.
4. Carry cream cheese separately.

Preparation on the Trail:
1. To prepare 2 servings, bring 4 cups water to boil in a cook pot.
2. Pour half of the hot water into a medium-size serving bowl (or second pot) along with contents from the bag of instant potatoes. Stir.
3. Add cream cheese to bowl and mix well.
4. Pour contents from bag of Crumbles mix into the 2 cups of hot water remaining in pot. Return to boiling while stirring.
5. Reduce heat, cover pot, and simmer for about 8 minutes until Crumbles rehydrate.
6. Pour Crumble mixture over rehydrated potatoes in bowl and serve.

Ken Harbison
Rochester, New York

GUITAR LAKE MELODY

Total Servings: 1
As Packaged for the Trail: 1 serving
Weight per Serving: 8 ounces
Preparation Time on the Trail: 30 minutes
Challenge Level: Easy

V-LO

"Yes, I've camped at Guitar Lake below Mount Whitney numerous times. And, yes, I really do carry a backpack guitar and often play it while waiting for dinner!"

Preparation at Home:
Combine all dry ingredients, including contents from ramen spice packet, in a pint-size ziplock bag.

Preparation on the Trail:
1. To prepare 1 serving, bring 2½ cups water to boil in a cook pot.
2. Add contents from the bag of ramen mixture. Stir.
3. Immediately remove pot from heat.
4. Cover pot and allow to stand for about 20 minutes before serving.

Marion "Llamalady" Davison
Apple Valley, California

1 (3-ounce) package mushroom flavored ramen

1 teaspoon curry powder

1 teaspoon dried minced onion

1 teaspoon dried vegetable flakes

⅓ cup beans, cooked and dried (your favorite)

¼ cup chopped unsalted cashews

¼ cup raisins

½ teaspoon Mrs. Dash Garlic and Herb seasoning blend

2½ cups water per serving, added on the trail

Required Equipment on the Trail:
Cook pot with lid

Nutritional Information per Serving:
Calories: 872
Protein: 24 g
Fat: 31 g
Carbohydrates: 128 g
Fiber: 10 g
Sodium: 1,689 mg
Cholesterol: < 1 mg

FLYIN' BRIAN'S GARLIC POTATOES

Total Servings: 1
As Packaged for the Trail: 1 serving
Weight per Serving: 8 ounces
Preparation Time on the Trail: 10 minutes
Challenge Level: Easy

V-LO

"This recipe's high fat content comes from the olive oil, healthy power fuel of long-distance backpackers."

1 cup instant mashed potato flakes

2 tablespoons granulated garlic

¼ cup instant dry nonfat milk

1 (0.75-ounce) package "chicken" flavored vegetarian gravy mix

¼ cup Kraft grated Parmesan cheese

¼ cup olive oil

2 cups water per serving, added on the trail

Required Equipment on the Trail:
Cook pot

Nutritional Information per Serving:
Calories: 1,067
Protein: 33 g
Fat: 66 g
Carbohydrates: 99 g
Fiber: 3 g
Sodium: 1,522 mg
Cholesterol: 26 mg

Preparation at Home:
1. Mix all dry ingredients together and carry in a pint-size ziplock bag.
2. Package olive oil separately.

Preparation on the Trail:
1. To prepare 1 serving, bring 2 cups water to boil in a cook pot, then remove pot from heat.
2. Stir potato mixture from the bag into the hot water along with ¼ cup olive oil.
3. Allow to cool for a few minutes before serving.

Brian "Flyin' Brian" Robinson
Mountain View, California

Instant potato flakes have a variety of uses: mashed potatoes, soup thickener, food breading, soup base, or even as a crust poured over soup. Formed into patties, they can be fried into potato pancakes. In an emergency, they can even be rolled into tiny balls and used as fish bait or as a soothing salve for bites and stings.

Traci Marcroft
Arcata, California

CEDAR GROVE COUSCOUS

Total Servings: 2
As Packaged for the Trail: 1 serving
Weight per Serving: 8 ounces
Preparation Time on the Trail: 20 minutes
Challenge Level: Moderate

V

Preparation at Home:
1. Thaw, chop, and dehydrate frozen vegetables.
2. Combine the now dried vegetables with vegetable recipe mix and TVP in a bowl.
3. Evenly divide mixture between 2 pint-size ziplock bags. Label these "Cedar Grove A."
4. Divide couscous between 2 more pint-size ziplock bags, labeling these "Cedar Grove B."
5. Pack 1 bag of "Cedar Grove A" and 1 bag of "Cedar Grove B" for 1 serving.

Preparation on the Trail:
1. To prepare 1 serving, bring 3 cups water to boil in a pot.
2. Add contents from a bag labeled "Cedar Grove A" to the pot. Stir.
3. Return water to a boil long enough for vegetables to become tender, about 5 to 10 minutes.
4. Add couscous from a bag labeled "Cedar Grove B."
5. Stir, remove pot from heat, and cover. Allow to stand for about 5 minutes before serving.

Heather Burror
Martinez, California

1 (16-ounce) package frozen vegetable mix

1 (1.4-ounce) package Knorr Vegetable Recipe mix

1 cup unflavored textured vegetable protein (TVP)

10 ounces plain couscous

3 cups water per serving, added on the trail

Required Equipment on the Trail:
Cook pot with lid

Nutritional Information per Serving:
Calories: 890
Protein: 52 g
Fat: 3 g
Carbohydrates: 162 g
Fiber: 22 g
Sodium: 1,613 mg
Cholesterol: 0 mg

LONE PINE LENTILS AND DUMPLINGS

Total Servings: 1
As Packaged for the Trail: 1 serving
Weight per Serving: 9 ounces
Preparation Time on the Trail: 30 minutes
Challenge Level: Moderate

¾ cup all-purpose wheat flour

1 teaspoon baking powder

¼ teaspoon granulated sugar

2 teaspoons dry instant soy milk

½ teaspoon garlic powder

½ cup dry brown lentils

½ teaspoon rosemary or sage

½ (0.7-ounce) package Hain vegetarian brown gravy mix

1 tablespoon vegetable oil

2¼ cups water per serving, added on the trail

Required Equipment on the Trail:
Cook pot with lid

Nutritional Information per Serving:
Calories: 617
Protein: 20 g
Fat: 15 g
Carbohydrates: 99 g
Fiber: 10 g
Sodium: 1,395 mg
Cholesterol: 0 mg

Preparation at Home:
1. Combine flour, baking powder, sugar, soy milk powder, and garlic powder in a pint-size ziplock bag.
2. In a separate pint-size bag, combine lentils, rosemary or sage, and gravy mix.
3. Package vegetable oil separately.

Preparation on the Trail:
1. To prepare 1 serving, pour lentil mix into 2 cups water in cook pot.
2. Bring lentils to boil, stirring occasionally, then reduce heat to a simmer.
3. Add 1 tablespoon vegetable oil and about ¼ cup water to the flour mixture in the bag.
4. Knead flour mixture to eliminate lumps, then spoon batter onto the lentils in 5 or 6 globs. The dumplings will be touching but should stay distinct.
5. Cover pot and continue to simmer for about 20 minutes, until lentils and dumplings are cooked through.
6. Hydrate lentil mix with small additions of water if it's drying out while cooking. See tip below for information about cooking at high altitude.

Tip: At high elevation, pre-soak the lentils to ensure they'll fully cook. Combining the lentils and some hot water in a wide-mouth water bottle in the morning will significantly shorten required cooking time at dinner. When using this method, package lentils separately and add the remainder of the ingredients at the time of cooking.

Suzanne Allen
Seattle, Washington

PINDOS MOUNTAIN PASTA

V-LO

Total Servings: 1
As Packaged for the Trail: 1 serving
Weight per Serving: 10 ounces
Preparation Time on the Trail: 15 minutes
Challenge Level: Easy

¼ cup chopped dried tomatoes

1 tablespoon dried basil

1 tablespoon balsamic vinegar

1 tablespoon olive oil

4 ounces whole wheat angel-hair pasta

4 ounces feta cheese

Slightly more than 2½ cups water per serving, added on the trail

Preparation at Home:
1. Place dried tomatoes and basil together in a pint-size ziplock bag.
2. Store vinegar and olive oil in a small plastic bottle.
3. Carry pasta and cheese in separate bags.

Preparation on the Trail:
1. To prepare 1 serving, pour a little water into the bag of tomato-basil mix to begin rehydration.
2. Bring 2½ cups water to boil in a cook pot.
3. Cook pasta until tender, about 5 to 10 minutes. Most of the water should be absorbed, requiring little draining.
4. Add tomato-basil mix to the pot along with the feta cheese and balsamic vinegar-oil mix. Toss and serve.

Tip: Feta cheese does not keep long if it remains unrefrigerated, so use early in the trip or substitute with a more durable hard cheese.

Katarina "Katgirl" Sengstaken
Hollis, New Hampshire

Required Equipment on the Trail:
Cook pot

Nutritional Information per Serving:
Calories: 961
Protein: 37 g
Fat: 43 g
Carbohydrates: 116 g
Fiber: 13 g
Sodium: 1,707 mg
Cholesterol: 60 mg

If having trouble chopping leather foods like dried spaghetti sauce or sun-dried tomatoes, try the following trick: First freeze the food for at least 10 minutes, then chop with a blender or knife.

Ken Harbison
Rochester, New York

BACKPACKER'S BOXTY

Total Servings: 4
As Packaged for the Trail: 2 servings
Weight per Serving: 3 ounces
Preparation Time on the Trail: 30 minutes
Challenge Level: Moderate

V-LO

"Boxty is a traditional Irish potato cake similar to a hash brown in texture. In Ireland, it's served as a side both at breakfast and dinner."

1 (4.2-ounce) package Hungry Jack Premium Hashbrown Potatoes

1/3 cup all-purpose flour

½ cup Betty Crocker Mashed Potato Buds

½ teaspoon garlic salt

1 tablespoon whole egg powder

¼ teaspoon ground black pepper

2 tablespoons olive oil

1 cup water per 2 servings, added on the trail

Required Equipment on the Trail:
Frying pan

Spatula

Nutritional Information per Serving:
Calories: 300
Protein: 6 g
Fat: 8 g
Carbohydrates: 45 g
Fiber: 2 g
Sodium: 773 mg
Cholesterol: 26 mg

Preparation at Home:

1. Combine hash brown potato mix, flour, Potato Buds, garlic salt, egg powder, and black pepper in a bowl. Mix well.

2. Evenly divide potato mix into 2 quart-size ziplock freezer bags, about 1 cup of mix into each. Each bag will provide 2 servings.

3. Pack oil separately for the trail, using 1 tablespoon for 2 servings.

Preparation on the Trail:

1. To prepare 2 servings, heat 1 cup water in a frying pan until hot but not boiling.

2. Pour hot water into a bag containing boxty mix.

3. Seal bag and knead periodically while potatoes rehydrate, about 10 to 15 minutes.

4. Wipe water from pan, then warm 1 tablespoon oil over low heat in the pan.

5. Cut a corner from bottom of bag of rehydrated potato mix and squeeze potato batter into pan as if making pancakes.

6. Flatten batter with spatula and allow to cook until bottom is golden brown.

7. Flip and cook until boxty is brown on opposite side.

8. Repeat with remaining batter.

Ken Harbison
Rochester, New York

AT **NCT**

MOUNTAIN GOAT QUESADILLAS

V-LO

Total Servings: 2
As Packaged for the Trail: 2 servings
Weight per Serving: 5 ounces
Preparation Time on the Trail: 30 minutes
Challenge Level: Moderate

Preparation at Home:

1. Sauté onions and mushrooms together with 1 teaspoon oil and the Worcestershire sauce.
2. Spread sautéed onions and mushrooms on a lined dehydrator tray and dry.
3. Place dried onion-mushroom mixture into a pint-size ziplock bag along with the sun-dried tomatoes. One bag produces 2 servings.
4. Carry goat cheese, tortillas, and olive oil separately.

Preparation on the Trail:

1. To prepare 2 servings, warm ¼ cup water in frying pan and add to bag of dried onions and mushrooms. Allow to rehydrate for a few minutes.
2. Wipe frying pan dry.
3. Add ¼ of the cheese and ¼ of the rehydrated onion-mushroom mix to 1 tortilla.
4. Fold tortilla over to enclose the mix and cheese.
5. Spread ½ tablespoon of oil on outside of tortilla.
6. Fry tortilla on both sides until cheese has melted.
7. Repeat steps 3 through 6 for the remaining 3 tortillas.

Tip: Goat cheese is delicious but doesn't keep long when unrefrigerated. So use it early on the trip or substitute with a more durable hard cheese.

Rachel Jolly
Burlington, Vermont

1 medium onion, finely chopped

1 (8-ounce) package fresh mushrooms, finely chopped

1 teaspoon vegetable oil

1 tablespoon vegetarian Worcestershire sauce

8 sun-dried tomatoes, chopped into small pieces

4 ounces goat cheese

4 medium-size flour tortillas

2 tablespoons olive oil

¼ cup water per 2 servings, added on the trail

Required Equipment on the Trail:
Frying pan

Nutritional Information per Serving:
Calories: 823
Protein: 27 g
Fat: 41 g
Carbohydrates: 86 g
Fiber: 6 g
Sodium: 1,276 mg
Cholesterol: 26 mg

NORTH MOUNTAIN OKONOMIYAKI

V-LO

Total Servings: 4
As Packaged for the Trail: 1 serving
Weight per Serving: 7 ounces
Preparation Time on the Trail: 30 minutes (plus 1 hour to rehydrate)
Challenge Level: Moderate

"There was a definitive moment that converted us from eating prefabricated backpacking meals to creating our own. Once while hiking on Manitou Island in Lake Michigan, the enchilada-mush-in-a-bag that was our dinner was very unfulfilling, and we had to squeeze the bag like a tube of toothpaste to suck out the remaining drops. We knew then that we had to either find better food or stop backpacking. We're still backpacking!"

1 (8-ounce) package fresh coleslaw vegetable mix

2 cubes vegan vegetable bouillon

4 cups all-purpose wheat flour

8 teaspoons ground ginger

8 teaspoons dried egg whites

4 tablespoons vegetable oil

4 tablespoons soy sauce

Slightly more than 1 cup water per serving, added on the trail

Required Equipment on the Trail:
Frying pan

Spatula

Nutritional Information per Serving:
Calories: 592
Protein: 18 g
Fat: 15 g
Carbohydrates: 99 g
Fiber: 2 g
Sodium: 2,287 mg
Cholesterol: < 1 mg

Preparation at Home:

1. Dry coleslaw mix on a lined dehydrator tray.
2. Divide dried coleslaw evenly into 4 pint-size ziplock freezer bags, about ¼ cup into each. Add ½ bouillon cube to each bag.
3. Into each of 4 separate pint-size ziplock bags, place 1 cup flour, 2 teaspoons ground ginger, and 2 teaspoons dried egg whites.
4. Pack oil and soy sauce separately, 1 tablespoon of each per serving.
5. When packing, 1 bag of dried slaw combined with 1 bag of flour mixture provides 1 serving.

Preparation on the Trail:

1. To prepare 1 serving, add ⅓ cup water to 1 bag of coleslaw mix and allow to rehydrate for about an hour. Ensure bouillon dissolves.
2. Add ¾ cup water to 1 bag of flour mix and knead to eliminate lumps.
3. Once coleslaw is rehydrated, add it to the flour batter and knead again.
4. Warm 1 tablespoon oil in pan over low heat.
5. Pour about ¼ cup of dough at a time into heated pan as you would for a pancake (exact amount depends on your pan size).
6. After edges are cooked, flip patty and fry until heated through.
7. Remove patty from pan and repeat as required for remainder of flour mixture.
8. Sprinkle patties with about 1 tablespoon soy sauce and serve.

Rebecca and Jim Spencer
Albany, California

Breads

HARDTACK

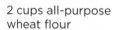

Total Servings: About 30 (1 square per serving)
As Packaged for the Trail: As required
Weight per Serving: 1 ounce
Preparation Time on the Trail: None
Challenge Level: Easy

"Hardtack was used as a basic ration during the early days of the United States. Hunters, explorers, and miners all carried hardtack. During the Civil War, it was issued by the U.S. government to its troops. Many soldiers disliked hardtack because it was, in fact, very hard. Sometimes referred to as 'teeth-dullers,' it often had to be broken with a rifle butt, rock, or blow of the fist. Soldiers sometimes softened hardtack by soaking it in coffee or a wet cloth, frying it in grease, or adding it to soup. They even discovered a way to make pudding by pouring boiling water over it and adding a little molasses or honey. Despite being the butt of jokes for centuries, hardtack remains one of the most pack-friendly trail breads."

2 cups all-purpose wheat flour

2 cups white whole wheat flour

1 teaspoon salt

2 tablespoons granulated sugar

1 cup and 1 tablespoon water

Required Equipment on the Trail:
None

Nutritional Information per Serving:
Calories: 56
Protein: 2 g
Fat: 1 g
Carbohydrates: 12 g
Fiber: 1 g
Sodium: 79 mg
Cholesterol: 0 mg

Preparation at Home:

1. Preheat oven to 300°F.

2. Mix flours, salt, and sugar in a large bowl.

3. Add water and knead mixture with your hands. Dough should eventually become firm and pliable.

4. Cut a sheet of parchment paper just large enough to fit a cookie sheet, then lay the paper on the sheet.

5. Using a rolling pin, flatten dough on the paper to about ¼-inch thick. Leave at least a half-inch of space between the dough and edges of the cookie sheet.

6. Cut dough into squares about 3 inches on a side. Score each square numerous times using a fork.

7. Bake 1½ to 2 hours, until dough is very hard and moisture completely gone.

8. Package for the trail in servings as required.

Preparation on the Trail:
None

Dave "Chainsaw" Hicks
Dublin, Virginia

OASIS FRUIT BARS

V-LO

Total Servings: 16 (1 bar per serving)
As Packaged for the Trail: As required
Weight per Serving: 2 ounces
Preparation Time on the Trail: None
Challenge Level: Easy

Preparation at Home:
1. Preheat oven to 325°F.
2. In a bowl, mix together the dried fruit, nuts, and 1 tablespoon of flour.
3. In a second bowl, cream the brown sugar with the butter, then add eggs, vanilla, and cardamom. Stir well.
4. Add ½ cup flour and the baking powder to the mixture in the second bowl.
5. Combine fruit and nut mix from the first bowl with dough in the second. Stir well once again.
6. Line a 13x9-inch baking pan with parchment paper.
7. Add dough to the pan, making sure it's evenly thick and pressed firmly against the sides.
8. Bake for 35 minutes.
9. Cool, then cut into 16 bars.
10. Package for the trail in servings as required.

Preparation on the Trail:
None

Barbara "Mule 2" Hodgin
Sacramento, California

1 cup chopped dates

1 cup chopped figs, stems removed

1 cup raisins

1⅓ cups walnuts, chopped

1⅓ cups pecans, chopped

1 tablespoon and ½ cup all-purpose wheat flour, divided

½ cup brown sugar

2 tablespoons butter, softened

2 eggs

2 teaspoons vanilla extract

1 teaspoon ground cardamom

½ teaspoon baking powder

Required Equipment on the Trail:
None

Nutritional Information per Serving:
Calories: 290
Protein: 4 g
Fat: 15 g
Carbohydrates: 38 g
Fiber: 8 g
Sodium: 33 mg
Cholesterol: 31 mg

POPPY FIELD BREAD

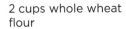

Total Servings: 24 (1 square per serving)
As Packaged for the Trail: As required
Weight per Serving: 2 ounces
Preparation Time on the Trail: None
Challenge Level: Easy

"When backpacking, I generally eat four pieces of bread each day, two in the late morning and two in the early afternoon. Using different bread recipes, I'm able to bring variety to my camping meals."

2 cups whole wheat flour

2 cups all-purpose flour

1 cup soy flour

1 tablespoon orange peel

½ teaspoon salt

½ teaspoon Nu-Salt

2 large eggs

2 (12.5-ounce) cans poppy seed filling

6 ounces frozen orange juice concentrate

½ cup honey

2 cups 1-percent milk

Required Equipment on the Trail:
None

Nutritional Information per Serving:
Calories: 242
Protein: 7 g
Fat: 5 g
Carbohydrates: 44 g
Fiber: 3 g
Sodium: 79 mg
Cholesterol: 19 mg

Preparation at Home:
1. Preheat oven to 250°F.
2. In a large bowl, mix all dry ingredients.
3. In a separate bowl, beat eggs, then add remainder of wet ingredients. Mix well.
4. Combine all ingredients in the large bowl and thoroughly mix.
5. Pour batter into a greased 11x17x1-inch jelly roll pan and smooth to an even depth.
6. Bake for 90 minutes, then poke bread with a fork to form vents. If batter sticks to the fork, bake for an additional 30 minutes. Bread is ready once fork comes from the bread clean.
7. Remove pan from oven, cool, then slice bread into 24 squares.
8. Separate pieces and dry in oven at lowest setting for about 6 hours. During the drying process, occasionally sample bread. Remove from oven before it becomes too tough to bite into.
9. Pack bread in ziplock bags in servings as required. Bread can be frozen until ready to use.

Preparation on the Trail:
None

Tip: The more moisture removed from the bread during the drying process, the longer it will keep in storage and the more durable it will become for the trail.

Fred "Greybeard" Firman
Columbia, Maryland

Greybeard has developed an exceptional number of trail bread recipes. We've included six of them in our book because each represents a unique taste experience. You'll find them all easy to prepare, very durable, full of flavor, and well balanced nutritionally. For long trips, consider Greybeard's advice and bring along a variety.

Christine and Tim Conners
Statesboro, Georgia

GINGER KICK BREAD

V-LO

Total Servings: 24 (1 square per serving)
As Packaged for the Trail: As required
Weight per Serving: 2 ounces
Preparation Time on the Trail: None
Challenge Level: Easy

2 cups whole wheat flour

1 cup cornmeal

1 cup soy flour

1 cup rye flour

⅔ cup raisins

⅔ cup chopped walnuts

½ cup brown sugar

2 teaspoons ground ginger

2 teaspoons ground cinnamon

½ teaspoon ground nutmeg

½ teaspoon salt

½ teaspoon Nu-Salt

2 large eggs

½ cup vegetable oil

1 cup dark molasses

2 cups 1-percent milk

Required Equipment on the Trail:
None

Nutritional Information per Serving:
Calories: 233
Protein: 7 g
Fat: 9 g
Carbohydrates: 28 g
Fiber: 4 g
Sodium: 78 mg
Cholesterol: 19 mg

Preparation at Home:
1. Preheat oven to 250°F.
2. In a large bowl, mix all dry ingredients.
3. In a separate bowl, beat eggs, then add remainder of wet ingredients. Mix well.
4. Combine all ingredients in the large bowl and thoroughly mix.
5. Pour batter into a greased 11x17x1-inch jelly roll pan and smooth to an even depth.
6. Bake for 90 minutes, then poke bread with a fork to form vents. If batter sticks to the fork, bake for an additional 30 minutes. Bread is ready once fork comes from the bread clean.
7. Remove pan from oven, cool, then slice bread into 24 squares.
8. Separate pieces and dry in oven at lowest setting for about 6 hours. During the drying process, occasionally sample the bread. Remove from oven before it becomes too tough to bite into.
9. Pack bread in ziplock bags in servings as required. Bread can be frozen until ready to use.

Preparation on the Trail:
None

Fred "Greybeard" Firman
Columbia, Maryland

GREYBEARD'S APRICOT-ALMOND BREAD

COOK

V-LO

Total Servings: 24 (1 square per serving)
As Packaged for the Trail: As required
Weight per Serving: 2 ounces
Preparation Time on the Trail: None
Challenge Level: Easy

Preparation at Home:

1. Preheat oven to 250°F.
2. In a large bowl, mix all dry ingredients.
3. In a separate bowl, beat eggs, then add remainder of wet ingredients. Mix well.
4. Combine all ingredients in the large bowl and thoroughly mix.
5. Pour batter into a greased 11x17x1-inch jelly roll pan and smooth to an even depth.
6. Bake for 90 minutes, then poke bread with a fork to form vents. If batter sticks to the fork, bake for an additional 30 minutes. Bread is ready once fork comes from the bread clean.
7. Remove pan from oven, cool, then slice bread into 24 squares.
8. Separate pieces and dry in oven at lowest setting for about 6 hours. During the drying process, occasionally sample the bread. Stop before it becomes too tough to bite into.
9. Pack bread in ziplock bags in servings as required. Bread can be frozen until ready to use.

Preparation on the Trail:
None

Fred "Greybeard" Firman
Columbia, Maryland

AT CDT

2 cups whole wheat flour

2 cups all-purpose wheat flour

1 cup soy flour

1½ cups chopped dried apricots (about 15 pieces)

1 cup sliced almonds

½ teaspoon salt

½ teaspoon Nu-Salt

2 large eggs

½ cup vegetable oil

½ cup honey

2 cups 1-percent milk

1 teaspoon vanilla extract

Required Equipment on the Trail:
None

Nutritional Information per Serving:
Calories: 219
Protein: 7 g
Fat: 9 g
Carbohydrates: 29 g
Fiber: 3 g
Sodium: 64 mg
Cholesterol: 19 mg

DUSTY ROADS DATE-N-WALNUT BREAD

V-LO

Total Servings: 24 (1 square per serving)
As Packaged for the Trail: As required
Weight per Serving: 2 ounces
Preparation Time on the Trail: None
Challenge Level: Easy

2 cups whole wheat flour

2 cups old-fashioned oats

1 cup soy flour

8 ounces chopped dates

1½ cups chopped walnuts

1 cup brown sugar

2 teaspoons ground cinnamon

½ teaspoon salt

½ teaspoon Nu-Salt

2 large eggs

½ cup vegetable oil

2 cups 1-percent milk

2 teaspoons vanilla extract

Required Equipment on the Trail:
None

Nutritional Information per Serving:
Calories: 220
Protein: 7 g
Fat: 10 g
Carbohydrates: 26 g
Fiber: 3 g
Sodium: 70 mg
Cholesterol: 19 mg

Preparation at Home:
1. Preheat oven to 250°F.
2. In a large bowl, mix all dry ingredients.
3. In a separate bowl, beat eggs, then add remainder of wet ingredients. Mix well.
4. Combine all ingredients in the large bowl and thoroughly mix.
5. Pour batter into a greased 11x17x1-inch jelly roll pan and smooth to an even depth.
6. Bake for 90 minutes, then poke bread with a fork to form vents. If batter sticks to the fork, bake for an additional 30 minutes. Bread is ready once fork comes from the bread clean.
7. Remove pan from oven, cool, then slice bread into 24 squares.
8. Separate pieces and dry in oven at lowest setting for about 6 hours. During the drying process, occasionally sample the bread. Remove from oven before it becomes too tough to bite into.
9. Pack bread in ziplock bags in servings as required. Bread can be frozen until ready to use.

Preparation on the Trail:
None

Fred "Greybeard" Firman
Columbia, Maryland

TRAVELER'S TAHINI-LEMON BREAD

V-LO

Total Servings: 24 (1 square per serving)
As Packaged for the Trail: As required
Weight per Serving: 2 ounces
Preparation Time on the Trail: None
Challenge Level: Easy

Preparation at Home:

1. Preheat oven to 250°F.
2. Thoroughly scrub the skin of the lemon.
3. In a large bowl, mix all dry ingredients.
4. In a separate bowl, beat eggs, then add remainder of wet ingredients. Include juice from the lemon along with its zest (i.e. fine shavings from the yellow part of the skin). Mix well.
5. Combine all ingredients in the large bowl and thoroughly mix.
6. Pour batter into a greased 11x17x1-inch jelly roll pan and smooth to an even depth.
7. Bake for 90 minutes, then poke bread with a fork to form vents. If batter sticks to the fork, bake for an additional 30 minutes. Bread is ready once fork comes from the bread clean.
8. Remove pan from oven, cool, then slice bread into 24 squares.
9. Separate pieces and dry in oven at lowest setting for about 6 hours. During the drying process, occasionally sample the bread. Remove from oven before it becomes too tough to bite into.
10. Pack bread in ziplock bags in servings as required. Bread can be frozen until ready to use.

Preparation on the Trail:
None

Fred "Greybeard" Firman
Columbia, Maryland

1 large lemon

2 cups whole wheat flour

2 cups all-purpose wheat flour

1 cup soy flour

½ teaspoon salt

½ teaspoon Nu-Salt

3 large eggs

1 (8-ounce) jar tahini

½ cup vegetable oil

1½ cups honey

1½ cups 1-percent milk

1 teaspoon vanilla extract

Required Equipment on the Trail:
None

Nutritional Information per Serving:
Calories: 264
Protein: 7 g
Fat: 11 g
Carbohydrates: 36 g
Fiber: 3 g
Sodium: 71 mg
Cholesterol: 27 mg

ALTITUDE BREAD

V-LO

Total Servings: 24 (1 square per serving)
As Packaged for the Trail: As required
Weight per Serving: 3 ounces
Preparation Time on the Trail: None
Challenge Level: Easy

3 cups whole wheat flour

2 cups all-purpose wheat flour

1½ cups soy flour

2 cups chopped dried apricots (about 20 pieces)

1 cup chopped almonds

¾ teaspoon salt

¾ teaspoon Nu-Salt

1 (8-ounce) can almond paste

2 large eggs

⅔ cup vegetable oil

⅔ cup honey

2½ cups 1-percent milk

1 teaspoon vanilla extract

Required Equipment on the Trail:
None

Nutritional Information per Serving:
Calories: 329
Protein: 10 g
Fat: 13 g
Carbohydrates: 47 g
Fiber: 6 g
Sodium: 133 mg
Cholesterol: 19 mg

Preparation at Home:
1. Preheat oven to 250°F.
2. In a large bowl, mix all dry ingredients and almond paste.
3. In a separate bowl, beat eggs, then add remainder of wet ingredients. Mix well.
4. Combine all ingredients in the large bowl and thoroughly mix.
5. Pour batter into a greased 11x17x1-inch jelly roll pan and smooth to an even depth.
6. Bake for 90 minutes, then poke bread with a fork to form vents. If batter sticks to the fork, bake for an additional 30 minutes. Bread is ready once fork comes from the bread clean.
7. Remove pan from oven, cool, then slice bread into 24 squares.
8. Separate pieces and dry in oven at lowest setting for about 6 hours. During the drying process, occasionally sample the bread. Remove from oven before it becomes too tough to bite into.
9. Pack bread in ziplock bags in servings as required. Bread can be frozen until ready to use.

Preparation on the Trail:
None

Fred "Greybeard" Firman
Columbia, Maryland

KENTUCKIANA LOGAN BREAD

V-LO

Total Servings: 16 (1 slice per serving)
As Packaged for the Trail: As required
Weight per Serving: 4 ounces
Preparation Time on the Trail: None
Challenge Level: Easy

Preparation at Home:
1. Preheat oven to 300°F.
2. Combine dry ingredients in a very large bowl, then add water, shortening, honey, and molasses. Mix well.
3. Divide dough evenly between 4 small loaf pans (5⅝x3x2 inches) and bake for 1 hour.
4. Allow loaves to cool before removing from pans.
5. Dry loaves in oven for about 5 hours at lowest heat setting with oven door slightly ajar. Once bread is very hard, it's ready for removal.
6. Cool and cut each loaf into 4 slices.
7. Package for the trail in servings as required.

Preparation on the Trail:
None

Peggy "Mama Llama" Kinnetz
Louisville, Kentucky

6 cups whole wheat flour
⅔ cup granulated sugar
¼ cup instant dry nonfat milk
½ teaspoon salt
1 teaspoon baking powder
1 cup chopped nuts, your choice
2 cups water
⅔ cup vegetable shortening, melted
¾ cup honey
¾ cup dark molasses

Required Equipment on the Trail:
None

Nutritional Information per Serving:
Calories: 391
Protein: 7 g
Fat: 14 g
Carbohydrates: 64 g
Fiber: 5 g
Sodium: 75 mg
Cholesterol: 1 mg

None of the bread recipes in our book produce a fluffy, yeast-raised loaf. Traditional breads can certainly be baked on the trail using a backpacking oven or wrapped in foil over coals. With care, slices of light and airy breads can even be dehydrated at home then successfully resurrected on the trail with a light sprinkling of water. However, for the rigors of the trail, this book places higher value on durability and storage life, and so you'll find breads that, once prepared, don't resemble bakery-bought loaves. Instead, they tend to be more dense and chewy.

Christine and Tim Conners
Statesboro, Georgia

MAMA LLAMA'S FRUIT BREAD

Total Servings: 12 (1 slice per serving)
As Packaged for the Trail: As required
Weight per Serving: 4 ounces
Preparation Time on the Trail: None
Challenge Level: Easy

1 cup granulated sugar

1½ cups all-purpose wheat flour

1 cup whole wheat flour

1 teaspoon baking soda

1½ teaspoons ground cinnamon

¼ teaspoon ground nutmeg

1 cup chopped walnuts

¾ cup chopped dried apricots

¾ cup raisins

½ cup date pieces

½ cup flaked sweetened coconut

¾ cup honey

1 cup boiling water

Required Equipment on the Trail:
None

Nutritional Information per Serving:
Calories: 375
Protein: 6 g
Fat: 7 g
Carbohydrates: 77 g
Fiber: 3 g
Sodium: 122 mg
Cholesterol: 0 mg

Preparation at Home:

1. Preheat oven to 325°F.
2. Combine sugar, flour, baking soda, cinnamon, nutmeg, and walnuts in a large bowl. Stir.
3. Add apricots, raisins, date pieces, and coconut to the bowl and stir again.
4. Pour honey and boiling water in the bowl, mixing well.
5. Line 3 small (5 5⁄8x3x2-inch) loaf pans with parchment paper.
6. Fill each pan about two-thirds full with batter.
7. Bake for 45 minutes.
8. Reduce oven temperature to 300°F, cover pans loosely with foil, then bake for an additional 30 minutes.
9. Cool and cut each loaf into 4 slices.
10. Store in refrigerator or freezer before packing for the trail.

Preparation on the Trail:
None

Peggy "Mama Llama" Kinnetz
Louisville, Kentucky

BROOKS RANGE BANNOCK

Total Servings: 1
As Packaged for the Trail: 1 serving
Weight per Serving: 4 ounces
Preparation Time on the Trail: 15 minutes
Challenge Level: Easy

"Also referred to as bush bread or grease bread, the outdoor use of this basic biscuit dates back hundreds of years. The beauty of the recipe is its flexibility: It can be served as a bread, dumpling, or, with a little additional water, even as a pancake."

Preparation at Home:
1. Mix dry ingredients in a bowl.
2. Blend in shortening using a pastry cutter or fork. Mixture should have the consistency of coarse cornmeal.
3. When finished, pour dough mixture into a pint-size ziplock bag.
4. Pack oil separately for the trail.

Preparation on the Trail:
1. To prepare 1 serving, add ¼ cup water to mixture in the ziplock bag. Knead until no large lumps remain. The goal is a soft dough. Add more water if needed, just a little at a time. Be careful not to use too much.
2. Warm 1 tablespoon oil in frying pan over low heat.
3. Flatten dough with the palm of hand, then fry, turning once with a spatula.

Options: *The recipe can be varied by adding fruit, nuts, sugar, or powdered buttermilk; using different flours; or topping with honey. The dough can also be wrapped around a dry stick and baked over a campfire.*

Dave "Chainsaw" Hicks
Dublin, Virginia

½ cup all-purpose wheat flour

1 teaspoon baking powder

1 dash salt

4 teaspoons vegetable shortening

1 tablespoon vegetable oil

¼ cup water per serving, added on the trail

Required Equipment on the Trail:
Frying pan

Spatula

Nutritional Information per Serving:
Calories: 467
Protein: 6 g
Fat: 30 g
Carbohydrates: 44 g
Fiber: 1 g
Sodium: 775 mg
Cholesterol: 0 mg

HOPI FRY BREAD

Total Servings: 1
As Packaged for the Trail: 1 serving
Weight per Serving: 8 ounces
Preparation Time on the Trail: 30 minutes
Challenge Level: Moderate

V

"I once was a teacher on the Hopi Indian Reservation. While there, the people taught me the art of cooking fry bread as a staple food and a means of sustenance on a low budget. During those days, fry bread and pinto beans became my primary means of survival."

½ cup all-purpose wheat flour

½ cup white whole wheat flour

2 teaspoons baking powder

¼ teaspoon garlic salt

2 teaspoons dried parsley flakes

Optional: bread-topping such as chopped nuts, Parmesan cheese, or herbs and spices

2 tablespoons vegetable oil

½ cup water per serving, added on the trail

Required Equipment on the Trail:
Frying pan

Nutritional Information per Serving:
Calories: 648
Protein: 14 g
Fat: 29 g
Carbohydrates: 90 g
Fiber: 6 g
Sodium: 902 mg
Cholesterol: 0 mg

Preparation at Home:
1. Combine flours and baking powder in a quart-size ziplock bag.
2. Place garlic salt, parsley, and any optional ingredients in a separate pint-size ziplock bag.
3. Pack oil separately.

Preparation on the Trail:
1. To prepare 1 serving, slowly add ½ cup water to the bag while kneading. Warm water works best.
2. Seal bag and continue to knead.
3. Remove dough from bag once it thickens, then continue kneading until the mixture forms an elastic ball of dough.
4. Allow dough to rest on a clean surface in the open air for about 5 minutes.
5. Heat 1 tablespoon oil in frying pan over medium heat until sizzling hot.
6. Split dough ball in two. Taking half, roll dough, then knead into a flat, waferlike tortilla approximately ½-inch thick. This can be done by repeatedly pinching the dough in circles in your hand or using a water bottle as a rolling pin.
7. Once dough has been thoroughly stretched, pinch a hole in the middle—like a flat doughnut.
8. Set dough carefully in the hot oil. Flip over once sides begin to brown.
9. Continue cooking for a few moments, then remove fry bread from pan and cover with about half of the contents of the bag of seasoning mix.
10. Using another tablespoon of oil, repeat with the remainder of dough and seasoning mix.

Therése Polacca
Mojave, California

SACAGAWEA CORN BREAD

Total Servings: 1
As Packaged for the Trail: 1 serving
Weight per Serving: 8 ounces
Preparation Time on the Trail: 30 minutes
Challenge Level: Moderate

V-LO

"Sacagawea was a Shoshone Native American who helped guide the Lewis and Clark expedition from the northern Great Plains to the Pacific Ocean. Sacagawea not only led the way through her own country, but she also taught the men how to gather edible plants in addition to serving as a translator with other native tribes. No other woman in American history has had as many streams, lakes, landmarks, parks, songs, poems, or monuments named in her honor."

Preparation at Home:
1. Combine all dry ingredients in a quart-size ziplock bag.
2. Pack cheese and oil separately.

Preparation on the Trail:
1. To prepare 1 serving, cut 1 ounce of cheddar cheese into small pieces.
2. Add 1 tablespoon oil and ⅓ cup water, along with the pieces of cheese, to the flour mixture in the ziplock bag. Be precise with the water: If too much is added, the corn bread will fall apart while cooking.
3. Thoroughly knead until a very stiff dough forms.
4. Heat 1 tablespoon vegetable oil over low flame in a nonstick frying pan.
5. Spread ½-inch-thick rounds of batter onto the cooking surface. Rounds can be of any manageable diameter.
6. Cook on low heat until the bottom of bread is browned and the top begins to lose its shine. It's important that the heat remains low; otherwise, the bread will burn.
7. Flip bread, flatten slightly, and continue cooking for a few moments until bottom is browned.
8. Repeat for any remaining batter.

Suzanne Allen
Seattle, Washington

⅔ cup cornmeal

⅓ cup all-purpose wheat flour

½ teaspoon baking powder

¼ teaspoon baking soda

1 teaspoon granulated sugar

1 dash ground cumin

1 pinch ground cayenne pepper

¼ teaspoon chili powder

1 ounce cheddar cheese, from block

2 tablespoons vegetable oil

⅓ cup water per serving, added on the trail

Required Equipment on the Trail:
Nonstick frying pan

Spatula

Nutritional Information per Serving:
Calories: 818
Protein: 19 g
Fat: 45 g
Carbohydrates: 101 g
Fiber: 4 g
Sodium: 846 mg
Cholesterol: 30 mg

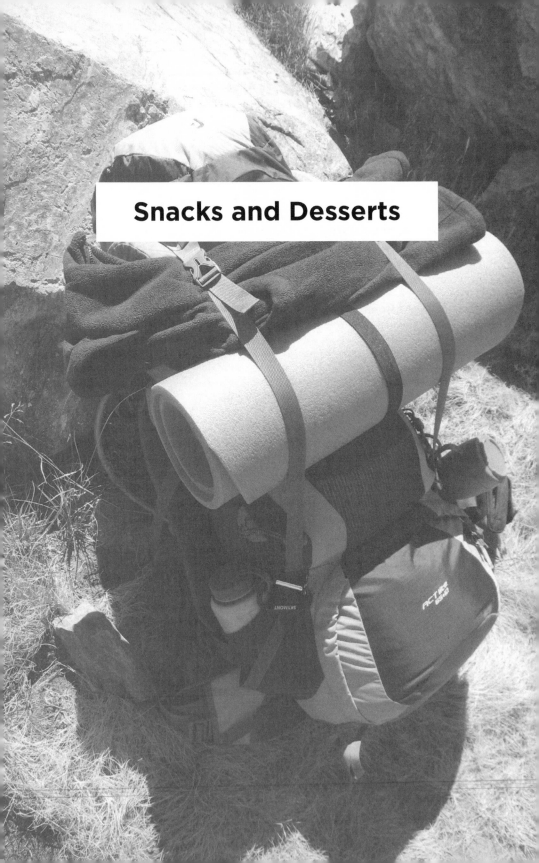

Snacks and Desserts

HALF DOMES

Total Servings: 72 (1 dome per serving)
As Packaged for the Trail: As required
Weight per Serving: 1 ounce
Preparation Time on the Trail: None
Challenge Level: Easy

V-LO

"I put these in care packages to my hiking friends when they are on long-distance trips."

Preparation at Home:
1. Preheat oven to 375°F.
2. In a large bowl, beat butter and sugars together until light and fluffy.
3. Add vanilla extract and eggs to bowl and continue to beat until combined.
4. In a separate large bowl, mix flour, oats, baking powder, and salt together, then add to the butter mixture.
5. Stir chocolate chips, walnuts, and cranberries into the batter.
6. Drop batter on baking sheets by the large teaspoonful.
7. Bake for 10 to 12 minutes. The cookies should be thoroughly cooked, but slightly chewy once cooled.
8. Package in ziplock bags as required for the trail.

Preparation on the Trail:
None

Beth Murdock
Portland, Oregon

 PCT

1 cup (2 standard sticks) butter, softened

1 cup brown sugar

1 cup granulated sugar

1 teaspoon vanilla extract

2 eggs

2 cups all-purpose wheat flour

2¼ cups old-fashioned oats

1 teaspoon baking powder

1 teaspoon salt

1 cup semisweet chocolate chips

½ cup chopped walnuts

½ cup dried cranberries

Required Equipment on the Trail:
None

Nutritional Information per Serving:
Calories: 82
Protein: 1 g
Fat: 4 g
Carbohydrates: 10 g
Fiber: 1 g
Sodium: 60 mg
Cholesterol: 13 mg

POINT PELEE PEACH LEATHER

V

Total Servings: 1
As Packaged for the Trail: 1 serving
Weight per Serving: 1 ounce
Preparation Time on the Trail: None
Challenge Level: Easy

5 fresh peaches

Required Equipment on the Trail:
None

Nutritional Information per Serving:
Calories: 185
Protein: 3 g
Fat: 1 g
Carbohydrates: 49 g
Fiber: 7 g
Sodium: 0 mg
Cholesterol: 0 mg

Preparation at Home:
1. Peel peaches and chop into small pieces.
2. Transfer chopped fruit to a pot of water.
3. Bring water to a brief boil.
4. Remove fruit and evenly spread over paper towels until well drained.
5. Puree fruit in a blender.
6. Spread puree on a lined dehydrator tray. Depth of puree should be no more than about ⅛-inch. Try to make the center of the puree pool a little thinner so that it will dry more evenly.
7. Dehydrate. The leather is ready once edges are no longer sticky to the touch.
8. Roll and package leather in a ziplock bag for the trail.

Preparation on the Trail:
None

Options: Nectarine, plum, or pear leather can be prepared using the same method.

Laurie Ann March
Guelph, Ontario, Canada

MOUNTAIN MANGO LEATHER

Total Servings: 4
As Packaged for the Trail: As required
Weight per Serving: 1 ounce
Preparation Time on the Trail: None
Challenge Level: Easy

Preparation at Home:

1. Peel and core mangos, then puree in blender along with the juice of the lime.
2. Divide mixture evenly between 2 lined dehydrator trays. Depth of puree should be no more than about ⅛-inch. Try to make the center of the puree pool a little thinner so that it will dry more evenly.
3. Dehydrate. The leather is ready once edges are no longer sticky to the touch.
4. Roll leather and package in ziplock bags for the trail. Each tray will provide 2 servings.

Preparation on the Trail:
None

Laurie Ann March
Guelph, Ontario, Canada

5 large mangos, very ripe
1 lime

Required Equipment on the Trail:
None

Nutritional Information per Serving:
Calories: 174
Protein: 2 g
Fat: 1 g
Carbohydrates: 46 g
Fiber: 5 g
Sodium: 5 mg
Cholesterol: 0 mg

ALGONQUIN APPLE LEATHER

Total Servings: 1
As Packaged for the Trail: 1 serving
Weight per Serving: 2 ounces
Preparation Time on the Trail: None
Challenge Level: Easy

1 pound apples,
thoroughly washed

1 lemon, juiced

2 tablespoons
granulated sugar

¼ teaspoon ground
cinnamon

Required Equipment on the Trail:
None

Nutritional Information per Serving:
Calories: 340
Protein: 1 g
Fat: 2 g
Carbohydrates: 89 g
Fiber: 11 g
Sodium: 3 mg
Cholesterol: 0 mg

Preparation at Home:
1. Remove cores from the apples.
2. Puree lemon juice together with the apples in a blender.
3. Mix sugar and cinnamon into the apple-lemon puree.
4. Spread puree on a lined dehydrator tray. Depth of puree should be no more than about ⅛-inch. Try to make the center of the puree pool a little thinner so that it will dry more evenly.
5. Dehydrate. The leather is ready once edges are no longer sticky to the touch.
6. Roll and package leather in a ziplock bag for the trail.

Preparation on the Trail:
None

Tip: The lemon juice is added to delay browning of the fruit leather.

Laurie Ann March
Guelph, Ontario, Canada

WILD BERRY FRUIT LEATHER

Total Servings: 2
As Packaged for the Trail: As required
Weight per Serving: 2 ounces
Preparation Time on the Trail: None
Challenge Level: Easy

Preparation at Home:

1. Puree berries in a blender. If you'd like to remove the seeds, strain the puree through cheesecloth.
2. Divide mixture evenly between 2 lined dehydrator trays. Depth of puree should be no more than about ⅛-inch. Try to make the center of the puree pool a little thinner so that it will dry more evenly.
3. Dehydrate. The leather is ready once edges are no longer sticky to the touch.
4. Roll leather and package in ziplock bags for the trail. Each tray will produce 1 serving.

Preparation on the Trail:
    None

Options: *Leather can also be made from your favorite combinations of blueberries, loganberries, boysenberries, and pitted cherries using the same method.*

Laurie Ann March
Guelph, Ontario, Canada

2 pounds fresh strawberries

Required Equipment on the Trail:
None

Nutritional Information per Serving:
Calories: 130
Protein: 3 g
Fat: 2 g
Carbohydrates: 30 g
Fiber: 11 g
Sodium: 5 mg
Cholesterol: 0 mg

APPLESAUCE LEATHER

Total Servings: 2
As Packaged for the Trail: As required
Weight per Serving: 2 ounces
Preparation Time on the Trail: None
Challenge Level: Easy

1 (24-ounce) jar
applesauce

Required Equipment on the Trail:
None

Nutritional Information per Serving:
Calories: 288
Protein: 0 g
Fat: 0 g
Carbohydrates: 66 g
Fiber: 3 g
Sodium: 0 mg
Cholesterol: 0 mg

Preparation at Home:
1. Divide applesauce evenly between 2 lined dehydrator trays. Depth of puree should be no more than about ⅛-inch. Try to make the center of the puree pool a little thinner so that it will dry more evenly.
2. Dehydrate. The leather is ready once edges are no longer sticky to the touch.
3. Roll leather and package in ziplock bags for the trail. Each tray will produce 1 serving.

Preparation on the Trail:
None

Laurie Ann March
Guelph, Ontario, Canada

FIREHOUSE APPLES

V

Total Servings: 2
As Packaged for the Trail: 1 serving
Weight per Serving: 2 ounces
Preparation Time on the Trail: None
Challenge Level: Easy

Preparation at Home:
1. In a large bowl, dissolve cinnamon imperials in the hot water.
2. Peel, core, and thinly slice the apples.
3. Soak sliced apples in the cinnamon solution for 5 to 10 minutes.
4. Dry apples in a dehydrator.
5. Divide dried apples between 2 pint-size ziplock bags. Each bag provides 1 serving.

Preparation on the Trail:
None

Phil "Scodwod" Heffington
Edmond, Oklahoma

⅔ cup cinnamon imperials (aka "red hots")

3 cups hot water

6 medium apples

Required Equipment on the Trail:
None

Nutritional Information per Serving:
Calories: 219
Protein: 1 g
Fat: 1 g
Carbohydrates: 57 g
Fiber: 7 g
Sodium: 0 mg
Cholesterol: 0 mg

WENDJIDU ZINZIBAHKWUD

Total Servings: 6 (1 piece per serving)
As Packaged for the Trail: As required
Weight per Serving: 2 ounces
Preparation Time on the Trail: None
Challenge Level: Easy

"Maple sugar was the basic seasoning for the Anishnabeg people and was used with grains, breads, berries, stews, teas, and vegetables. So important was the making of this sugar that the several weeks of spring, during which the maple syrup was boiled down, were referred to as the 'moon month of boiling.' In summer they dissolved the syrup in water to make a cooling drink. In the winter it was added to various leaf, root, and bark teas. This recipe can be used as a seasoning or eaten like a candy."

2 cups 100 percent pure maple syrup

Required Equipment on the Trail:
None

Nutritional Information per Serving:
Calories: 267
Protein: 0 g
Fat: 0 g
Carbohydrates: 71 g
Fiber: 0 g
Sodium: 1 mg
Cholesterol: 0 mg

Preparation at Home:
1. Set a muffin pan in the freezer and allow to chill.
2. Bring maple syrup to boil, stirring constantly and watching closely to be sure it doesn't boil over. The syrup will eventually take on a milky appearance, indicating that it's almost ready to set.
3. Continue to boil until syrup reaches 236°F, measured using a candy thermometer, or, alternately, until the syrup reaches the "hardball" stage. The "hardball" method requires placing a small drop of syrup into a glass of cold water. If syrup solidifies into a little hard ball, it's ready to remove from the heat. If it dissipates into the water, continue stirring until a drop eventually forms a solid ball in the water.
4. Once ready, pour syrup into 6 individual cups in the now-chilled muffin pan. Or, for smaller pieces, use a mini muffin pan or pour smaller amounts into more standard size cups.
5. Return pan to freezer and allow to chill for about 30 minutes.
6. Remove candy from pan and wrap in parchment paper for the trail.

Preparation on the Trail:
None

Tip: A double boiler is useful for helping to prevent the syrup from overheating.

Laurie Ann March
Guelph, Ontario, Canada

BLUEBERRY NIAN-GAO RICE CAKE

V-LO

Total Servings: 24 (1 cake per serving)
As Packaged for the Trail: As required
Weight per Serving: 2 ounces
Preparation Time on the Trail: None
Challenge Level: Easy

"Don't expect these rice cakes to resemble the bland, low-calorie versions found at the grocery store. These are a dense, durable, sweet-tasting treat."

Preparation at Home:
1. Preheat oven to 375°F.
2. In a large bowl, combine all dry ingredients and stir.
3. In a separate bowl, beat eggs, then add oil and water. Stir well.
4. Combine wet and dry ingredients in the large bowl and mix again.
5. Pour rice cake batter into 24 greased muffin pan cups.
6. Bake for 30 minutes or until golden brown. A knife poked into the middle should come out clean.
7. Package in ziplock bags in quantities as required for the trail.

Preparation on the Trail:
   None

Tip: Sweet rice flour can be found in Oriental food stores.

Christine and Tim Conners
Statesboro, Georgia

3 cups sweet rice flour

1¼ cups granulated sugar

1⅓ cups dried blueberries

3 eggs

¾ cup vegetable oil

1½ cups water

Required Equipment on the Trail:
None

Nutritional Information per Serving:
Calories: 214
Protein: 2 g
Fat: 8 g
Carbohydrates: 34 g
Fiber: 1 g
Sodium: 12 mg
Cholesterol: 27 mg

WHITEWATER MOON PIE

Total Servings: 4
As Packaged for the Trail: 1 serving
Weight per Serving: 3 ounces
Preparation Time on the Trail: 5 minutes
Challenge Level: Easy

V-LO

"This recipe is named for Miami-Whitewater Park, a beautiful hardwood enclave west of Cincinnati. During our time in Ohio, we repeatedly hoofed the park's trails. It was here that our kids gained their walking legs as toddlers and learned to click off distances measured in miles. It isn't the John Muir Wilderness, but because of the foresight of those who set aside this wonderful parcel of land to protect it from urban sprawl, our kids were able to learn at a very young age to love the outdoors."

⅔ cup instant dry nonfat milk

1 (3.4-ounce) package vanilla-flavored instant pudding

1 cup shredded sweetened coconut

20 vanilla wafers

½ cup cold water per serving, added on the trail

Required Equipment on the Trail:
None

Nutritional Information per Serving:
Calories: 358
Protein: 7 g
Fat: 13 g
Carbohydrates: 51 g
Fiber: 2 g
Sodium: 545 mg
Cholesterol: 5 mg

Preparation at Home:
1. Combine dry milk, pudding mix, and coconut in a bowl. Stir well.
2. Divide mixture evenly between 4 pint-size ziplock bags.
3. Place 5 vanilla wafers into each of 4 separate pint-size ziplock bags. At this point, you'll have a total of 8 bags equaling 4 servings.

Preparation on the Trail:
1. To prepare 1 serving, add ½ cup cold water to 1 bag pudding mix.
2. Seal bag and shake vigorously until mixture thickens. This may take a few minutes.
3. Crush cookies in a bag of wafers, then pour broken wafers into the bag of pudding.
4. Knead pudding mix and cookies, then serve straight from the bag.

Christine and Tim Conners
Statesboro, Georgia

GREEN MOUNTAIN GRASSHOPPER

Total Servings: 3
As Packaged for the Trail: 1 serving
Weight per Serving: 4 ounces
Preparation Time on the Trail: 15 minutes
Challenge Level: Easy

V-LO

Preparation at Home:
1. Into each of 3 separate pint-size ziplock bags place about 3 tablespoons pudding mix and ¼ cup instant dry milk. Each bag provides 1 serving.
2. Pack cookies and crème de menthe separately, using 3 Oreo cookies and 2 teaspoons crème de menthe per serving.

Preparation on the Trail:
1. To prepare 1 serving, add ½ cup cold water to a bag of pudding mixture.
2. Seal bag, then knead and shake vigorously for 1 to 2 minutes.
3. Set bag, aside to rest for at least 5 minutes.
4. Either in the bag or in a cup, top pudding with 3 broken Oreo cookies and 2 teaspoons crème de menthe.

Option: For a nonalcoholic version, use crushed mint candies or substitute Mint Creme Oreo cookies.

Tip: It's important to use cool water with recipes containing thickened instant pudding. If the water is too warm, the mix won't congeal properly.

Ken Harbison
Rochester, New York

1 (3.4-ounce) package pistachio-flavored instant pudding

¾ cup instant dry nonfat milk

9 Oreo cookies, broken into pieces (or 1 cup Mini Oreo cookies)

2 tablespoons crème de menthe liqueur

½ cup cold water per serving, added on the trail

Required Equipment on the Trail:
None

Nutritional Information per Serving:
Calories: 450
Protein: 8 g
Fat: 11 g
Carbohydrates: 70 g
Fiber: 2 g
Sodium: 760 mg
Cholesterol: 6 mg

SKIDAWAY BANANA PUDDING

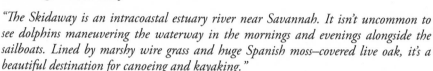

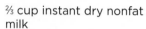

Total Servings: 2
As Packaged for the Trail: 1 serving
Weight per Serving: 6 ounces
Preparation Time on the Trail: 5 minutes
Challenge Level: Easy

"The Skidaway is an intracoastal estuary river near Savannah. It isn't uncommon to see dolphins maneuvering the waterway in the mornings and evenings alongside the sailboats. Lined by marshy wire grass and huge Spanish moss–covered live oak, it's a beautiful destination for canoeing and kayaking."

⅔ cup instant dry nonfat milk

1 (3.4-ounce) package banana cream-flavored instant pudding

20 vanilla wafers

1 cup banana chips

1 cup water per serving, added on the trail

Required Equipment on the Trail:
None

Nutritional Information per Serving:
Calories: 708
Protein: 17 g
Fat: 15 g
Carbohydrates: 105 g
Fiber: 0 g
Sodium: 1,051 mg
Cholesterol: 6 mg

Preparation at Home:
1. Combine dry milk with pudding mix in a bowl. Stir well.
2. Divide mixture evenly between 2 pint-size ziplock bags.
3. Crush vanilla wafers and banana chips into pieces, then divide evenly into 2 separate pint-size ziplock bags. At this point, you'll have a total of 4 bags equaling 2 servings.

Preparation on the Trail:
1. To prepare 1 serving, add 1 cup cold water to a bag of pudding mix.
2. Seal bag and shake vigorously until mixture thickens. This may take a few minutes.
3. Add contents from a bag of crushed wafer-banana chips to the bag of pudding.
4. Knead wafer-banana-pudding mix and serve straight from the bag.

Christine and Tim Conners
Statesboro, Georgia

DIRTY SOCKS PEACH COBBLER

Total Servings: 2
As Packaged for the Trail: 2 servings
Weight per Serving: 4 ounces
Preparation Time on the Trail: 15 minutes
Challenge Level: Easy

"Yes, it looks a little like dirty hiking socks once it's finished cooking, but it really does taste great!"

Preparation at Home:

1. Drain peaches and cut into thin slices.
2. Dry peaches on a lined dehydrator tray.
3. Pack dried peaches in a small ziplock bag.
4. Combine remainder of dry ingredients in a pint-size ziplock bag.

Preparation on the Trail:

1. To prepare 2 servings, pour ¼ cup water along with dried peaches into a nonstick cook pot or frying pan.
2. Bring water to boil, then reduce heat to a simmer.
3. Add ¼ cup water to the bag containing Bisquick mixture and knead.
4. Cut a corner from bottom of the bag and squeeze Bisquick mixture onto the peaches. Scramble mixture in the pot until batter is fully cooked.

Option: *Two ounces commercially dried peaches can be substituted for the can of peaches.*

Christine and Tim Conners
Statesboro, Georgia

1 (15-ounce) can sliced peaches in heavy syrup

½ cup Bisquick

¼ cup granulated sugar

¼ cup brown sugar

¼ teaspoon ground cinnamon

½ cup water per 2 servings, added on the trail

Required Equipment on the Trail:

Nonstick cook pot or frying pan

Nutritional Information per Serving:

Calories: 496
Protein: 3 g
Fat: 5 g
Carbohydrates: 113 g
Fiber: 2 g
Sodium: 396 mg
Cholesterol: 0 mg

CHOCOLATE RASPBERRY INDULGENCE

V-LO

Total Servings: 2
As Packaged for the Trail: 2 servings
Weight per Serving: 4 ounces
Preparation Time on the Trail: 10 minutes
Challenge Level: Moderate

1 (3.5-ounce) package Jell-O Cook & Serve chocolate pudding

⅔ cup instant dry nonfat milk

1 ounce Just Raspberries–brand dried raspberries

2 cups water per 2 servings, added on the trail

Required Equipment on the Trail:
Cook pot

Nutritional Information per Serving:
Calories: 310
Protein: 10 g
Fat: 1 g
Carbohydrates: 68 g
Fiber: 4 g
Sodium: 345 mg
Cholesterol: 5 mg

Preparation at Home:
Each item can be packed and carried separately, or the pudding mix and the powdered milk can be combined in a pint-size ziplock bag and the dried raspberries carried separately.

Preparation on the Trail:
1. To prepare 2 servings, combine 2 cups water with pudding mix and powdered milk in a pot. Stir well.
2. Heat pudding over medium flame until mixture comes to full boil, stirring constantly. For stoves with poor heat control, it's helpful to use a heat disperser between pot and flame to minimize chance of scorching.
3. Divide raspberries between 2 cups, bowls, or ziplock bags.
4. Pour cooked chocolate pudding over raspberries.

Tip: This recipe recommends the use of a 'heat disperser' for stoves that tend to scorch foods while cooking. You can make your own from the top of a large (3-pound) can of coffee. Remove the top using a smooth-edge can opener, one that cuts just below the rim, leaving a safe, non-jagged edge.

*Ken Harbison
Rochester, New York*

FABULOUS FRY BROWNIES

V-LO

Total Servings: 6
As Packaged for the Trail: 1 serving
Weight per Serving: 3 ounces
Preparation Time on the Trail: 15 minutes
Challenge Level: Easy

Preparation at Home:
1. Combine flour, cocoa, sugar, baking powder, salt, and powdered milk in a bowl. Stir well.
2. Add chocolate chips and walnuts to the bowl, then stir well once again.
3. Pour about ½ cup brownie mixture into each of 6 pint-size ziplock bags. Each bag provides 1 serving.
4. Pack oil separately for the trail, 2 teaspoons per serving.

Preparation on the Trail:
1. To prepare 1 serving, warm 1 teaspoon oil in a frying pan over low heat.
2. To 1 bag of brownie mixture, add a second teaspoon of oil and 2 tablespoons water.
3. Knead mixture in the bag.
4. Once pan is hot, scoop small, spoon-size mounds of batter into the pan or cut a corner from the bag and squeeze out small brownie batter blobs.
5. Cook until bottoms are browned and tops are no longer shiny.
6. Flip with a spatula, flatten, and brown the other sides.

Option: Carob chips can be substituted for the chocolate chips.

Suzanne Allen
Seattle, Washington

1 cup all-purpose wheat flour

¼ cup unsweetened baking cocoa

¾ cup granulated sugar

1 teaspoon baking powder

¼ teaspoon salt

2 tablespoons instant dry nonfat milk

½ cup mini chocolate chips

¼ cup walnuts

4 tablespoons vegetable oil

2 tablespoons water per serving, added on the trail

Required Equipment on the Trail:
Frying pan

Spatula

Nutritional Information per Serving:
Calories: 363
Protein: 5 g
Fat: 18 g
Carbohydrates: 53 g
Fiber: 3 g
Sodium: 187 mg
Cholesterol: < 1 mg

CHOCOLATE CHIP FRY COOKIES

V-LO

Total Servings: 4
As Packaged for the Trail: 1 serving
Weight per Serving: 3 ounces
Preparation Time on the Trail: 15 minutes
Challenge Level: Easy

1 cup all-purpose wheat flour

¼ cup granulated sugar

1 teaspoon baking powder

¼ teaspoon salt

Optional: ¼ teaspoon ground cinnamon, cloves, or nutmeg

½ cup mini chocolate chips

¼ cup chopped walnuts

4 teaspoons vegetable oil

2 tablespoons water per serving, added on the trail

Required Equipment on the Trail:
Frying pan

Spatula

Nutritional Information per Serving:
Calories: 400
Protein: 5 g
Fat: 17 g
Carbohydrates: 63 g
Fiber: 2 g
Sodium: 267 mg
Cholesterol: < 1 mg

Preparation at Home:
1. In a bowl, combine flour, sugar, baking powder, salt, and any optional spices. Thoroughly mix.
2. Add chocolate chips and walnuts to the bowl and mix again.
3. Place about ½ cup cookie mix into each of 4 pint-size ziplock bags. Each bag provides 1 serving.

Preparation on the Trail:
1. To prepare 1 serving, warm 1 teaspoon oil in a frying pan over low heat.
2. Add 2 tablespoons water to a bag of cookie mix.
3. Knead mixture in the bag.
4. Once pan is hot, scoop small, spoon-size mounds into the pan or cut a corner from the bag and squeeze out small cookie batter blobs.
5. Cook until bottoms are browned and tops are no longer shiny.
6. Flip with a spatula, flatten, and brown the other sides.

Suzanne Allen
Seattle, Washington

Drinks

GROOOVY SMOOOTHIE

V-LO

Total Servings: 8
As Packaged for the Trail: 8 servings
Weight per Serving: 1 ounce
Preparation on the Trail: 5 minutes
Challenge Level: Easy

1 (3.4-ounce) package vanilla-flavored instant pudding

½ cup instant dry orange drink mix

½ cup Better Than Milk original-flavor soy drink mix

1 cup cold water per serving, added on the trail

Required Equipment on the Trail:
Drinking cup

Nutritional Information per Serving:
Calories: 133
Protein: 1 g
Fat: 1 g
Carbohydrates: 30 g
Fiber: 0 g
Sodium: 300 mg
Cholesterol: 0 mg

Preparation at Home:
Combine all dry ingredients in a pint-size ziplock bag and shake well.

Preparation on the Trail:
To prepare 1 serving, add 3 tablespoons drink mix to 1 cup cold water. Stir.

Richard "Ranger Rick" Halbert
Traverse City, Michigan

On cold nights, pour hot water in your water bottle, seal it tightly to ensure that it doesn't leak, and place it in the bottom of your sleeping bag to warm your feet. This also keeps the water warmer than it would if it was left out in the cold all night, so in the morning it won't take as long to boil water for a hot breakfast.
Rebecca Spencer
Albany, California

SWITCHBACK SMOOTHIE

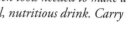

Total Servings: 7
As Packaged for the Trail: 1 serving
Weight per Serving: 2 ounces
Preparation Time on the Trail: 30 minutes
Challenge Level: Easy

"With a blender and a dehydrator, you have all the kitchen tools needed to make a portable, durable, and great-tasting version of this wonderful, nutritious drink. Carry extra to help you up those final switchbacks!"

Preparation at Home:

1. Combine all ingredients in a blender. Be careful not to include the 1 cup water, needed instead on the trail.
2. Puree, then evenly spread about 1 cup of mixture over each of 7 lined dehydrator trays.
3. Dry, rotating trays periodically to improve evenness of drying. The smoothie mixture is ready once it becomes leathery.
4. Each tray provides 1 serving. Store each in its own pint-size ziplock bag.

Preparation on the Trail:

1. Tear 1 serving of leather into very small pieces and add to a wide-mouth bottle containing 1 cup cold water.
2. Allow mixture to dissolve for about 30 minutes, periodically shaking vigorously to help speed the process.

Option: The fruit leather itself is very tasty and can be eaten as is.

Christine and Tim Conners
Statesboro, Georgia

1 (16-ounce) package frozen blueberries, thawed

1 (16-ounce) package frozen fruit blend (such as strawberries, mango, and pineapple), thawed

2 bananas

2 cups almond milk

½ cup honey

2 tablespoons lemon juice

1 cup cold water per serving, added on the trail

Required Equipment on the Trail:
Wide-mouthed water bottle

Nutritional Information per Serving:
Calories: 231
Protein: 2 g
Fat: 1 g
Carbohydrates: 59 g
Fiber: 3 g
Sodium: 33 mg
Cholesterol: 0 mg

WHOPPER MALT BRIBE

V-LO

Total Servings: 6

As Packaged for the Trail: 6 servings

Weight per Serving: 2 ounces

Preparation Time on the Trail: 5 minutes

Challenge Level: Easy

"Once while we were hiking the AT approach trail in northern Georgia, our daughter, Maria, generally an agreeable little girl, refused to take another step. With the narrow trail hemmed in high on both sides by nettles, we were out of options. So our two-year-old went to the top of already-heavy backpacks, bulging with extra gear for not only Maria but also her two little brothers. We became much wiser after that and began stocking the larder with a variety of goodies designed solely to move kids' feet. Whopper Malt Bribe was one of the tricks, but it's great for adults too. You just might use it to coerce your feet into taking those last few thousand steps of the day!"

1 cup crushed Whoppers malted milk candies

1 cup Ovaltine chocolate malt mix

1 cup instant dry nonfat milk

1 cup cold water per serving, added on the trail

Required Equipment on the Trail:
Drinking cup

Nutritional Information per Serving:
Calories: 174
Protein: 5 g
Fat: 3 g
Carbohydrates: 31 g
Fiber: 0 g
Sodium: 197 mg
Cholesterol: 2 mg

Preparation at Home:
Combine all dry ingredients in a quart-size ziplock bag and shake well.

Preparation on the Trail:
To prepare 1 serving, add ½ cup drink mix to 1 cup cold water in a mug. Stir.

Option: *Hot water can be substituted for the cold to make a great warm drink.*

Christine and Tim Conners
Statesboro, Georgia

EARTH SMOOTHIE

Total Servings: 2
As Packaged for the Trail: 1 serving
Weight per Serving: 3 ounces
Preparation Time on the Trail: 5 minutes
Challenge Level: Easy

"One evening, while backpacking in Hawaii, I fell asleep on the beach. I woke up to the dark night sky, and above me was a huge comet, its tail nearly filling the entire sky. What does this have to do with a smoothie? Nothing at all!"

Preparation at Home:
1. Crush dried raspberries in a plastic bag.
2. Into each of 2 small ziplock bags place 2 heaping tablespoons crushed raspberries, 2 heaping tablespoons SuperFood, 1 heaping tablespoon rice protein powder, and 1 heaping tablespoon flaxseed. Shake well. Each bag provides 1 serving.

Preparation on the Trail:
1. To prepare 1 serving, pour mixture from a bag of drink mix into a wide-mouth water bottle.
2. Add 2 cups water to bottle and shake vigorously until well mixed.

Tip: SuperFood is a nutritious natural drink mix that includes spirulina, algae, seaweed, chlorella, barley, wheat grass, alfalfa, and spinach leaf. It has a pronounced seaweed flavor, which for some can be an acquired taste. If this is true for you, any type of drink mix made from greens, such as barley grass, may be substituted. Any vegetable-based protein powder can be substituted for the rice powder as well.

Jason Rumohr
Seattle, Washington

1½ ounces Just Raspberries–brand dried raspberries

4 tablespoons Dr. Schulze's SuperFood Plus drink mix

2 tablespoons rice protein powder

2 tablespoons ground flaxseed

2 cups water per serving, added on the trail

Required Equipment on the Trail:
Quart-size wide-mouth water bottle

Nutritional Information per Serving:
Calories: 169
Protein: 20 g
Fat: 5 g
Carbohydrates: 17 g
Fiber: 6 g
Sodium: 39 mg
Cholesterol: 0 mg

CLOUDY MOUNTAIN LATTE

V-LO

Total Servings: 1
As Packaged for the Trail: 1 serving
Weight per Serving: 3 ounces
Preparation Time on the Trail: 5 minutes
Challenge Level: Easy

"This recipe was born from my love of decent trail coffee as well as an aversion to cooking when I solo-hike. It's a quick way to get a lot of calories, calcium, and a morning caffeine fix without a stove. Nestlé Nido, at almost 150 calories per ounce, is a great energy-dense trail food."

⅔ cup Nestlé Nido or instant dry whole milk

3½ teaspoons instant coffee crystals

Optional: granulated sugar to taste

2 cups water per serving, added on the trail

Required Equipment on the Trail:
Quart-size wide-mouth water bottle

Nutritional Information per Serving:
Calories: 300
Protein: 16 g
Fat: 18 g
Carbohydrates: 24 g
Fiber: 0 g
Sodium: 230 mg
Cholesterol: 60 mg

Preparation at Home:
Combine dry ingredients in a pint-size ziplock bag and shake well.

Preparation on the Trail:
1. To prepare 1 serving, pour 1 cup water into a rigid wide-mouth bottle.
2. Add latte mix to bottle and shake vigorously for about 10 seconds once per minute for 3 to 5 minutes, by which point the coffee and milk will have dissolved.
3. Add remaining cup of water and shake again.

Tip: Nestlé Nido is a whole-fat powdered milk product. It has almost twice the calories of nonfat or low-fat powdered milk. It's creamy and delicious and a tasty alternative to regular powdered milk for cereals and drinks. It also mixes more easily than most brands. Nido can be found in Latino markets as well as in the international food section of larger grocery stores.

Alan "Adventure Alan" Dixon
Arlington, Virginia

ELECTRO-TEA

Total Servings: 1
As Packaged for the Trail: 1 serving
Weight per Serving: < 1 ounce
Preparation Time on the Trail: 10 minutes
Challenge Level: Easy

Preparation at Home:
Pack Electro-C mix, tea bag, and honey separately for the trail.

Preparation on the Trail:
1. To prepare 1 serving, heat 1 cup water in a cook pot.
2. Pour hot water in a mug containing ½ teaspoon Electro-C mix and 1 teaspoon honey.
3. Stir and immediately add a ginger tea bag to the hot water.
4. Allow tea to steep for a few minutes before serving.

Tip: Electro-C is a nutritional supplement in drink-mix form that contains natural vitamin C and mineral electrolytes and is sweetened with stevia. Because it is a dietary supplement, it should be used with prudence.

Jack Young and Jo Crescent
Winters, California

½ teaspoon lemon-flavored Nutribiotic Electro-C mix

1 ginger tea bag

1 teaspoon honey

1 cup water per serving, added on the trail

Required Equipment on the Trail:
Cook pot

Nutritional Information per Serving:
Calories: 61
Protein: 0 g
Fat: 0 g
Carbohydrates: 6 g
Fiber: 0 g
Sodium: 0 mg
Cholesterol: 0 mg

HURRICANE HILL HOT CHOCOLATE

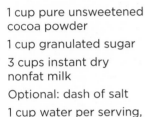

V-LO

Total Servings: 15
As Packaged for the Trail: As required
Weight per Serving: 1 ounce
Preparation Time on the Trail: 5 minutes
Challenge Level: Easy

1 cup pure unsweetened cocoa powder

1 cup granulated sugar

3 cups instant dry nonfat milk

Optional: dash of salt

1 cup water per serving, added on the trail

Required Equipment on the Trail:
Cook pot

Nutritional Information per Serving:
Calories: 115
Protein: 6 g
Fat: 1 g
Carbohydrates: 25 g
Fiber: 0 g
Sodium: 82 mg
Cholesterol: 3 mg

Preparation at Home:
1. Combine all dry ingredients together in a bowl.
2. Partition ingredients into small ziplock bags, ⅓ cup per bag per serving, or bring in bulk to divide on the trail.

Preparation on the Trail:
1. To prepare 1 serving, bring 1 cup water to boil in a cook pot.
2. Pour ⅓ cup hot chocolate mix into a mug.
3. Add hot water to mug and stir well.

Ramona Hammerly
Anacortes, Washington

Pero is an instant grain beverage that contains roasted barley, rye, and chicory. It makes for a nice drink in cold weather. There are many sorts of tea, both traditional and herbal. The most interesting I've had is red mellow bush, or rooibos, from southern Africa. It has a powerful taste, and one bag can make several cups.

Ramona Hammerly
Anacortes, Washington

MOO-LESS HOT CHOCOLATE

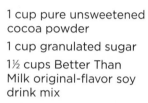

Total Servings: 14
As Packaged for the Trail: As required
Weight per Serving: 1 ounce
Preparation Time on the Trail: 5 minutes
Challenge Level: Easy

"This is an excellent-tasting vegan version of the Hurricane Hill Hot Chocolate recipe. Note that the amount of dry powder mix used per serving in this recipe is less than in the dairy-based version."

Preparation at Home:
1. Combine all dry ingredients together in a bowl. Stir well.
2. Partition ingredients into small ziplock bags, ¼ cup per bag per serving, or bring in bulk to divide on the trail.

Preparation on the Trail:
1. To prepare 1 serving, bring 1 cup water to boil in a cook pot.
2. Pour ¼ cup hot chocolate mix into a mug.
3. Add hot water to mug and stir well.

Ramona Hammerly
Anacortes, Washington

1 cup pure unsweetened cocoa powder

1 cup granulated sugar

1½ cups Better Than Milk original-flavor soy drink mix

1 cup water per serving, added on the trail

Required Equipment on the Trail:
Cook pot

Nutritional Information per Serving:
Calories: 101
Protein: 1 g
Fat: 1 g
Carbohydrates: 23 g
Fiber: 0 g
Sodium: 36 mg
Cholesterol: 0 mg

WHITE BEAR MOCHA

Total Servings: 16
As Packaged for the Trail: 16 servings
Weight per Serving: 1 ounce
Preparation Time on the Trail: 5 minutes
Challenge Level: Easy

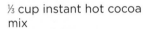

V-LO

"The Tsimshian Native Americans believed the raven descended from the heavens to an earthly world of white. He used his spiritual powers to turn the land green. As a reminder of the precious gift from the spirits and the harsh climate that once was, the raven made some of the bears white. First Nations people believe that this bear is sacred, and the Tsimshian call him moskgm'ol, meaning 'white bear.' This drink is named for this special albino bear."

⅓ cup instant hot cocoa mix

¾ cup instant dry whole milk

½ cup granulated sugar

½ cup instant coffee crystals

1 cup water per serving, added on the trail

Required Equipment on the Trail:
Cook pot

Nutritional Information per Serving:
Calories: 55
Protein: 1 g
Fat: 2 g
Carbohydrates: 9 g
Fiber: 0 g
Sodium: 26 mg
Cholesterol: 4 mg

Preparation at Home:
Place all dry ingredients in a quart-size ziplock bag and shake well.

Preparation on the Trail:
1. To prepare 1 serving, bring 1 cup water to boil in a cook pot.
2. Pour hot water into a cup, then add 2 tablespoons mocha mixture to cup and stir.

Tip: Due to its lower acid content, Kava is less bitter than many instant coffees and makes for a smoother tasting drink.

Laurie Ann March
Guelph, Ontario, Canada

LIGHTNING COFFEE

Total Servings: 6
As Packaged for the Trail: 6 servings
Weight per Serving: 1 ounce
Preparation Time on the Trail: 5 minutes
Challenge Level: Easy

V-LO

"This recipe is sure to zap the ice off your tent in the morning!"

Preparation at Home:

1. Place 20 candies in a ziplock bag, then seal bag and gently hammer candies into small chips.
2. Combine candy chips, dry instant coffee, and malted milk powder in a pint-size ziplock bag, then shake well.

Preparation on the Trail:

1. To prepare 1 serving, bring 1 cup water to boil in a cook pot.
2. Pour hot water in a cup, then add 3 tablespoons coffee mixture to cup and stir.

Christine and Tim Conners
Statesboro, Georgia

20 hard peppermint candies

½ cup Kava instant coffee

½ cup instant dry Carnation malted milk

1 cup water per serving, added on the trail

Required Equipment on the Trail:
Cook pot

Nutritional Information per Serving:
Calories: 213
Protein: 3 g
Fat: 1 g
Carbohydrates: 47 g
Fiber: 0 g
Sodium: 49 mg
Cholesterol: 2 mg

ALASKAN WINTER COFFEE

Total Servings: 10
As Packaged for the Trail: 10 servings
Weight per Serving: 1 ounce
Preparation Time on the Trail: 5 minutes
Challenge Level: Easy

V-LO

½ cup pure unsweetened cocoa powder

½ cup original flavor Coffee Mate powdered creamer

½ cup Kava instant coffee

½ cup granulated sugar

¼ teaspoon ground nutmeg

1 teaspoon ground cinnamon

1 cup water per serving, added on the trail

Preparation at Home:
Combine all dry ingredients in a quart-size ziplock bag and shake well.

Preparation on the Trail:
1. To prepare 1 serving, bring 1 cup water to boil in a cook pot.
2. Pour hot water into a mug, then add 3 tablespoons coffee mixture and stir.

Christine and Tim Conners
Statesboro, Georgia

Required Equipment on the Trail:
Cook pot

Nutritional Information per Serving:
Calories: 91
Protein: 1 g
Fat: 2 g
Carbohydrates: 17 g
Fiber: 0 g
Sodium: 25 mg
Cholesterol: < 1 mg

> For vanilla coffee, split open 1 or more vanilla beans. Place beans in the bag along with the coffee mix. After a few days, the mix will pick up the hint of vanilla flavor. Toss the beans before preparing the coffee.
>
> *Laurie Ann March*
> *Guelph, Ontario, Canada*

FOUR MOONS CHOCOLATE COFFEE

Total Servings: 1
As Packaged for the Trail: 1 serving
Weight per Serving: 1 ounce
Preparation Time on the Trail: 5 minutes
Challenge Level: Easy

V-LO

Preparation at Home:
Combine all dry ingredients in a small ziplock bag.

Preparation on the Trail:
1. To prepare 1 serving, bring 1 cup water to boil in a cook pot.
2. Pour hot water into a mug, then add contents from a bag of coffee mix. Stir well.

Christine and Tim Conners
Statesboro, Georgia

1 packet Starbucks Via instant coffee

2 tablespoons Ovaltine chocolate malt mix

4 balls Whoppers malted milk candy

1 cup water per serving, added on the trail

Required Equipment on the Trail:
Cook pot

Nutritional Information per Serving:
Calories: 60
Protein: 0 g
Fat: 2 g
Carbohydrates: 17 g
Fiber: 0 g
Sodium: 92 mg
Cholesterol: < 1 mg

MOONLIGHT MINT TEA

Total Servings: 2
As Packaged for the Trail: 2 servings
Weight per Serving: 1 ounce
Preparation Time on the Trail: 10 minutes
Challenge Level: Easy

"Thanks to Sana Al-Arashi for providing the idea for our delicious Mediterranean tea recipes: Moonlight Mint and Shawnee Sage."

2 standard-size bags black tea

¼ cup granulated sugar

2 heaping tablespoons dried whole mint or peppermint leaves

4 cups water per 2 servings, added on the trail

Required Equipment on the Trail:
Cook pot

Nutritional Information per Serving:
Calories: 97
Protein: 0 g
Fat: 0 g
Carbohydrates: 25 g
Fiber: 0 g
Sodium: 8 mg
Cholesterol: 0 mg

Preparation at Home:
Pack dry ingredients separately for the trail.

Preparation on the Trail:
1. To prepare 2 servings, bring 4 cups water to boil in a cook pot.
2. Add ¼ cup sugar to pot, then immediately remove pot from heat.
3. Stir, then add tea bags and mint or peppermint leaves.
4. Allow tea to steep for several minutes, then remove black tea bags from pot to keep tea from becoming bitter.

Tip: If the mint or peppermint leaves are grown fresh, do not water the plant for at least two days prior to picking the leaves.

Christine and Tim Conners
Statesboro, Georgia

I find that peppermint, spearmint, and lemon mint leaves make a refreshing tea after they float in my water bottle for a few hours.
From her book, Walking Home: A Woman's Pilgrimage on the Appalachian Trail.
Kelly "Amazin' Grace" Winters
Bayville, New York

SHAWNEE SAGE TEA

Total Servings: 2
As Packaged for the Trail: 2 servings
Weight per Serving: 1 ounce
Preparation Time on the Trail: 10 minutes
Challenge Level: Easy

"The Shawnee Trail is a beautiful 46-mile loop trail in the tree-covered hill country of south-central Ohio where I hiked as a boy and where our kids learned to backpack."

Preparation at Home:
Pack dry ingredients separately for the trail.

Preparation on the Trail:
1. To prepare 2 servings, bring 4 cups water to boil in a cook pot.
2. Add ¼ cup sugar to pot, then immediately remove pot from heat.
3. Stir, then add tea bags and sage leaves.
4. Allow tea to steep for several minutes, then remove black tea bags from pot to keep tea from becoming bitter.

Tip: If sage leaves are grown fresh, do not water the plant for at least two days prior to picking the leaves.

Christine and Tim Conners
Statesboro, Georgia

2 standard-size bags black tea

¼ cup granulated sugar

2 heaping tablespoons dried whole sage leaves

4 cups water per 2 servings, added on the trail

Required Equipment on the Trail:
Cook pot

Nutritional Information per Serving:
Calories: 97
Protein: 0 g
Fat: 0 g
Carbohydrates: 25 g
Fiber: 0 g
Sodium: 8 mg
Cholesterol: 0 mg

GOAT DANCE BRANDY

Total Servings: 1
As Packaged for the Trail: 1 serving
Weight per Serving: 2 ounces
Preparation Time on the Trail: 5 minutes
Challenge Level: Easy

"I learned about this drink from my sister-in-law, who taught climbing on Mt. Rainier. It has great powers of recuperation and relaxation after a hard day of almost anything outdoors. On the trail I have to ration this drink, or the goat-packer's club that I hike with will drink it all the first night."

3 tablespoons Jeannie strawberry jelly dessert mix

1 tablespoon peach brandy (or to taste)

1 cup water per serving, added on the trail

Required Equipment on the Trail:
Cook pot

Nutritional Information per Serving:
Calories: 138
Protein: 0 g
Fat: 0 g
Carbohydrates: 30 g
Fiber: 0 g
Sodium: 15 mg
Cholesterol: 0 mg

Preparation at Home:
Pack dessert mix and brandy separately for the trail.

Preparation on the Trail:
1. To prepare 1 serving, bring 1 cup water to boil.
2. Pour hot water into a mug.
3. Add 3 tablespoons dessert mix and 1 tablespoon brandy to the mug. Stir until mix is dissolved.

Carolyn "Dances with Goats" Eddy
Estacada, Oregon

PANAMINT PEPPERMINT COOLER

Total Servings: 5
As Packaged for the Trail: 5 servings
Weight per Serving: 2 ounces
Preparation Time on the Trail: 15 minutes
Challenge Level: Easy

"This drink has an amazing sequence of aftertastes, all of them intriguing. It starts with the sharp hit of mint and then smoothly rolls into a series of sweet, fruity nuances. No, it's not fine wine, but not bad for a quick and easy trail beverage."

Preparation at Home:

1. Combine cherry- and lemonade-flavored Kool-Aid mixes in a pint-size ziplock freezer bag.
2. Carry tea bags separately.

Preparation on the Trail:

1. To prepare 1 large serving, bring 2 cups water to boil in a cook pot.
2. Remove pot from heat and add 4 peppermint tea bags to the hot water. Let steep for 6 minutes before removing bags.
3. Add ¼ cup Kool-Aid mix to pot and stir until dissolved.
4. Allow water to cool, then add 2 more cups cold water. For an on-the-trail treat, pour into a water bottle for later enjoyment.

Christine and Tim Conners
Statesboro, Georgia

5 ounces (1 full container cap) cherry-flavored sweetened Kool-Aid mix

5 ounces (1 full container cap) lemonade-flavored sweetened Kool-Aid mix

1 (20-bag) package Celestial Seasonings peppermint tea

4 cups water per serving, added on the trail

Required Equipment on the Trail:
Cook pot

Nutritional Information per Serving:
Calories: 208
Protein: 0 g
Fat: 0 g
Carbohydrates: 78 g
Fiber: 0 g
Sodium: 0 mg
Cholesterol: 0 mg

Vegetarian and Vegan Meal System Examples

Meal systems, when compared to stand-alone recipe-based menus, offer an interesting, alternate approach to dining on the trail. With meal systems, a predetermined amount of bulk staples are used to mix and match to taste once on the trail. This approach can simplify planning, reduce packaging waste, and, if carefully applied, offer a very wide range of meal variety in the wilderness.

While attractive for these reasons, meal systems should nevertheless be used with caution. For one, it's easy to over- or under-pack when using a system filled with food choices with which you don't have previous experience. And, in odd contrast to their promise of providing nearly unlimited variety, meal systems are vulnerable to just the opposite if the types of foods selected aren't sufficiently different in flavor, type, and texture. Before using any meal system with which you're unfamiliar, test it out at home for a couple of weeks before taking it on a long trek.

Use the following three examples—one each for breakfast, lunch, and dinner—for ideas on building and customizing your own system.

BREAKFAST 101 HOT CEREAL SYSTEM

Category 1: Cereals
Bulgur wheat

Cream of Wheat

Farina

Granola (uncooked)

Grits

Malt-O-Meal

Quick oats

Category 2: Seasonings and Condiments
Allspice

Brown sugar

Butter Buds Sprinkles

Ground cinnamon

Ground cloves

Ground nutmeg

Instant dry milk

Salt

Category 3: Dried Fruit
Apples

Apricots

Blueberries

Cherries

Coconut (flaked or shredded)

Cranberries

Dates

Peaches

Pineapple

Raisins

Strawberries

Required Equipment on the Trail:
Cook pot

Preparation at Home:
Select items from each of the following three categories and pack them separately for the trail. The amount needed for each meal will vary depending on the type of cereal selected and, of course, your individual appetite, but expect to average between 3 to 5 ounces of ingredients per serving per meal.

Preparation on the Trail:
Begin by cooking the cereal using an appropriate amount of water. Continue by adding to taste from the list of seasonings and condiments. Finally, toss in a handful of chopped, dried fruit.

Tip: Be careful when using seasonings, especially with cereal, because odd combinations or excessive quantities can quickly ruin the meal. Add a little at a time, stirring well, then sample before adding more.

Options: *This system has fruit as the crowning finale, but a whole range of chopped nuts could be used in place of, or in addition to, the fruit: almonds, chia, flax, macadamias, peanuts, pecans, pine, pistachios, poppy, pumpkin, sesame, sunflower, and walnuts.*

Rick Bombaci
Enterprise, Oregon

SIMPLE LUNCH SYSTEM

Preparation at Home:
As with the breakfast system, select items from each of the following categories and pack separately for the trail. Expect to carry about 4 to 6 ounces of ingredients per serving per meal.

Preparation on the Trail:
Combine items from each category, first rehydrating any dried ingredients, if required. To round out your lunch, serve with trail mix, snack bars, or fruit leathers.

Rick Bombaci
Enterprise, Oregon

Category 1: Breads
Bagels

English muffins

Pita

Tortillas

Triscuits

Wheat Thins

Category 2: Fillings
Bean mix (rehydrated on trail)

Cheese (block)

Honey

Hummus mix (rehydrated on trail)

Jam and jelly

Nature's Burger mix (rehydrated on trail)

Peanut butter

Tahini

Category 3: Seasonings and Condiments
Ground black pepper

Dill weed

Catsup (in condiment packets)

Mayonnaise (in condiment packets)

Prepared mustard (coarse ground, Dijon, or yellow)

Olive oil

Red pepper flakes

Salt

Required Equipment on the Trail:
None

624 VEGAN DINNER SYSTEM

Category 1: Dehydrated Vegetables
Black beans

Broccoli

Butter beans

Corn

Green beans

Kidney beans

Lima beans

Onions

Peas

Pinto beans

Stir-fry vegetable blend

Category 2: Carbohydrates
Bulgur

Couscous

Grits (regular)

Hash browns (dried)

Noodles

Potato flakes

Rice

Category 3: Seasonings
Ground black pepper

Vegan vegetable bouillon cubes

Curry powder

Garlic powder

Italian seasoning

Lemon pepper seasoning

Onion powder

Red pepper flakes

Dried sage

Dried salsa (rehydrated on trail)

Salt

Required Equipment on the Trail:
Cook pot

Preparation at Home:
A very large variety of dinner meals can be produced from the following three-category system of vegetables, carbs, and seasonings. For each meal select one or more items from each category, packing each separately for the trail. Use about ½ cup ingredients from the list of vegetables, about 1 cup from the carbs, and to taste from the seasonings. Expect to carry about 5 to 7 ounces of food per serving per meal.

Preparation on the Trail:
To prepare a single serving, bring 3 cups water to a boil, then add ½ cup dried vegetables, and about 1 cup carbs to the pot. Stir, then reduce heat to a simmer. Add seasonings to taste, cover, and continue to cook for about 5 minutes before serving.

Charlie Thorpe
Huntsville, Alabama

APPENDIX A: COMMON MEASUREMENT CONVERSIONS

United States Volumetric Conversions

1 smidgen	$\frac{1}{32}$ teaspoon
1 pinch	$\frac{1}{16}$ teaspoon
1 dash	$\frac{1}{8}$ teaspoon
3 teaspoons	1 tablespoon
48 teaspoons	1 cup
2 tablespoons	$\frac{1}{8}$ cup
4 tablespoons	$\frac{1}{4}$ cup
5 tablespoons + 1 teaspoon	$\frac{1}{3}$ cup
8 tablespoons	$\frac{1}{2}$ cup
12 tablespoons	$\frac{3}{4}$ cup
16 tablespoons	1 cup
1 ounce	2 tablespoons
4 ounces	$\frac{1}{2}$ cup
8 ounces	1 cup
$\frac{5}{8}$ cup	$\frac{1}{2}$ cup + 2 tablespoons
$\frac{7}{8}$ cup	$\frac{3}{4}$ cup + 2 tablespoons
2 cups	1 pint
2 pints	1 quart
1 quart	4 cups
4 quarts	1 gallon
1 gallon	128 ounces

Note: Dry and fluid volumes are equivalent for teaspoon, tablespoon, and cup.

International Metric System Conversions

Volume and Weight

United States	Metric
¼ teaspoon	1.25 milliliters
½ teaspoon	2.50 milliliters
¾ teaspoon	3.75 milliliters
1 teaspoon	5 milliliters
1 tablespoon	15 milliliters
1 ounce (volume)	30 milliliters
¼ cup	60 milliliters
½ cup	120 milliliters
¾ cup	180 milliliters
1 cup	240 milliliters
1 pint	0.48 liter
1 quart	0.95 liter
1 gallon	3.79 liters
1 ounce (weight)	28 grams
1 pound	0.45 kilogram

Temperature

°F	°C
175	80
200	95
225	105
250	120
275	135
300	150
325	165
350	175
375	190
400	205
425	220
450	230
475	245
500	260

British, Canadian, and Australian Conversions

1 teaspoon . . . . approx. 1 teaspoon
(Britain, Canada, Australia)   (United States)

1 tablespoon . . . . approx. 1 tablespoon
(Britain, Canada)   (United States)

1 tablespoon . . . . 1.35 tablespoons
(Australia)   (United States)

1 ounce . . . . 0.96 ounce
(Britain, Canada, Australia)   (United States)

1 gill . . . . 5 ounces
(Britain)   (Britain, Canada, Australia)

1 cup . . . . 10 ounces
(Britain)   (Britain, Canada, Australia)

1 cup . . . . 9.61 ounces
(Britain)   (United States)

1 cup . . . . 1.20 cups
(Britain)   (United States)

1 cup . . . . 8.45 ounces
(Canada, Australia)   (United States)

1 cup . . . . 1.06 cups
(Canada, Australia)   (United States)

1 pint . . . . 20 ounces
(Britain, Canada, Australia)   (Britain, Canada, Australia)

1 Imperial gallon . . . . 1.20 gallons
(Britain)   (United States)

1 pound . . . . 1 pound
(Britain, Canada, Australia)   (United States)

Equivalent Measures*

16 ounces water. . . . . .1 pound
2 cups vegetable oil . . . . .1 pound
2 cups or 4 standard sticks butter . . . . . . .1 pound
2 cups granulated sugar. . . . . .1 pound
3 ½ to 4 cups unsifted confectioners' sugar . .1 pound
2 ¼ cups packed brown sugar . . . . .1 pound
4 cups all-purpose wheat flour . . . . .1 pound
3 ½ cups whole wheat flour . . . . .1 pound
8–10 egg whites. . . . . .1 cup
12–14 egg yolks. . . . . .1 cup
1 whole lemon, squeezed . . . . .3 tablespoons juice
1 whole orange, squeezed . . . . .⅓ cup juice
* Approximate

Drying Conversions*

Undried Item	Dried Volume	Dried Weight
1 tablespoon fresh herbs	.1 teaspoon. .	less than 1 ounce
1 tablespoon mustard.	.1 teaspoon. .	less than 1 ounce
1 garlic clove, minced.	.⅛ teaspoon powder . . .	less than 1 ounce
1 pound frozen peas	.1 cup	4 ounces
1 pound cooked and sliced carrots	.½ cup	2 ounces
1 pound boiled and sliced potatoes	.1½ cups . . .	4 ounces
1 pound diced onions.	.1 cup	1 ounce
1 pound frozen French-sliced green beans	.2 cups	1½ ounces
1 pound diced celery	.⅓ cup	½ ounce
1 pound sliced fresh mushrooms	.2½ cups . . .	1 ounce
1 pound fresh green bell pepper.	.¾ cup	1½ ounces
1 pound fresh jalapeño peppers	.1⅓ cups . . .	1 ounce
1 pound frozen mixed vegetables	.¾ cup	3½ ounces
1 15-ounce can mixed vegetables	.½ cup	1½ ounces

1 6-ounce can medium diced olives. . . . .½ cup . . . . 1 ounce

1 15-ounce can pinto beans. . . . . .1 cup . . . . 2½ ounces

1 15-ounce can black beans. . . . . .1 cup . . . . 2½ ounces

1 15-ounce can kidney beans . . . . .1¼ cups . . . 3½ ounces

1 pound steamed and chopped
   zucchini . . . . .⅓ cup . . . . ½ ounce

1 pound frozen sliced broccoli . . . . . . .1 cup . . . . 1 ounce

1 pound sliced Roma tomatoes . . . . . . .1 cup . . . . 1 ounce

1 6-ounce can tomato paste. . . . . .leather roll. . 1½ ounces

1 pound salsa . . . . .½ cup . . . . ½ ounce

1 pound sliced apples . . . . .1½ cups . . . 3 ounces

1 pound sliced bananas . . . . .1½ cups . . . 4 ounces

1 20-ounce can diced pineapple . . . . . .¾ cup . . . . 2 ounces

1 pound trimmed watermelon . . . . . . .1 cup . . . . 1 ounce

1 pound frozen cherries. . . . . .½ cup . . . . 2 ounces

1 cup whole milk . . . . .½ cup
                            instant dry. . 2 ounces

* Volumes and weights may vary slightly from those shown here due to a variety of factors, including brand selection, depth of cut, dehydrating method, and equipment.

APPENDIX B: SOURCES OF EQUIPMENT AND SUPPLIES

AlpineAire

www.alpineaire.com

A good source for freeze-dried, ready-to-eat instant meals, AlpineAire's products are available through outfitters as well as at their online store.

Amazon

www.amazon.com

It's well known that Amazon sells an enormous array of products. But it might come as a surprise nevertheless that it also hosts a very large number of vendors who sell exotic food ingredients difficult to find in your local grocery store. Check out Amazon if you're stumped when trying to find an ingredient.

Asian Food Grocer

www.asianfoodgrocer.com

A wide selection of difficult-to-find Asian ingredients, including dried tofu and mushrooms, are available at Asian Food Grocer.

Backpacker's Pantry

www.backpackerspantry.com

Backpacker's Pantry is a well-known brand name at outdoor retailers, but their online store is also a very good source of freeze-dried meals as well as single-serving condiments like peanut butter, salsa, and jelly. Backpacker's Pantry also carries a selection of organic products.

Barry Farm Foods

www.barryfarm.com

Barry Farm offers an amazing selection of dry ingredients, including foods you might not believe could even be dried, such as sour cream and yogurt.

Bulk Foods

www.bulkfoods.com

Here you'll find an enormous selection of dried fruits, spices, grains, and nuts sold in a variety of sizes and quantities.

Campmor

www.campmor.com

Campmor's online catalog has one of the most comprehensive selections of gear available anywhere for backpacking and cooking on the trail.

Eden Foods

www.edenfoods.com

An interesting array of Japanese foods can be found at Eden, including dried tofu, seaweed, spices, and mushrooms, as well as exotic and organic bulk goods.

Emergency Essentials

www.beprepared.com

A good source for dried goods sold in bulk, including whole egg powder and the like.

Fantastic World Foods

www.fantasticfoods.com

A culinary voyage across continents and cultures, Fantastic World Foods's Internet store offers many dried products useful for backpacking, such as refried beans, falafel, hummus, and tabouli mixes.

Fastachi

www.fastachi.com

A wonderful selection of excellent nut and seed products, including mixes and nut butters, can be found at Fastachi.

Harmony House Foods

www.harmonyhousefoods.com

Harmony House carries a large selection of dried vegetables and fruits in bulk.

Harvest Foodworks

www.harvestfoodworks.com

A wide range of freeze-dried and dehydrated meals for the outdoors can be found at Harvest Foodworks.

Just Tomatoes, Etc!

www.justtomatoes.com

A wonderful source for bulk individual freeze-dried vegetables and fruits, Just Tomatoes doesn't offer just tomatoes. Their products are so tasty, you can eat them dry, right out of the bag.

King Arthur Flour

www.kingarthurflour.com

Popular at the grocer, King Arthur's online retail store offers not only flour but also a diverse selection of difficult-to-find ingredients, including whole egg powder, dried cheese, whole milk powder, and more.

Mountain Equipment Co-op

www.mec.ca

MEC is a large Canadian cooperative that specializes in outdoor gear via an extensive online catalog and through more than a dozen retail stores located across Canada.

Mountain House

www.mtnhse.com

Mountain House is well known at outdoor retailers for their freeze-dried meals, but online they also offer a good selection of discounted bulk dried items such as vegetables, eggs, and premade entrees.

My Spicer

www.myspicer.com

An enormous selection of exotic dried vegetables and spices from around the world can be found at My Spicer.

Nuts.com

www.nuts.com

More than just nuts, this proprietor stocks a fantastic assortment of food items ideal for backpacking, including dehydrated and freeze-dried fruits and vegetables.

PackitGourmet

www.packitgourmet.com

PackitGourmet stocks a large and unique selection of items with the backpacker in mind, including restaurant condiment packets in smaller lots and powdered citrus drinks.

REI

www.rei.com

REI is a membership cooperative that carries a large array of trail gear and freeze-dried foods online but also retails through dozens of super-stores located throughout the United States, providing the opportunity to see before you buy. Be prepared to be bitten by the backpacking bug once you step foot in an REI.

Sport Chalet

www.sportchalet.com

Sport Chalet is a major outdoor recreation retailer in the southwestern United States. Like REI, this is an excellent place to go to see backpacking gear in general, and trail kitchen equipment and freeze-dried foods in particular, firsthand.

SunOrganic Farm

www.sunorganic.com

This retailer carries a good selection of organic dried fruits and vegetables as well as seasonings, beans, nuts, and sprouting seeds.

SunRidge Farms

www.sunridgefarms.com

A large variety of nuts, seeds, and dried fruit can be found at SunRidge, including wonderfully creative trail mixes. Many of their products are organic.

Suttons Bay Trading Company

www.suttonsbayspices.com

Suttons Bay Trading offers a large selection of dried fruit and vegetables, including an interesting assortment of flavored powders such as horse-radish, yogurt, and even honey, which is impossible to dry in a home dehydrator.

APPENDIX C: ADDITIONAL READING AND RESOURCES

Books and Periodicals
Cook's Illustrated and *Cook's Country*
www.cooksillustrated.com and *www.cookscountry.com*

These outstanding periodicals from America's Test Kitchen turn common recipes into wonderful re-creations but with a minimum of effort. Along the way, the reader learns how and why the recipes work. *Cook's Illustrated* explores fewer dishes but in more detail than *Cook's Country*, its sister publication, which comes in a larger format and full color. These are magazines for the home kitchen. But what you'll learn indoors will prove invaluable on the trail.

FalconGuides
www.falcon.com

FalconGuides is the top outdoor recreation publisher in the country with an extensive catalog of books for every outdoor activity, covering most states and geographical regions in the United States as well as many of the most popular National Parks.

Lipsmackin' Backpackin', Christine and Tim Conners, FalconGuides
A close sibling to the book you hold, the second edition of *Lipsmackin' Backpackin'* is also filled with recipes well suited for backpacking trips of longer duration. Nearly two-thirds of the recipes in *Lipsmackin' Backpackin'* are vegetarian or vegan, and those that are have been clearly marked for easy location.

On Food and Cooking: The Science and Lore of the Kitchen, Harold McGee, Scribner
This is an excellent resource for understanding the science behind cooking. When chefs decipher why recipes work the way they do, they become much more effective at adapting recipes in a pinch or creating new ones on the fly. Be forewarned: This is not a cookbook, much less an outdoor cookbook. But if science interests you, this book will too.

Preserve It Naturally, Excalibur/KBI Inc.
A very good compendium of tips and tricks to make you a wizard with your kitchen dehydrator.

Trail Food, Alan Kesselheim, Ragged Mountain Press
This little classic is an excellent reference for those who desire to master the art of drying foods for any outdoor excursion.

Informational Websites

American Hiking Society

www.americanhiking.org
The mission of the American Hiking Society is to be the national voice of those who use and love this country's foot trails. The AHS champions conservation issues, builds partnerships, and provides resources to plan, fund, and develop foot trails. Go to their website to find out more about the work of the AHS and the local organizations whose efforts preserve and protect the trails in your neck of the woods.

Backpack Gear Test

www.backpackgeartest.com
Contemplating the purchase of expensive equipment? This is the place to go to see thorough reviews of the performance of gear in the field.

Backpacking Light

www.backpackinglight.com
A very good reference for those who want to learn more about how to safely reduce that heavy load on their back.

Epicurious

www.epicurious.com
You won't find much on trail cooking at Epicurious. But if you're looking to hone your basic cooking skills and could use many hundreds of vegetarian and vegan recipes for practice, this is a good resource.

Exploratorium

www.exploratorium.edu/cooking
Exploratorium makes cooking fun by putting emphasis on the science behind it. Even if you're not the scientist type, you'll enjoy this site. Quirky yet practical, recipes flow down the page with relevant science posted in the sidebar.

Gourmet Sleuth
www.gourmetsleuth.com
A good kitchen measurement conversion calculator can be found at this website. Included is the ability to convert between US and British measurement units.

Leave No Trace (LNT) Center for Outdoor Ethics
www.LNT.org
The Center for Outdoor Ethics has been a leader and respected voice in communicating why and how our outdoor places require responsible stewardship. The LNT outdoor ethics code is becoming standard practice in the wilderness. More information about the organization is available at their website, and specific information about outdoor ethics principles, especially as applied to cooking, can be found in Appendix D of this book.

APPENDIX D: LOW-IMPACT COOKING

The Leave No Trace Center for Outdoor Ethics provides a set of principles that are becoming increasingly well-known and applied by those who visit the wild places of the world.

There are seven core principles of Leave No Trace:

- Plan ahead and prepare

- Travel and camp on durable surfaces

- Dispose of waste properly

- Leave what you find

- Minimize campfire impacts

- Respect wildlife

- Be considerate of other visitors

Careful planning, especially with respect to food preparation, is critical to successfully following the principles of Leave No Trace. When preparing for an upcoming outing, consider the following list of application points as you evaluate your food and cooking options.

Decide how you'll prepare your food.

Some methods of cooking, such as the use of pack stoves, create less impact than others, such as open fires. When using open fire to cook, follow local fire restrictions and use an established fire ring instead of creating a new one. Keep fires small. Collect wood from the ground rather than from standing trees. To avoid creating barren earth, find wood farther away from camp. Select smaller pieces of wood and burn them completely to ash. Afterward, be sure the fire is completely out, then scatter the ashes. Learn how to use a mound fire to prevent scorching the ground and blackening rocks.

Carefully select and repackage your food to minimize trash.

Tiny pieces of trash easily become litter. Avoid bringing small, individually packaged candies and other such food items on the trail. Twist ties and bread clips are easily lost when dropped. Remove the wrappers and repackage such foods into ziplock bags before leaving home; or use knots, instead of ties and clips, to seal bags and the like.

Metal containers and their lids, crushed beverage cans, and broken glass can easily cut or puncture trash sacks. Wrap these carefully before placing them in thin-wall trash bags. Minimize the use of glass on the trail. Scan your trail camp carefully when packing up to ensure that no litter is left behind.

Minimize leftovers and dispose of food waste properly.

Leftover food makes for messier trash and cleanup. If poured on open ground, it is unsightly and unsanitary. If buried too close to the surface, animals may dig it up. Leftovers encourage problem animals if not properly managed. Carefully plan your meals to reduce leftovers.

Dispose of used wash and rinse water, also called "gray water," in a manner appropriate for your area. Before disposal, remove or strain food chunks from the gray water and place these with the trash. Dispose of gray water in a cat hole covered by several inches of soil in an area free of sensitive vegetation and at least 200 feet from streams and lakes. Avoid excessive suds by using only the amount of detergent necessary for the job. Bring only biodegradable soap on the trail.

Protect your food, trash, and other odorous items from animals.

Consider avoiding the use of very aromatic foods that can attract animals. Store food, trash, and other odorous items where animals won't be able to get to them. Besides being potentially dangerous to the animal, and inconvenient for the backpacker, trash is often spread over a large area once the animal gains access. Follow local regulations regarding proper food storage, such as the use of bear-bagging techniques or bear-proof food canisters.

Avoid collecting wild foods.

Don't harvest wild foods, such as berries, if these are not plentiful in the area you're visiting. Such foods are likely to be a more important component of the local ecosystem when scarce.

These are only a few of the practical considerations and potential applications of the principles of Leave No Trace. Visit www.LNT.org for additional information and ideas.

APPENDIX E: THE NATIONAL SCENIC TRAILS SYSTEM

Looking for some of the most challenging, beautiful, and inspiring places to apply your hiking skills? Perhaps you've had a taste of the spectacular majesty of the mountains and are now contemplating where to go next for more? If this is you, then look no further than the National Scenic Trails System.

Created by an Act of Congress to protect corridors of high scenic value, the National Scenic Trails System comprises a masterwork of eleven long footpaths distributed across the United States. Each of these trails is an unparalleled scenic gem. Now spanning more than 18,000 trail miles, they were created to provide ultimate access to the country's most awesome wild places. Each trail presents a challenge like no other.

The following list contains basic information about each of the trails, including length and location. You will probably recognize some of the names. In fact, you may have walked at least a portion of one of these trails in the past. But were you aware of the others? Did you realize just how truly massive this network of long trails is? The opportunities for exploring are nearly endless.

The National Park Service maintains ultimate oversight of the National Scenic Trails System. But day-to-day trail stewardship is accomplished through volunteer organizations that work closely with federal and state government bureaus. These volunteer organizations are often the best source for up-to-date information, and so web links to these have been provided where applicable in the list below. The Partnership for the National Trails System at www.pnts.org is also a good launching point to those organizations directly associated with each of the National Scenic Trails.

And while the National Scenic Trails may be the most famous of the long trails, they are by no means the only ones. Information regarding other backpacking options can be found through the National Park Service at www.nps.gov/nts, the US Forest Service at www.fs.fed.us/recreation/programs/trails, and the Bureau of Land Management at www.blm.gov.

So keep on challenging yourself. Browse the list below, follow the associated web links to learn more about our incredible long trails, and be inspired.

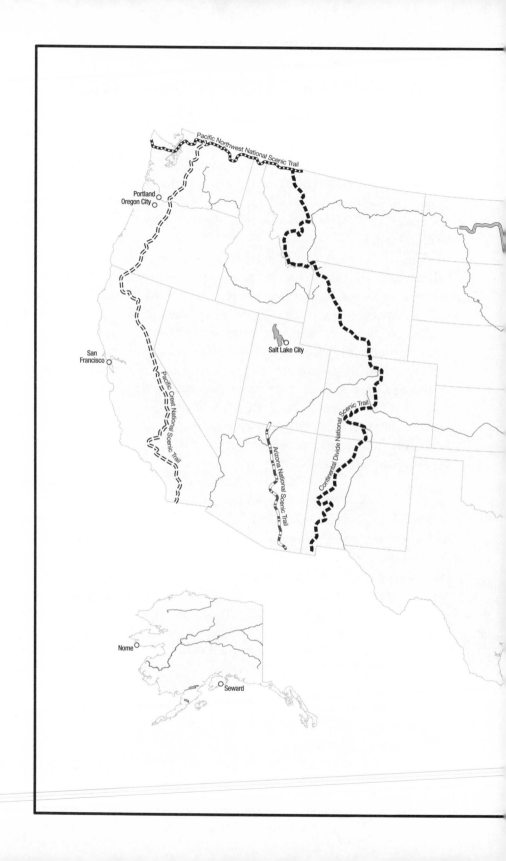

North Country National Scenic Trail

Ice Age National
Scenic Trail

New England
National
Scenic Trail

Council Bluffs

St. Joseph

Kansas City

St. Louis

Appalachian National Scenic Trail

Washington, D.C.

Potomac Heritage
National Scenic Trail

Natchez Trace National Scenic Trail

Selma   Montgomery

Florida National Scenic Trail

N

0   5   600 miles

Appalachian
2,174 miles, Georgia to Maine
Appalachian Trail Conservancy
www.appalachiantrail.org

Arizona
807 miles, Mexico–Arizona border to Utah–Arizona border
Arizona Trail Association
www.aztrail.org

Continental Divide
3,100 miles, Mexico–New Mexico border to Canada–Montana border
Continental Divide Trail Society
www.cdtsociety.org

Florida
1,400 miles, entirely within the state of Florida
Florida Trail Association
www.floridatrail.org

Ice Age
1,200 miles, entirely within the state of Wisconsin
Ice Age Trail Alliance
www.iceagetrail.org

Natchez Trace
65 miles, four segments in Mississippi and Tennessee
National Park Service
www.nps.gov/natt/index.htm

New England
220 miles, Connecticut to Massachusetts
Connecticut Forest and Park Association and Appalachian Mountain Club
www.newenglandnst.org

North Country
4,600 miles, New York to North Dakota
North Country Trail Association
www.northcountrytrail.org

Pacific Crest
2,638 miles, Mexico–California border to Canada–Washington border
Pacific Crest Trail Association
www.pcta.org

Pacific Northwest
1,200 miles, Montana to Washington
Pacific Northwest Trail Association
www.pnt.org

Potomac Heritage
830 miles, Virginia to Pennsylvania
Potomac Heritage Trail Association
www.potomactrail.org

INDEX

ABOUT THE AUTHORS

Experienced backpackers, campers, and outdoor chefs, Christine and Tim Conners are the authors of the nationally popular *Lipsmackin'* outdoor cookbook series, including the titles *Lipsmackin' Backpackin'*, *Lipsmackin' Vegetarian Backpackin'*, and, the latest entry to the series, *Lipsmackin' Car Campin'*.

Specifically for the Scouting world, Tim and Christine have produced *The Scout's Cookbook* series: *The Scout's Campfire Cookbook for Kids, The Scout's Outdoor Cookbook, The Scout's Dutch Oven Cookbook, The Scout's Large Groups Cookbook,* and *The Scout's Backpacking Cookbook*. Each title in *The Scout's Cookbook* lineup is a collection of unique and outstanding recipes from Scout leaders across the United States.

Christine and Tim have been testing outdoor recipes for twenty years. At the invitation of Boy Scouts of America, the Conners have served several times as judges for *Scouting* magazine's prestigious national camp food cooking contest.

The Conners have four children—James, Michael, Maria, and David—all of whom stay busy in the outdoors by backpacking on the Appalachian Trail, camping and day hiking in the local state parks, and kayaking on the region's lakes and rivers . . . when they aren't writing cookbooks!

Stop by www.lipsmackincampin.com to say howdy.